GARLAND STUDIES IN

THE HISTORY OF AMERICAN LABOR

edited by

STUART BRUCHEY
ALLAN NEVINS PROFESSOR EMERITUS
COLUMBIA UNIVERSITY

A GARLAND SERIES

THE ASSIMILATION OF IMMIGRANTS IN THE U.S. LABOR MARKET

EMPLOYMENT AND LABOR FORCE TURNOVER

MICHAEL E. HURST

GARLAND PUBLISHING, INC.
A MEMBER OF THE TAYLOR & FRANCIS GROUP
NEW YORK & LONDON / 1998

Library of Congress Cataloging-in-Publication Data

Hurst, Michael E., 1952–
    The assimilation of immigrants in the U.S. labor market :
employment and labor force turnover / Michael E. Hurst.
        p.   cm. — (Garland studies in the history of American
labor)
    Includes bibliographical references.
    ISBN 0-8153-3225-4 (alk. paper)
    1. Alien labor—United States. 2. Labor turnover—United
States. 3. Assimilation (Sociology)—United States. I. Title.
II. Series.
HD8081.A5H87 1998
331.6'2'0973—dc21
                                                                98-37496

Printed on acid-free, 250-year-life paper
Manufactured in the United States of America

Contents

Figures   ix
Tables   xi
Acknowledgments   xiii

I. Introduction   3
    1.1 Background   4
    1.2 Issues of Immigration   7
    1.3 Focus of the Dissertation   9

II. Theories of Immigration   11
    2.1 The Decision to Migrate to a Foreign Country   11
    2.2 Assimilation and Self-Selection Hypotheses   15
    2.3 The Cohort Quality Hypothesis   19

III. Models of Labor Turnover and Unemployment   21
    3.1 Issues of Measurement—Stocks and Flows   22
    3.2 Causes of Unemployment—Turnover vs. Lack of
        Jobs   25
    3.3 Types of Unemployment   27
    3.4 Causes of Unemployment—Job Search, Rigid Wages,
        Disequilibria   28
    3.5 Search Theories   28
       A. Overview   28
       B. Search Strategies   30
       C. Voluntary Quits   31
       D. Criticisms   32
    3.6 Reservation Wages   32

3.7 Firm-Specific Human Capital   33
3.8 Employer Behavior   33
   A. Implicit Contracts   34
   B. Efficiency Wages   35
   C. Insider/Outsider Models   36
3.9 Efficient Turnover   36

IV. Empirical Evidence in the Literature   39
4.1 Immigrant Labor Market Adjustment   39
4.2 Unemployment and Labor Market Turnover   44
   A. Demographic Groups   45
   B. Unemployment Rates   46
   C. Separation Rates   46
   D. Quit Rates   47
   E. Labor Force Movement of Youth   47
   F. Efficiency Wages and Firm-Specific Human
     Capital   49

V. The Theory of Immigrant Unemployment and Turnover,
   and Hypotheses   51

VI. Data Sources   59
6.1 Current Population Survey   59
   A. Basic Survey Questions   60
   B. Supplements   60
6.2 Survey of Income and Education   61
6.3 The Combined Database   62
6.4 Data Limitations   62

VII. The Model, Estimating Equations, and Methodology   65
7.1 Functional Form and Dependent Variables   65
7.2 Explanatory Variables   68
   A. Postmigration Acquisition of Labor Market Skills   68
   B. Wage Distribution, and the Cost of Search   68
   C. Local Labor Market Conditions   70
   D. Other Regional Effects   70
   E. Individual Value of Non-market Work   70
   F. Period Effects   71
   G. Other Individual Level Effects   72

VIII. Employment, Unemployment, Out of the Labor Force   83
    8.1 Basic Model Variables, Coefficients   83
    8.2 The Foreign Born Variables   99
    8.3 Disaggregation by Racial/Ethnic Group   110
    8.4 Summary of Chapter 8   123

IX. Job Losers, Job Leavers, Labor Force Entrants   125
    9.1. The Basic Model   126
    9.2 The Foreign Born Variables   136
    9.3 Summary of Chapter 9   147

X. Search Duration—Weeks Looking for Work   149
    10.1 Description of Model, and Problems   149
    10.2. Empirical Results—Basic Model   154
    10.3. The Foreign Born Variables   166
    10.4 Summary of Chapter 10   168

XI. Adjusting Unemployment Probabilities for Duration of
        Unemployment   171
    11.1. Derivation of the Estimating Equations   172
    11.2. The Basic Model   177
    11.3 The Foreign Born Variables   181
    11.4 Summary of Chapter 11   182

XII. Summary, Conclusions, Policy Implications   185
    12.1. The Assimilation Hypothesis   185
    12.2. Labor Force Hypotheses, and Study Design   186
    12.3 Summary of Findings, Base Variables   189
    12.4 Summary of Findings, Foreign Born Variables   191
    12.5. Discussion   194
    12.6 Policy Implications and Conclusion   196

Notes   201
Appendices   203
    Appendix A.
Cited References   207

Figures

2.1	Earnings Profile by Years Since Migration	17
2.2	Cross-Section Age-Earnings Profile of Immigrants	19
3.1	Job Search	29
4.1	Cross-Section Age-Earnings Profiles, Foreign Born and Native Born Adult Men, United States, 1970 and 1990 Censuses	40
8.1	Effect of Experience on Labor Force Probabilities, Pooled Sample of Native Born and Foreign Born Adult Men, Ceteris Paribus	93
8.2	Probabilities of Being Out of the Labor Force, Adult Foreign Born Men (Native Benchmark)—Continuous and Incremental YSM	108
8.3	Probabilities of Being Unemployed, Adult Foreign Born Men (Native Benchmark)—Continuous and Incremental YSM	108
8.4	Probabilities of Being Employed, Adult Foreign Born Men (Native Benchmark)—Continuous and Incremental YSM	109
10.1	Frequency of Weeks Unemployed, Native Born	153
10.2	Frequency of Weeks Unemployed, Foreign Born	153

Tables

7.1 Independent Variables : Names, Descriptions, and Expected Signs of Partial Effects   74

7.2 Means and Standard Deviations of Independent and Dependent Variables 1976-94, Native Born, Foreign Born, and Pooled, Men Ages 25-64   76

7.3 Means and Standard Deviations of Independent and Dependent Variables 1979-91, Pooled, Men Ages 25-64, by Racial Group   79

7.4 Means and Standard Deviations of Independent and Dependent Variables 1976-94, Pooled, Men Ages 25-64, by Labor Force/Employment Status   81

8.1 Multinomial Logit Coefficients of Employment, Unemployment, and NILF States Native Born and Foreign Born Adult Men, All Races   85

8.2 Estimated Probabilities for Changes in Explanatory Variables   88

8.3 Differentials in Estimated Probabilities for Changes in Explanatory Variables Native Born and Foreign Born Adult Men, All Races   90

8.4 Multinomial Logit Coefficients and Probabilities of Labor Force States, Foreign Born and Years Since Migration Variables   101

8.5 Multinomial Logit Estimates of Employment, Unemployment, and NILF States Pooled Sample of Native Born and Foreign Born Adult Men, by Racial Group   111

8.6   Estimated Probabilities for Changes in Explanatory
      Variables—by Racial Group   117
9.1   Multinomial Logit Coefficients of Unemployment
      States Native Born and Foreign Born Adult Men, All
      Races   127
9.2   Estimated Probabilities for Changes in Explanatory
      Variables Native Born and Foreign Born Adult Men,
      All Races   130
9.3   Multinomial Logit Coefficients, and Probabilities, of
      Unemployment States Foreign Born and Years Since
      Migration   137
9.4   Estimated Total Probabilities of Unemployment, Table
      9.4 Applied to Unemployment in Table 8.4 Pooled and
      Foreign Born Samples of Adult Men, All Races   142
9.5   Estimated Percentage Differentials in Total
      Probabilities in Table 9.4, Pooled and Foreign Born
      Samples of Adult Men, All Races   144
9.6   Estimated Percentage Differentials in Total
      Probabilities in Table 9.2 Pooled and Foreign Born
      Samples of Adult Men, All Races   146
10.1 Regression Analysis of Weeks Unemployed, Weeks
      Ratio, and Ln Weeks Basic Model, Native Born and
      Foreign Born Adult Men   155
10.2 Regression Analysis of Ln Weeks Unemployed, Pooled
      and Foreign Born Samples of Adult Men   157
10.3 Regression Analysis of Ln Weeks Unemployed, Pooled
      Samples of Adult Men, by Racial Group   161
10.4 Regression Analysis of Ln Weeks Unemployed, Pooled
      Samples of Adult Men, by Category of Unemployment   164
10.5 Regression Analysis of Ln Weeks Unemployed,
      Duration Variables Only Shown, Pooled Samples of
      Adult Men, by Racial Group and by Unemployment
      Category   169
11.1 Percent Differentials in Unemployment Probabilities
      Adjusted for Percent Differentials in Unemp. Duration   178

Acknowledgments

This book is essentially a revision of my doctoral dissertation, which was completed in May, 1997. The most important factors contributing to this book were my committee members, who were invaluable for their helpful suggestions and comments. I'd like to thank: Richard E. Barrett for his unique sociological perspectives and expertise with U.S. Census data; Carmella U. Chiswick for her initial guidance and her instruction on proper research design; and Houston H. Stokes for teaching me the econometric skills I needed for the analysis. I'd especially like to thank Evelyn L. Lehrer for her careful reading of earlier drafts, and for holding my feet to the fire on many important technical points.

This book would not have been possible without the suggestions of Barry R. Chiswick, as well as his insightful comments on the various drafts. Beyond that, however, I owe Dr. Chiswick a world of gratitude for the knowledge I have gained in working with him over the past few years. His support, guidance, and mentoring were critical for my completion of the book.

I appreciate the support of the graduate college for helping me present my early results at various conferences and the UIC Scholarship Association for the various invaluable awards and financial support I received through the years, which made it possible for me to do my research.

I'd like to thank Professor Ann Merle Feldman for her proofreading efforts and other writing advice, as well as her patience, support, and friendship. I'd like to thank my family for all of their support and encouragement. I especially appreciate my mother waiting patiently so long for her son to become a doctor. And I want to acknowledge the sacrifices made by my two lovely daughters, Taprine and Briana, in putting up with me through the whole process.

Although this book benefited from contributions from many quarters, any errors of omission or commission in gathering the data or analyzing the results are strictly my own.

The Assimilation of
Immigrants in the
U.S. Labor Market

CHAPTER 1
Introduction

The immigration of foreign-born persons into the United States has become a topic of increasing interest since passage of the Immigration Act in 1965, and has taken on an almost urgent tone since the passage of California's Proposition 187 in 1994. Proposition 187 and subsequent provisions in the welfare reform bill passed by the U.S. Congress in 1996 prohibit non-emergency public benefits to illegal immigrants, and will have an important impact on legal immigrants as well. Proposed legislation in the U.S Congress would further cut public assistance to many legal immigrants.

One of the public's concerns about immigrants is their economic adjustment process after they arrive in the United States. One hypothesis argues that immigrants arrive with disadvantages relative to the native-born population but acquire skills over time and eventually converge in earnings and other labor market outcomes to the levels of the native born, even surpassing the native born in many cases. An alternative viewpoint argues that the skills of immigrants have been decreasing in recent decades, which will lead to slower and less complete assimilation.

This book focuses on the labor market processes and outcomes of foreign-born persons in the United States, such as unemployment, quit rates, job finding rates, and rates of leaving the labor force. One of the major implications of the assimilation hypothesis is that immigrants acquire skill by experiencing many employers—thus the labor market experience of recently migrated foreign-born persons is hypothesized to be characterized by many short spells of unemployment. This model is compatible with frictional, or turnover, models of unemployment. An alternative, "lack of jobs" model argues that most unemployment is concentrated in relatively few individuals with long spells. The higher rate of unemployment and fewer weeks worked for foreign-born persons compared to native-born persons could be compatible with either the turnover or lack of jobs models. A third model could also explain higher rates of unemployment and lower weeks worked for recent migrants—higher unemployment may be the result of a large pool entering the U.S. labor force for the first time prior to obtaining employment, and lower weeks worked could be the result of higher rates for recent immigrants of being out of the labor force.

Reconciling these differences is a primary goal of this book. The theoretical foundation is a combination of immigration hypotheses and theories of labor turnover, prime among which are search models. The database is a pooled cross-section time series assembled from various supplements to the Current Population Survey plus the 1976 Survey of Income and Education. Tests are run on various determinants of relative differences in quit rates, layoff rates, job finding rates, and entry and exit from the labor force. Key among the explanatory variables is the duration of time in the U.S. of foreign-born men, as well as a series of socio-economic and demographic variables.

Chapter 1 provides the framework for the book—Section 1.1 provides the background on immigration issues, while Section 1.2 provides further detail about the issues. Chapter 2 introduces immigration theory. Chapter 3 introduces a few of the key models of labor turnover. Chapter 4 reviews the empirical evidence of the models developed in Chapters 2 and 3. Chapter 5 combines the theoretical models of Chapters 2 and 3 into testable hypotheses. Chapter 6 describes the data sources and limitations. Chapter 7 develops the estimating equations and the methodology, and defines the explanatory variables. Chapters 8 - 11 provide the empirical analysis. Chapter 12 summarizes and discusses the results.

1.1   BACKGROUND

Immigration has been an important public policy issue since before the passage of the Alien and Sedition Act of 1789, although its importance peaked and ebbed periodically through the 18th and 19th centuries. Between 1875 and 1965 immigration policy was based on the exclusion of "undesirables," defined primarily by country of origin (Cafferty, 1984). Much of the debate on immigration has been fomented by "waves" of mass immigration: 1830s-1860s, 1860s-1880s,

1880s-1890s, 1901-1914 (Briggs, 1992). Exclusionary legislation in the 1920s and during the Great Depression drastically reduced immigration until the 1960s, although mass migration of U.S. blacks from southern rural areas to the north has been considered as another great "wave" (Muller, 1985).

There are four main reasons that the immigrant issue has grown in importance recently. The first is an increase in the flow of legal immigration and in the stock of legal immigrants. Inflows of immigrants began to increase after World War II, accelerated in the mid 1960s and again in the late 1970s; in 1992 over 800,000 immigrants were legally admitted for permanent resident status into the United States, not counting those legalized under the Immigration Reform and Control Act (IRCA) of 1986 (Fix and Passel, 1994). In 1990 the U.S. Census counted almost 20 million foreign-born residents, the highest in absolute numbers in U.S. history. About 40% of current U.S. population growth can be attributed to persons born outside the United States.

Second, the number of aliens who reside in the United States illegally—without documentation—has mushroomed in recent decades. The Immigration and Naturalization Service (INS) apprehended about 1.2 million illegal aliens in 1991, compared to about 89,000 in 1961 (Briggs, 1992). Estimates of the growth of the illegal alien population are about 200,000-300,000 per year in the 1990s with about 3 million residing in the United States in 1992 (Bean, 1990; Warren, 1993).

Third, in recent decades there has been a change in the composition of the flow of foreign-born persons into the United States. Until the 1960s over two thirds of immigrants came from Europe or Canada; during the 1980s only 13% of immigrants were from Europe or Canada, with the bulk of the difference being large increases from developing countries, primarily Latin America (mostly Mexico) and Asia. Of the top ten countries sending legal immigrants in 1960, only Mexico was in the top ten in 1990 (Fix and Passel, 1994). The change in origin, plus the higher fertility rate of some foreign-born groups has had a dramatic impact on the racial/ethnic composition of the U.S. population and the racial distribution of the minority population (Passel and Edmonston, 1994, Clark 1996a). This causes concerns to some about the dilution of "American" culture, language, and values (Cornelius, 1982; Bean, Cushing, Haynes, and Van Hook, 1997). An important part of the recent debate has focused on recent declines in immigrant "quality," as measured by education, language, skills, or earnings, with implications for increased poverty and inequality, and lower degrees of assimilation (Borjas, 1994, 1985; Chiswick, 1986).

Fourth, the increased mass immigration of low-skilled workers is expected to have increasing impact because of changes in the U.S. economy over the past few decades. The economic structure in the United States (as well as most of developed economies) today is far more service and knowledge oriented, with a greater reliance on advanced technology. High skilled labor is in demand, while relatively the demand for low-skilled labor has been declining (Briggs, 1992). Thus some expect that the capacity of the economy to "absorb" increases in low-skilled labor will diminish in the future, depressing the wages of native-born low-skilled workers, increasing their unemployment rates, or increasing wage inequality. Many analyses have refuted or found support for this hypothesis in the U.S. and other countries, and the research continues (Topel, 1997; Pischke and Velling, 1997; Dorantes and Huang, 1997; Camarota, 1997; Clark and Schultz, 1997). It is notable that, in contrast to fears of low-skilled immigrant displacement effects, in March 1998 the United States Senate Judiciary Committee nearly doubled (from 65,000 to 115,000) the number of H1-B visas, which allow highly skilled foreigners to work in the U.S. for up to six years.

Large increases in foreign-born flows can be of major concern for population control, crime prevention, environmental protection, and other social issues. Massive inflows can strain public services and budgets, cause congestion on highways and other public places, and overburden institutions such as schools and hospitals. Growth in illegal immigration and the percentage not speaking English, as well as a growing tendency for immigrants to cluster in enclaves, increases social tensions and resentments among some segments of the native population. Higher proportions of immigrants with low skills may cause increases in transfer payments, particularly SSI (Bean, Van Hook, and Glick, 1997).

On the other hand, most analysts will acknowledge that overall immigrants have been a positive force for the United States throughout its history. As a "nation of immigrants," we have developed a rich ethnic and cultural diversity. Historically immigrants have been self-selected as the "best and brightest" of their origin countries, and have usually been very successful economically (Chiswick, 1979). In addition, they have contributed greatly to U.S. economic growth and prosperity, in terms of aggregate income (Council of Economic

Advisors, 1986), returns to capital (Chiswick, 1982b), the capital-labor ratio (Vedder, Galloway, and Moore, 1990), and employment growth (Enchautegui, 1997).

Both sides of the immigration debate have ardent supporters, and the debate is often heated. An example is a recent book by Vernon Briggs of Cornell University and Stephen Moore of the Cato Institute (Briggs and Moore, 1994). Briggs calls for an extensive restructuring of immigration policy, to both reduce the absolute numbers of immigrants and to substantially reduce the number of low-skilled immigrants, focusing on the recent changing composition of immigrants and the changes in the U.S. economic structure. Moore, on the other hand, calls for a liberalization of immigration policy, an increase in immigration even of low-skilled workers. He downplays the impacts of immigrants on low-skilled, native-born workers, focusing instead on the positive net impacts to the U.S. economy. This book illustrates how the issue of immigration can become polarized, and often the same set of data can be used to bolster the arguments of either side. Interestingly both Briggs and Moore were presenters at a conference of the Association for Public Policy and Management in 1994, and both publicly opposed California's Proposition 187.

1.2   ISSUES OF IMMIGRATION

For the purpose of this book, issues of immigration can be classified into economic and noneconomic. One useful description of noneconomic impacts is that used by Fix and Passel (1994). They define four broad noneconomic goals of U.S. immigration policy: 1) social—unifying U.S. citizens and legal residents with their families; 2) cultural—promoting ethnic diversity; 3) moral—promoting human rights; 4) national and economic security—controlling illegal immigration. Fix and Passel state that "The current debate tends to focus on the economic outcomes and neglect the social, cultural and moral goals. Thus, many critiques of immigration policies ignore the intent of their framers." (page 13)

Each of these "noneconomic" goals has economic implications, however. Increased immigration because of family unification, as opposed to skill-based immigration, reduces the proportion of immigrants who are producers, and increases demands on social services and institutions, particularly schools (Chiswick, 1986b). Promoting diversity can increase the proportion of immigrants with less labor market-transferable skills and less English-language fluency, reducing the overall effect of immigrant assimilation (Cafferty, 1984). A similar effect results from protecting human rights, which partially results in increasing the number of noneconomic political refugees, who have been shown to have more divergence from native-born workers in many aspects (Chiswick, 1979).

The economic issues can be classified as (labor) market and nonmarket issues. Nonmarket issues include such factors as social transfers (welfare, unemployment compensation), taxes, crime, and consumption of social services (schools, hospitals, roads). There are two important aspects of nonmarket issues. Social transfers to natives are an important distributional tool to alleviate the negative impacts of immigration on some groups of native-born workers. On the other hand, social transfers to immigrants can reduce the positive benefits of increased aggregate income for natives. It is conceivable that such transfers caused by immigration, for natives and immigrants combined, can exceed the benefits.

Market issues can be further classified into three concerns: the effects of immigrants on the wages and employment of certain groups of native-born workers; the effects of immigrants on the aggregate income and social welfare of the native population; and the experience of immigrants in the labor market, particularly their degree of assimilation. The degree of assimilation has important implications for the long-term distribution of income in the U.S., and for the presumptions of U.S. citizens that immigrants may send substantial U.S.-earned wealth to foreign countries (Cafferty, 1984). The effect of immigrants on native income and wealth has important implications for the long-term growth and prosperity of the United States and is a critical argument for proponents of increased immigration (Vedder, Galloway, and Moore, 1990). Finally, the effect of immigrants on the wages and employment of natives is probably the most heatedly-debated of the immigration issues. Even if the aggregate impact is positive overall and incomes of skilled natives increase, if a large influx of low-skilled immigrants depresses the wages or increases unemployment of low-skilled native-born workers, inequality of income will increase, influencing the debate about income transfers; since the United States is apparently reassessing its policies regarding such transfers, this issue becomes even more pertinent today.

1.3 FOCUS OF THE BOOK

All of the above issues are important in the immigration debate, and each would benefit from continued study. This book will focus entirely on the experiences of immigrants and their assimilation into the labor market. Particularly, the key interest is in the degree of labor turnover of immigrants, the components and causes of such turnover, and how it impacts their ability or speed of assimilation.

CHAPTER 2

Theories of Immigration and Assimilation

This chapter will outline the basic theoretical models of immigration that underlie the analysis of this book. The models presented in this chapter are well established in the literature although some of the exposition here may be somewhat unique. Some modifications will be made later when defining the methodology used in this book. This chapter focuses primarily upon one main issue of immigration: the labor market adjustments made by the foreign born in the destination and their earnings and unemployment experiences over time. In the process some related concepts will be discussed, such as the determinants of immigration and the endogenous effects of native worker internal migration.

2.1 THE DECISION TO MIGRATE TO A FOREIGN COUNTRY

Before adressing any of the above issues, the most basic questions must be asked: why do people migrate between countries, and what factors increase or decrease the incentives to migrate? The answers to these questions have a direct bearing on the other issues addressed in this book.

A simple economic migration model defines a person's decision to migrate as a function of the expected difference in wages between the origin and the destination and the expected costs of the migration. Following Chiswick (1978), define W_o as expected wages in the origin, and W_d as expected wages in the destination. Let C_D represent direct costs, such as transportation costs, visas and fees, and psychic costs of moving to an unfamiliar area; let C_O represent opportunity cost, primarily foregone wages during the migration period and before finding employment in the destination. Then we can define person l's return, r_l, to migration as:

$$r_l = \frac{W_{d,l} - W_{o,l}}{C_{O,l} + C_{D,l}}$$

2.1

Clearly the greater the difference in wages between the origin and the destination, or the lower the direct or opportunity costs, the greater the return to migration.

An important use of the above model is explaining the favorable self-selection of immigrants, which is well established in the literature as a major reason for the foreign born having higher income than the native born after being in the destination country for a period of time. There are two main types of self-selection. Immigrants may be self-selected on the basis of skills, such as education. Another hypothesis says that for the same education, age, language skills, and other demographic variables, immigrants will have a higher level of innate ability (intelligence, ability to learn, allocative skills) and motivation to work and make investments in the labor market. A parallel type of self-selection that receives less attention is that those with higher ability have higher incomes in the origin, increasing their wealth, thus lowering the direct costs (C_D) of migration.

Even if we hold direct costs constant, however, the above model can still be used to show that the returns to migration are greater for those with greater skills or ability. The critical factor is the ratio of direct costs to opportunity costs. The lower the ratio, the greater is the incentive to migrate for higher ability persons relative to lower ability persons. Again following Chiswick (1978), let the subscript h represent persons with high skill or ability, l persons with low skill or ability. Equation 2.1 defines the return to migration for person l. Suppose greater ability results in higher incomes for person h by an amount k, so that $W_{o,h} = (1 + k) W_{o,l}$; then the return to migration for h can be defined as:

$$r_h = \frac{(1+k)W_{d,l} - (1+k)W_{o,l}}{(1+k)C_{O,l} + C_{D,l}},$$

2.2

which reduces to:

$$r_h = \frac{W_{d,I} - W_{o,I}}{C_{O,I} + \frac{C_{D,I}}{(1+k)}}$$

2.3

Clearly, the return to migration for persons of higher ability, rh is greater than for persons of lower ability, r_l, ceteris paribus. Immigrants, then, should theoretically come from the upper tail of the skill and ability distribution, which is the self-selection hypothesis, discussed further below.

However, it is not consistently true that workers will always migrate from low-income to high-income areas, or that high skilled workers migrate and low skilled workers do not, and this inconsistency is not explained by the above model. Part of this is an information problem. If origin wages decline, workers know about it, but they may not know if wages are the same or higher in a destination area. Workers decide to migrate on the basis of expected wages, not differences in average wages. In addition, a reduction in wages in the origin reduces not only income but also wealth; the wealth effect reduces resources, saved or borrowed, that are available for migration purposes, thus increasing direct costs.

A general equilibrium model developed by Oded Galor (1986) proposes that immigrants will flow from high time-preference (low wage) countries to low time-preference (high wage) countries if there is underinvestment in capital in both countries; if there is overinvestment, the flow could go the other way. Also, if preferences are heterogeneous, it is the high time-preference persons who will tend to migrate from a high time-preference country.

An alternative form of the self-selection hypothesis, Roy's Sectoral Model, is described in the general framework of an occupational sector assignment model by Sattinger (1993), and reevaluated from the standpoint of immigration self-selection by Borjas (1987;1994). The key variables are ρ, which is the correlation between skills in the origin and host country (or between the log of worker outputs for Sattinger), and $\sigma 1$ and $\sigma 0$, which are the variance in the log of wages in the destination and origin areas respectively. While Sattinger and Borjas differ in the detail of the explanations, they both conclude that immigrants can be negatively or positively self-selected depending upon the strength of the correlation in skills between the areas and the dispersion in incomes in each country. Specifically, if the correlation in skills is sufficiently high, immigrants will be positively self-selected (the more skilled workers will migrate) if the dispersion in wages is higher in the destination than in the origin, and will be negatively self-selected (less skilled workers migrate) if the dispersion in wages is higher in the origin.

This model would predict that more highly skilled workers would migrate from countries such as Sweden with socialized wage structures, and that low skilled workers would come from countries such as Mexico, where the wage dispersion is much higher than the U.S. If the correlation in skills is low, Borjas predicts a "refugee sorting" model where high skilled workers with low incomes in the origin will have high incomes in the destination; Sattinger predicts simply that if the correlation is negative, migration will be very low.

An important consideration in the decision to migrate is whether the pull factor (increased wages in the destination) or the push factor (decreased wages in the origin) is strongest. In the above model, an increase in Wd should have no effect on costs, resulting in an unequivocal increase in returns to migration. If, instead, W_o decreased by the same amount, and if there were no effect on costs, we would have the same increase in returns. However, the effect is ambiguous in this case, because opportunity costs may be higher or lower, and direct costs will probably be higher. First we can think of opportunity costs as an increasing function of wages in the origin or a decreasing function of unemployment rates in the origin ($C_o = p_1 W_o - p_2 U_o$). The higher the fractions, p_1 or p_2, the greater the effect a change in wages or unemployment rates in the origin will have on costs. A decrease in W_o, or an increase in U_o will reduce the denominator in the above model, increasing the returns to migration, and ceteris paribus, the "push" will be stronger than the "pull" for persons with higher levels of p_1 or p_2 respectively. Thus, persons who are more likely to be employed have a greater reduction in C_o with a reduction in W_o. This would increase the return to migration resulting from the push factor to a greater extent for persons who are more likely to be employed. Offsetting the smaller opportunity costs, however, is the wealth effect, which will reduce the returns to migration. So while the pull is unambiguously positive, the push could be positive or negative, increasing the likelihood that the pull factor will be stronger than the push factor.

Age and education are also important determinants in the push scenario. It has been shown (Sjaastad, 1962; Schwartz, 1976) that migration diminishes with age. Sjaastad shows a substantial reduction in net outmigration from rural areas in the upper Midwest U.S. after age 20. Schwartz shows that the rate of migration diminishes with age at a rate that increases with education. Schwartz cites one important reason for this result as the increase in transportation costs with age, i.e. an increase in C_D. Education may also become less transferable across regions with increasing age. In addition, age (to a point) and education both tend to reduce the probability of being unemployed (a smaller p_2 in the previous paragraph). These above effects could together partly explain the increase in low skilled, less educated, and younger immigrants from Mexico and other Latin American countries. This effect could have important implications for public policy.

Other factors that influence the decision to migrate between two countries are examined by Greenwood and McDowell (1982). Besides the factors considered above—age, wage differentials, and education – other important factors include distance (a proxy for direct money and nonmoney costs) and population size in the destination country (which affects labor market opportunities). Other factors include occupational distributions in the two countries, the relative proportions of males of working age in the two countries, the dominant languages in the two countries, and the hemispheres of the origin and destination countries.

2.2 ASSIMILATION AND SELF-SELECTION HYPOTHESES

Immigrants often arrive at a destination with distinct disadvantages in human capital specific to the destination labor market. Probably the most important is lack of fluency in the dominant language of the destination country. Also important are labor market skills and human capital specific to the destination, such as job search techniques and information, knowledge of rules and regulations, and occupational licenses. In addition, while many immigrants are highly educated, such education is often general in nature; in other words, immigrants often lack firm-specific, or even occupation-specific training. Thus the occupation or earnings position of foreign-born persons is often much lower than that of similar native-born persons upon arrival in the destination. This is a well accepted part of immigrant theory (Chiswick, 1979).

The experience of immigrants after arrival, how well they adjust to the social and economic conditions of the host country, is less certain. Earlier theories held that immigrants would continue to be at a disadvantage throughout their lives in the destination country, and relative economic status would improve for successive generations, converging to the native average after two or three generations following immigration (Carliner, 1980).

While this trend may have been observed frequently in the early immigrant waves, three significant contradictions were observed after World War II. First, improvement in earnings across generations tended to peak with the second generation, the children of immigrants (Nam, 1959; Chiswick, 1977), exceeding the earnings of later generations for many groups of immigrants. Second, earnings of immigrants rose rapidly with duration in the destination, more rapidly than the earnings of the native born (Chiswick, 1978; 1979). Third, after a period of time in the destination, earnings of immigrants often exceeded the earnings of the native born for many groups.

Chiswick (1978) proposed two hypotheses to explain these three observations. The rapid rise in earnings with duration is addressed by the assimilation hypothesis. Over time, human capital differences between native-born workers and immigrants narrow as the immigrants learn the dominant language, become educated about the labor market, and acquire local education, firm-specific training, and seniority. Their earnings will increase at a faster rate than the native born because they start from a lower base and are investing in and acquiring human capital at a faster rate. In addition, because many are positively self-selected, as explained below, their ability to acquire new skills may be greater than that of natives on average. Thus, the assimilation of immigrants into the native society and labor market accounts for much of the rapid increases in wages and occupational attainment.

Such assimilation and its results are not uniform across groups, however. The motivation for immigration and the transferability of initial skills are two important differences between groups. If an immigrant has skills in the origin country that are easily transferred to the destination, such as in medicine or bricklaying, as opposed to skills that are specific to the origin, such as in law or certain crafts, then the absorption into the destination economy will be more rapid. Immigrants that are motivated to migrate because of economic reasons are generally more skilled and their skills are more readily transferable than immigrants who come for non-economic reasons, such as political refugees or tied movers. Political migrants or tied movers probably did not plan to migrate and therefore made fewer preparatory investments in destination-specific human capital.

Immigrants from countries such as Canada and from Western Europe will generally fall under the economic/high transferability category; a physicist from the U.S.S.R. might be a non-economic/high transferability immigrant; immigrants from Mexico are often economic with low transferable skills, while those from Laos might be refugees with low transferable skills. These differences are illustrated in Figure 2.1, which shows the earnings profiles over time of various groups of immigrants relative to the earnings of immigrants (Chiswick, 1978).

Figure 2.1
Earnings Profile by Years Since Migration

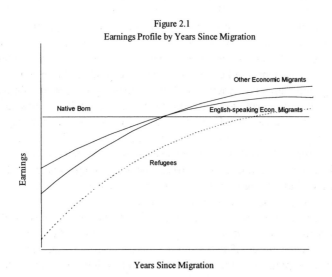

Roy's sectoral model, explained above, categorizes immigrants differently. The prediction for refugees with Roy's model is for a much faster rate of convergence than with the model above. Roy's model would also predict that immigrants with low skills would have a low rate of convergence, while the model above predicts that non-refugee immigrants with less transferable skills will have a faster rate of convergence, but from a lower base.

Studies for the U.S. and Canada show that some long-duration immigrants earn more than the native born, ceteris paribus. These results are not explained by the assimilation hypothesis. The assimilation hypothesis predicts only a steeper slope for immigrants than for native-born workers, but there should be a limit to the faster rate of acquisition of language and labor market capital for immigrants, holding ability constant.

The self-selection hypothesis can explain the crossover in three ways. First, we can think of immigrants as self-selected by any combination of three criteria—skills, for example measured by education; ability, holding skills constant; and motivation. If immigrants are self-selected by education, they have an initial advantage in general training, but a disadvantage in firm-specific or labor market-specific skills. As specific skills are acquired, the advantage in general skills can give them an overall productivity advantage. Education and experience, as well as innate ability, also contribute to allocative efficiency, which can result in a greater acquisition of labor market-specific human capital, a faster rate of learning, and a greater capacity for decision-making—a greater "ability to deal with equilibria" (Schultz, 1975). Finally, even for immigrants with the same level of education and ability as the native born, a greater degree of motivation could cause them to work longer hours, take less time off, and also to reinvest earnings to acquire physical capital at a greater rate than natives. The latter might explain why immigrants have a higher rate of self-employment in the service and trade industries (non-professional, non-farm).

Assimilation causes a faster rate of growth in earnings; self-selection then can result in earnings moving beyond convergence to actually exceed those of native-born workers. But self-selection can also partly explain why the first generation of children of immigrants often earn more than the children of native-born workers, ceteris paribus. First, many of the same advantages in motivation, allocative efficiency, and general skills may be passed on to the children of immigrants, who will also suffer less of a human capital disadvantage than their parents from migration. Second, children are a time-intensive good, and the quality/quantity tradeoff hypothesis says that parents motivated to achieve success in the labor market will have fewer children, allowing more resources to be devoted to each child (Becker, 1982). Some of the most successful groups of immigrants in the United

States have been shown to have smaller families than less successful groups (Chiswick, 1988).

2.3   THE COHORT QUALITY HYPOTHESIS

Finally, an alternative explanation of the rapid convergence of wages is the "cohort quality" hypothesis (Borjas, 1985, 1994). Chiswick (1980) pointed out that the use of cross-section data to illustrate trends over time could be somewhat misleading. Borjas contends that the use of decennial census data overestimates wage convergence. As Borjas explains, if natives and immigrants actually had the same rate of increase over time within the same cohorts, but the quality of the immigrant (and not native) cohorts decreased over time, a cross-section analysis would appear to show a higher rate of increase in immigrant wages than actually existed. This can be seen in Figure 2.2, taken from Borjas (1994).

Figure 2.2.

Cross-Section Age-Earnings Profile of Immigrants

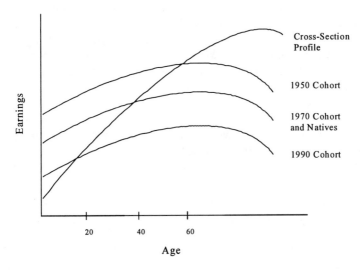

Each cohort of immigrants in Figure 2.2 has the same age-earnings profile, which is also the same, in slope, as that of native born workers, with the 1970 cohort drawn to coincide with the native profile. Each succeeding cohort in this model arrives in the destination with lower "quality"—less human capital specific to the labor market. A cohort might have a lower quality because of a decline of the economy in the origin, or many other reasons. A cross-section profile measures each cohort at the same time, but the relative positions of separate cohorts appear as the progress of individual cohorts over time. With the assumption of declining quality over time a cross-section will overestimate the slope of the earnings profiles of individual cohorts. It is an empirical quesion whether there has been a decline in quality and how much overestimation there is in the cross-section profile.

The description thus far of theories of immigration have considered only the effects of assimilation, self-selection, and cohort quality on earnings. There are also important differences between the native born and foreign born in their experiences with employment and unemployment. Much of the pattern of unemployment for immigrants is hypothesized, with some empirical support, to follow that of earnings, except with opposite signs—higher levels of unemployment for recent immigrants, converging over time asymptotically to the levels of natives. It is the dynamics of this process that is the interest of this book. Specifically, immigrants are hypothesized to have higher unemployment during the early years in the destination country because of higher turnover—more frequent quits and greater susceptibility to layoffs, much of which is due to low market-specific and firm-specific skills and the adjustments made to acquire such skills. This will be explained more fully in Chapter 4 below. First, however, theories of labor turnover will be breiefly reviewed to add to the theoretical background of assimilation.

CHAPTER 3

Models of Labor Turnover and Unemployment

In a perfectly competitive market, with perfect information, free mobility of factors of production, flexible prices, and no barriers to trade, a Walrasian equilibrium is characterized by a clearing of all markets for desirable goods. Since unemployment is typically defined in labor economics literature as the lack of market employment for persons desiring to work, Walrasian equilibrium by definition precludes unemployment. Yet the existence and persistence of unemployment is irrefutable.

Early explanations of unemployment focused on the effects of minimum wages or labor unions. These are unlikely to be major causes of unemployment—minimum wages affect a small portion of the labor force, and the large size of nonunionized sectors (the majority of U.S. workers) limits the effects of unions. Other early explanations emphasized the impact of rigid wages, which implies market disequilibria. More recent considerations drop one or more of the assumptions leading to market clearing, such as perfect information, or instantaneous matching. This section will describe some of the models that can help to explain the unemployment experience of immigrants. This book focuses primarily on search models, including key approaches such as reservation wages and variations such as job matching and signaling. Other models with applications to immigrant experiences attempt to explain employer behavior. The employer behavior models considered here are implicit contract models, insider/outsider models, and efficiency wage models.

3.1   ISSUES OF MEASUREMENT—STOCKS AND FLOWS

Before the theories are discussed, some basic definitions and key concepts will be established. Most of this is standard labor economics and can be found in any labor economics textbook, such as Ehrenberg and Smith (1994). Definitions provided here about the labor force and unemployment are standard ones used by the U.S. government.

The labor force at time t (L_t) is defined as all persons age 16 and over who are either employed, actively seeking employment, or awaiting recall from a layoff—they are either working or able, available, and willing to work. Those members of the labor force not employed at time t are considered unemployed (U_t). Persons who are not working but are not looking for work or are unable to accept employment are considered out of the labor force. The unemployment rate (u_t) is the fraction of the labor force that is unemployed, $u_t = U_t / L_t$. The equilibrium unemployment rate is defined as not changing over time ($\Delta u = 0$ or $u_t = u_{t-1}$), which can occur from no changes in unemployment or from the labor force growing at the same rate as unemployment.

This book defines the following categories, based on flows into or out of the state of unemployment. Flows into unemployment at time t can occur from employed workers who quit a job (Q_t) or are separated from either layoffs or discharges (D_t), or from new entrants or reentrants to the labor force (UNE_t) who have not yet found work. Flows out of unemployment come from unemployed persons who find work (F_t) by being newly hired or recalled by an employer, or from unemployed persons who retire or otherwise drop out of the labor force (UR_t). Flows into the labor force are determined by the number of new entrants and reentrants who are unemployed (UNE_t) plus those who begin working immediately (ENE_t). Flows out of the labor force are determined by the number of "retirements" from employment (ER_t) out of the labor force, including those who lose a job, and retirements out of unemployment (UR_t).

Equilibrium unemployment can be derived from the following equations. First, it can be shown (Davidson, 1990) that for small time periods the rate of growth of the unemployment rate is approximately equal to the difference between the rate of growth of unemployment and the rate of growth of the labor force:

$$\Delta u/u = \Delta U/U - \Delta L/L. \qquad \textbf{3.1}$$

Next, at any point in time, the labor force can be represented as the labor force in the previous period plus new entrants and reentrants in the current period minus "retirees" in the previous period:

$$L_t = L_{t-1} + UNE_t + ENE_t - UR_{t-1} - ER_{t-1}. \qquad 3.2$$

Finally, at any point in time unemployment can be represented by unemployment in the previous period plus new entrants and reentrants into unemployment this period, plus quits and separations in the previous period, minus "retirees" from unemployment and those who move into employment from unemployment in the previous period:

$$U_t = U_{t-1} + UNE_t + Q_{t-1} + D_{t-1} - UR_{t-1} - F_{t-1}. \qquad 3.3$$

Now to simplify, we can express each of these terms as fractions of either the labor force or of unemployment. Let r represent the proportions of the labor force that "retire" or leave the labor force from unemployment or from employment: $UR_{t-1} = r_u[U_{t-1}]$ and $ER_{t-1} = r_e[L_{t-1} - U_{t-1}]$. Similarly, let b stand for "births", the proportions of the labor force that are new entrants or reentrants into either unemployment or employment: $UNE_t = b_u[L_{t-1}]$ and $ENE_t = b_e[L_{t-1}]$. Let q and d stand for the proportions of the employed labor force that either quit or are discharged, respectively: $Q_{t-1} = q[L_{t-1} - U_{t-1}]$ and $D_{t-1} = d[L_{t-1} - U_{t-1}]$. Finally, let e represent the proportion of the unemployed labor force that finds employment: $F_{t-1} = e[U_{t-1}]$.

As a major simplification, Davidson (1990) sets $r_e = r_u$, and $b_e = b_u$, assuming labor force exit rates to be independent of a worker's employment status and assuming all entry to be into unemployment. With these simplifications, if we substitute these proportions into equations 3.2 and 3.3, then substitute into equation 3.1 and set Δu equal to zero and solve, we get an expression for equilibrium unemployment:

$$u^* = \frac{b + q + d}{b + q + d + e}. \qquad 3.4$$

Equation 3.4 expresses the equilibrium unemployment rate as a function of various flow rates into or out of the state of employment or into the labor force; flows into the labor force (b) increase unemployment, but flows out (r) have no effect in Davidson's formulation. A simpler model (Karras, 1994; McCafferty, 1990), derived with a differential equation process, and holding constant flows into the labor force as well, is:

$$u^* = \frac{q+d}{q+d+e} \cdot \qquad\qquad 3.5$$

McCafferty notes that the equilibrium unemployment rates experienced since World War II have been generally higher than equation 3.5 would predict, and references the argument of Clark and Summers (outlined below) as an explanation. However, if we include entry into the labor force as in equation 3.4, the increases in the labor force due to the baby boom generation coming of age and the increase in female labor force participation can explain part of the difference.

For the purposes of this book, assumptions that rates of flows out of the labor force are equal whether from employment or unemployment, or assumptions that entry rates are always into unemployment, are not acceptable. Flows into the labor force will have different origination between the foreign born and the native born: a higher percentage of the native born may enter because of positive economic information, resulting in very short or even non-existent unemployment spells, whereas a high percentage of the foreign born enter because they have just arrived in the United States. Likewise, dropping out of the labor force from employment may be for completely different reasons than from unemployment, where discouraged workers become a problem. Marston (1976) derives a similar definition of unemployment rates as above, although Marston's formula is somewhat more complex:

$$u^* = \frac{1}{\frac{(be + bu)e + beru}{(be + bu)(q + d) + bure}} \cdot \qquad\qquad 3.6$$

Equations 3.4, 3.5, and 3.6, although different in complexity, imply similar relationships between the separate flow rates of unemployment and the unemployment rate. Equation 3.6, however provides a complete view. Some of the relationships are intuitively obvious—increasing the quit rate or separation rates (q and d) will, *ceteris paribus*, increase the equilibrium unemployment rate, as will increases in the proportion of persons entering the labor force prior to employment (b_u), while increasing the rate of job finding (e) or of persons dropping out of the labor force from unemployment (r_u) will reduce the equilibrium unemployment rate. Not as obvious is the result that increases in the rate of persons entering the labor force into employment (be) will reduce the equilibrium unemployment rate, while increases in the rate of persons leaving the labor force out of employment (re) will increase the equilibrium unemployment rate. Both of these last two effects operate through increasing or decreasing the labor force without directly affecting unemployment—increasing or decreasing the denominator in the formula for unemployment rates without affecting the numerator. Equation 3.6 also provides a mathematical representation of relative flow rates, or ratios: equilibrium unemployment increases if the flows into the labor force into unemployment exceed such flows into employment, if flows out of the labor force from employment exceed such flows from unemployment, and if the rate of job separations exceeds the rates of job finding.

The flow rates of equation 3.6 are percentages from an aggregate point of view, but they represent hazard rates from an individual point of view, the per-period probability of a transition from one employment/labor force status into another. The transition probabilities provide information that is hidden in the statistics on unemployment rates. It is important to distinguish the relative effects of incidences of unemployment from the duration of spells of unemployment. For example, if the rate of job finding (e) is low relative to some comparative point, then the unemployment rate would be relatively high, and the higher unemployment rate would derive from greater duration for persons unemployed. If e were relatively high, however, but so were q and s, and if ru were relatively high (unemployed persons drop out of the labor force rapidly), then higher unemployment would derive from entrants into the labor force, but would be accompanied by low duration. These two scenarios suggest different implications for social welfare and public policy.

3.2 CAUSES OF UNEMPLOYMENT—TURNOVER VS. LACK OF JOBS

An important debate in the literature has focused around the issue of duration versus incidence. Conventional wisdom (Feldstein, 1973) has for many years held that most unemployment was of short duration and was a normal part of labor market adjustments (the turnover model). Viewed from one angle, the facts are that in 1990 the average duration of unemployment was 12.1 weeks, and about 78% of the unemployed were unemployed for less than 15 weeks, while about 10% were unemployed more than 27 weeks (Statistical Abstract, 1992). In addition, measures of spells underestimate the unemployment of persons, since many have more than one spell—while the average duration of a spell of unemployment in 1977 was 9.5 weeks, the average duration for persons with single spells was 13.6 weeks, and the average over the whole year for persons with multiple spells was 18 weeks (Akerlof and Main, 1980). Counting all persons and their total duration throughout the year, about 61% were unemployed less than 15 weeks and about 15% were unemployed more than 27 weeks (Blaustein, 1993). These are still relatively short durations, however, and lend support to the turnover hypothesis of unemployment. The turnover model suggests that unemployment is not a serious social issue and is largely voluntary. The public policy in this view is to improve information and mobility to reduce friction, which means that cyclical demand management is unnecessary.

An alternative view, while accepting that most spells of unemployment are of short duration, holds that most unemployment can be accounted for by relatively few persons with long durations, who are unemployed because of a lack of available jobs. Two complications suggest that standard calculations of duration can lead to underestimates. First, almost half of transitions out of unemployment are by persons leaving the labor force, ru (Summers, 1990a). About half of these express that they "want a regular job now." "Indomitable seekers", unemployed persons who do not drop out of the labor force, experienced average durations in 1975 almost twice as long as the average duration for all completed spells. Second, a longer duration of unemployment leads to a greater probability of unemployment during any given month. Thus, at any point in time the population of the unemployed will consist of a significant share who are long-term unemployed. As an example, while half of completed spells of unemployment in 1974 for adult males ended within one month, half of all unemployment for adult males in 1974 was accounted for by men who eventually would be unemployed for 4 months or more. Between 1948 and 1978, the average duration of unemployment for "currently unemployed" persons was between 10 and 30 weeks, about three times the duration for the average spell (Akerlof and Main, 1981). Again, the flows into and out of unemployment and the labor force can tell us more about the true unemployment picture than unemployment rates or average durations.

3.3   TYPES OF UNEMPLOYMENT

Before describing the theoretical models of labor turnover, it is necessary to provide a few more definitions. We define here four types of unemployment. Frictional unemployment can occur when the economy is technically at full employment levels, where labor demand equals labor supply. It arises from the dynamic nature of the labor market in which there are flows into and out of the state of employment, but because of imperfect information (asymmetric between employers and employees) and imperfect mobility of workers (between firms) at prevailing wages, it takes time for employees and employers to become matched. Frictional unemployment is often considered voluntary, since, theoretically, an individual could reduce his or her reservation wage and receive an immediate offer of employment. Frictional unemployment occurs within sectors (occupational, industrial, geographical); frictional imbalances between sectors are usually considered structural. Frictional unemployment will be a major focus of this book, as will be explained in Chapter 4.

Structural unemployment also is derived from imbalances and imperfect information and mobility, and can be thought of as a long-term form of frictional unemployment. Structural unemployment, however, occurs between sectors—if workers were perfectly mobile between occupations, industries, or geographic areas (through the ability to acquire education, for example), and if they had advance notice of impending changes in their current sector, adjustments could be made so that structural unemployment would not exist. Structural unemployment is generally long term in nature, and is often associated with plant closings and mass layoffs.

Cyclical unemployment, often called demand-deficient unemployment, primarily occurs because of fluctuations in business activity and rigid wages. When aggregate demand declines, if wages are inflexible downward demand for labor declines as well. Cyclical unemployment occurs across sectors—if unemployment increased because of deficient demand within a sector, it would be considered structural. This book will test, among other effects, differential impacts of cyclical unemployment between immigrants and native-born workers.

Seasonal unemployment is a form of short-term cyclical unemployment, with the difference that it occurs on a regular basis and can be reasonably anticipated. Seasonal unemployment will be important in this book primarily when considering different degrees of sensitivity to seasonal factors between foreign-born and native-born workers.

3.4   CAUSES OF UNEMPLOYMENT—JOB SEARCH, RIGID WAGES, DISEQUILIBRIA

The causes of the various types of unemployment have been widely debated. Already discussed is whether the causes of unemployment are from many persons experiencing frequent but short spells of unemployment, or from relatively few persons experiencing spells of long duration. Both views have merit and the answer is a matter of emphasis. Another part of the debate about the causes of unemployment focuses more directly on individual behavior of workers and firms. A large number of models have been developed that attempt to explain why there is unemployment at all, why persons will accept unemployment rather than reduced wages, and why dispersion in wages persists. There are several bodies of literature that have sprung up from these attempts, and many summaries, which often differ widely in how the models are grouped together or how they are described. It is beyond the scope of this book to address all models or to describe them in complete detail. Instead, a thumbnail sketch of the most salient features will be provided here, of the models that seem to hold the most promise for addressing immigrant unemployment.

3.5   SEARCH THEORIES

A. Overview

One of the common assumptions about frictional unemployment is that workers choose to remain unemployed for a period of time, often while professing to "want a job now", while searching for the best job match. Job search unemployment can result from either voluntary unemployment (quits) or involuntary unemployment (layoffs or discharges). In a framework suggested by Parsons (1977), the optimal job search depends on the worker's objectives and on the job search environment. The job search environment includes: the distribution of wage offers; the costs of search; the explicit or implicit job duration; the worker's state of knowledge of market conditions; and the terms normally encountered when contracting with employers. If employed, the search environment also includes the ability to search while on the job. The worker's objectives should include non-pecuniary benefits and should account for the worker's degree of risk aversion, but in most studies the wage is considered the sole objective. While Parsons considers duration as an environment variable, it should also be considered as an objective. If the worker is maximizing the utility of lifetime income, the duration of a job (the inverse of the probability of future unemployment) is a critical factor in the job search.

Figure 3.1 Job Search

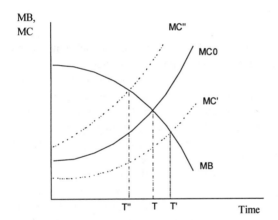

In the most fundamental description of job search, first proposed by Stigler (1962), workers continue searching until the marginal cost of additional search just equals the marginal benefit, as illustrated in Figure 3.1. In Figure 3.1 the marginal cost of search slopes upward because direct costs (travel expenses, agency fees) increase as more difficult search is undertaken, and opportunity costs of foregone earnings increase as search time increases. The marginal benefits of search slope downward because the worker contacts the most promising employers first, so the probability of receiving a better offer than one already received declines with further search. Optimum search time is the amount T. While very simple, this model provides some useful ways to illustrate the effects of public policies. For instance, an increase in unemployment insurance benefits lowers the marginal cost, shifting the curve out to MC'—reservation wages and subsequently search times will theoretically increase (Feldstein, 1973). Similarly, reemployment subsidies paid to unemployed workers who find jobs within a specified period (Woodbury, 1987) , or wage subsidies paid to dislocated workers (Davidson and Woodbury, 1995), increase the value of each wage offer received, increasing the cost of rejecting a wage offer, shifting the marginal cost curve in Figure 3.1 up, reducing the reservation wage and optimal search time.

B. Search strategies

Many of the earlier search models focused on the optimum search technology, primarily from the standpoint of an unemployed worker; the emphasis in these models is on e, the job finding rate, and generally ignore quit behavior. Stigler's model specified the search process as a batch process—workers estimated the optimal amount of search time prior to searching, then contacted N number of employers, accepting the best offer received over the period. This is a suboptimal process, since if the best offer was received first, the maximum benefit would be received by accepting the offer, ending the search process. McCall (1965; 1970) developed the hypothesis of "optimal stopping rules," wherein an unemployed worker searches sequentially, deciding after each job offer whether or not to continue searching. McCall developed more fully the concept of reservation wages, which can be represented in Figure 3.1 if we change the X axis to wages rather than time; marginal cost can be represented as the wage minus unemployment compensation benefits minus the value of leisure (ignoring direct costs of search). The optimal equilibrium level is still where the marginal benefit equals marginal cost, but this modification defines the reservation wage rather than the search endpoint.

Several other papers attempted to describe more realistically the individual search process. Salop (1973) proposed that workers search sequentially by contacting progressively less attractive employers and accepting the first job offer; since the best prospects are contacted first, reservation wages decline with additional search. Benhabib and Bull (1983) and Burdett and Judd (1983} combine the Stigler and McCall model to suggest a series of nonsequential periods that are searched sequentially, which allows for a more optimal process than Stigler's but also allows for the simultaneous consideration of multiple job offers. Gronau (1971) adds a fixed labor force endpoint, which lowers the value of job offers (the importance of duration as a motive), a change that is most valuable as a model of older workers. Mortensen (1970) finds that an employed worker will have a reservation wage higher than the current wage, and that search duration rises with the level of unemployment compensation and falls with higher interest rates.

C. Voluntary Quits

Some search models also address voluntary quit behavior. One model (Mortensen, 1970) suggests that both unemployed workers and employed workers search for jobs, but that unemployed workers have lower reservation wages. This model does not account for quits that lead to unemployment. Alchian (1970) suggests that it is a necessary condition of unemployment that search is more efficient when unemployed while searching. Matilla (1969) presents a model in which a worker maximizes utility by remaining employed while searching when the cost of searching while unemployed exceeds the additional benefit of being able to search more intensely.

Jovanovic (1979) extends Nelson's (1970) work on consumer behavior to the labor market; Nelson proposed a concept of search goods, the qualities of which people have knowledge of a priori, and experience goods which people learn about only with consumption. Jovanovic presents a model of job matching, in which information available to the worker about the qualities of the job, and information available to the employer about the qualities of the worker, are not available prior to the worker being hired by the firm. If the match between worker and job is good, the worker stays employed. If not, the employer terminates the match by lowering the worker's wages inducing him to seek other employment. Although the worker is allowed to search while employed in this model, if the wage has dropped low enough the benefit of a more intense job search while unemployed may outweigh the costs, inducing a quit.

D. Criticisms

Two major lines of criticism have been offered about search theories such as the ones presented above. Summers and Clark (1990a) contend that most unemployment stems from long-term spells. They rightly point out that the search theories described thus far address only short-term frictional unemployment and cannot account for prolonged unemployment. Davidson (1990) emphasizes that the search theories above are "partial-partial equilibrium" approaches, in that they address only the supply side of unemployment and ignore both unemployment due to firm behavior (layoffs, discharges) and the effects of the above worker actions on the behavior of firms.

3.6   RESERVATION WAGES

One branch of search theory proposes that high and/or inflexible reservation wages of individual workers can account for a large portion of unemployment. Central to this theory is that workers reject job offers if they do not meet their reservation wages. Reservation wage hypotheses are still in the class of search theory, but they at least partially meet the objections of Summers and Clark and Davidson. Presumably, if workers maintain constant high reservation wages, then the probability of leaving unemployment may be independent of duration, unless they are close to retirement (low job duration) or liquidity constrained (high search costs). High reservation wages may alter firm behavior; in addition, if workers reject some wage offers and not others, then it is a necessary condition that firms must be offering different wages at equilibrium. Unemployment is driven by the interactions of the distribution of reservation wages and the distribution of wage offers.

Davidson provides a brief history of the reservation wage literature. Essentially, early studies attempted to deal with the dilemma posed by early attempts to "tack on" firm behavior to basic search theory: the early results predicted that all firms would offer the same wage (the monopsony wage) and all offers would be accepted. The attempts to find a solution to this problem generally added heterogeneity in productivity between both firms and workers. The major contributors were Reingenum (1979), Albrecht and Axell (1984), and Burdett and Judd (1983). The details of the studies will not be dealt with here. In brief, the reservation wage models did provide an explanation for the coexistence of unemployment with wage dispersion in equilibrium. On the other hand, Davidson points out that these models tend to be difficult to characterize, are intractable, and seldom lead to clean solutions. The importance of the reservation wage approach will be addressed in Chapter 4 below describing empirical results.

3.7 FIRM-SPECIFIC HUMAN CAPITAL

A well-accepted part of labor market theory, first made prominent by Becker (1975), argues that, unlike general training which is portable and is therefore financed solely by the worker, investment in firm-specific human capital is often borne by both the firm and the worker, since such capital is not easily marketed to other firms. This specification relates turnover to firm-specific human capital in two ways. First, workers are more willing to invest in firm-specific training if the probability of layoff is lower; and firms are more willing to invest in firm-specific training if the probability of a quit is lower. Thus, investment in firm-specific human capital is negatively related to the probability of turnover. Second—the other side of the coin—once the investment is made workers have less incentive to quit, and employers have less incentive to lay off such workers.

The human capital model, as simple as it is, has clear and important ramifications for immigrant labor market adjustment. Upon arrival in the U.S., foreign-born workers will by definition have lower firm-specific human capital, as well as labor-market specific human capital. As explained previously, this results in greater incentives for foreign-born workers to quit their current employer than for native-born workers, and for employers to discharge or lay off foreign-born workers at a higher rate; the human capital model then clearly predicts higher turnover from both sides for newly arrived immigrants. After a period of time in the U.S., more labor market specific and firm specific human capital is acquired, and turnover rates should decline.

3.8 EMPLOYER BEHAVIOR

Search theories, reservation wages, and part of the human capital model focus upon the behavior of workers, which is an attempt to explain voluntary unemployment. Voluntary unemployment, however, accounts for only a small fraction of unemployment—only 10-15% of new unemployment is due to quits, and quit unemployment is of shorter duration than layoff unemployment. In contrast, half of the unemployment rate in 1985 was attributable to job losers (Summers and Clark, 1990a). If involuntary unemployment is considered to be the result of the behavior of employers (a point with some contention, as discussed later), then some attention must be given to the theories of the employer behavior that causes such unemployment.

This section will briefly describe three of the theories of employer behavior: implicit contracts, efficiency wages, and insider-outsider models. All three take as a starting point the human capital model—implicit in each is the assumption that firms wish to maintain stability in their labor force, due to investments made in firm-specific human capital. Each is also an attempt to apply the concept of wage rigidities as explanations of unemployment, an attempt to provide a microeconomic foundation to macroeconomic theories dealing with Keynesian models.

A. Implicit Contracts

Implicit contract models are based on the premise that workers are risk averse while firms are risk neutral. Because of this differential, contracts (explicit or implicit) are possible, in which workers are willing to accept some lower wage in good economic times in trade for a guaranteed wage during bad economic times. Because of their risk aversion, they are thus able to maximize their utility. Employers can accept a greater degree of risk, and can maximize their profits over time.

In early models, implicit contracts were used to explain wage rigidity, and without the ability to adjust wages, adjustments were made through increasing layoffs during economic downturns. However, as Davidson (1990) summarizes, these models have several problems in trying to explain unemployment. If workers are risk averse, they could adjust the terms of the contracts to guarantee employment as well as wages. Further, early models did not account for flexibility in hours of employment. In general, the basic implicit contract models do not explain unemployment well. Attempts to improve the models included adding asymmetric information and enforcement provisions as modifiers.

The importance of implicit contract models to the immigrant adjustment model stems from the risk aversion of workers. Almost by definition, newly arrived foreign-born workers probably have different levels of risk aversion than similar native-born workers. Aside from the obvious implications of their taking the risk to migrate in the first place, the fact that they desire to acquire human capital at a faster rate would make them more apt to quit, but perhaps more averse to layoffs. If this were true, recent immigrants might be more willing to accept wage cuts in economic downturns, and therefore be less desirous of guaranteed-wage contracts, explicit or implicit. Implicit contract theory would then predict a lower layoff rate for recently arrived foreign-born workers.

B. Efficiency Wages

According to efficiency wage models, workers' productivities depend positively, or firms costs negatively, on wages. Workers' productivity may increase with wages because of factors such as improved nutrition, which is most important in underdeveloped countries (Bose, 1997), greater morale, or through greater effort due to a sense of loyalty or gratitude toward the firm (Salop, 1979; Akerlof, 1982; Akerlof, 1984; Yellen, 1984). Firms may also raise wages in order to have a wider pool of applicants during recruitment (Weiss, 1980). Because such "efficiency wages" are above market clearing levels, the hypotheses are consistent with the persistence of involuntary unemployment—even without artificial constraints on wage flexibility; the profit maximizing wage for a firm is independent of labor supply conditions. Chiswick (1986), in fact, shows that surplus labor is a necessary condition for efficiency wages; also necessary, however, are zero economic rent for at least one group of workers and constant marginal costs for at least one sector or quality attribute—greater restrictions than other authors had assumed.

It is not clear how the above views of efficiency wages affect the immigrant model. It would seem that employers who employ large numbers of immigrants would have a wide pool of applicants and would not need to raise wages. Surveys of employer attitudes imply that immigrant workers are considered to be hard workers and are actually preferred by some employers, reducing the incentive to pay efficiency wages to immigrants in order to induce greater effort. The part of efficiency wage theory that is most directly applicable to the immigrant model is the notion that efficiency wages are paid in order to reduce turnover for the most productive workers. Turnover is reduced by either reducing layoffs because the higher cost of a layoff to a worker elicits greater effort (Shapiro, 1984), or by reducing quits

(Salop, 1973). Because the cost of turnover (recruiting, screening, and training) can be high, firms can pay wages higher than market clearing wages. Yet recent immigrants receive little firm-specific training, and wages are lower on average than for other groups. The implication is that efficiency wages are paid to immigrants at a lower rate than to native-born workers, which in turn implies that turnover should be higher for foreign-born workers.

C. Insider/Outsider models (discrimination)

Insider/outsider models assume that wokers can be divided into two separate groups—insiders, those who are currently working at a firm, and outsiders, those who are unemployed and willing to offer their services to the firm. Market power of the insiders, based on situations such as union contracts, concentrations of firm-specific human capital, or threats of intimidation, allows them to exact concessions from the employer, such as higher wages or greater severance pay, which the reduces the employer's ability to hire outsiders. Thus unemployment is higher due to wage rigidity, not for the insiders, but for the outsiders.

Insider/outsider models would appear to bear directly upon the immigrant adjustment experience. Immigrants are, by definition, outsiders when they first arrive in the U.S., and if outsider status is tied to seniority, for some time after that. This would imply higher unemployment rates for recent immigrants, expressed through longer duration of unemployment spells rather than higher quit or layoff rates.

3.9   EFFICIENT TURNOVER

Search models usually focus on worker behavior as an explanation for unemployment, with inflexible or high reservation wages as a prime cause; most unemployment in these models is based on quits, voluntary to the worker but involuntary to the firm. Employer behavior models focus on layoffs as a major cause of unemployment, voluntary to the firm but involuntary to the worker. A more recent model (McLaughlin, 1991) suggests that the distinction between layoffs and quits is overemphasized in the literature and that both determinants of turnover, or separations, are efficient tools for adjusting to changes in relative productivities in workers and firms. In McLaughlin's model, a separation is worker-initiated if the wage that a worker can get at another firm is greater than what his current firm is willing to offer. A separation is employer-initiated if the wage that the worker demands is greater than his productivity in the firm. In a basic model, firms are willing to pay the worker his marginal productivity, but workers and firms are heterogeneous, so a worker may have different productivities at different firms, hence different wage offers. Information about productivities and wage offers is perfect for both workers and firms. In a less restricted model, firms are willing to pay a portion of "match rents" generated from different productivities—in a two-firm case, a firm will pay a percentage (η) of the worker's productivity, plus a percentage ($1-\eta$) of the worker's productivity in a rival firm. McLaughlin contends that his model is an efficient allocation of labor across firms, and leads to the solutions that quits are decreasing in current wages, increasing in outside offers, are procyclical, and result in wage increases, while layoffs have just the opposite of each of these effects. In addition, McLaughlin includes the value of non-market work in the hypothetical model, and defines separations to the non-market sector as layoffs, rather than quits.

Unfortunately, the McLaughlin model does not account for unemployment. Quits and layoffs in this model should always lead directly to employment in another firm, since in the case of quits a worker already has a better offer, and in the case of layoffs the worker refuses to take a pay cut because he knows he can get a higher wage in another firm. However, it would not be difficult to extend this model to allow for search time unemployment. Part of search theory suggests that workers do not know a priori which individual firms will make specific wage offers, but they do know the distribution of wage offers, and thus can assess the probability (ρ) of receiving an outside wage offer of, say W_x. Thus, the expected wage would be $E(W_x) = \rho W_x$. If the worker then demanded $E(W_x)$ from his current employer and was refused because of McLaughlin's rules, a quit would result; the same logic would apply to employer initiated wage cuts leading to layoffs. But if ρ was less than unity, the worker may spend some time unemployed while searching for work. If probabilities are assessed correctly, then this is still efficient by McLaughlin's standards, and we have "efficiency unemployment". One important aspect of McLaughlin's model for this book is that it accounts for efficient turnover when productivities of workers are increasing, a major point of the assimilation hypothesis.

CHAPTER 4
Empirical Evidence in the Literature

The previous chapters provided a brief overview of the basic hypotheses and theoretical models underlying the issues of immigrant labor market adjustment and causes of unemployment. An important feature of these theoretical models is that they do not predict unambiguously the direction or magnitude of the variables in question. Much of the debate has focused, therefore, on testing various hypotheses empirically. This chapter will review the relevant findings of the empirical research that is available in the literature.

4.1 IMMIGRANT LABOR MARKET ADJUSTMENT

The theoretical models of the experiences of immigrants in the destination country are largely developed to help explain the results of empirical analysis and stylized facts. The most basic model explains the facts very well, perhaps because of its derivation from the facts, or perhaps because it is the true model.

As noted above, it is expected that on average immigrant earnings increase at a faster pace than for native-born workers. The two key empirical questions are, how much steeper will the age/earnings profiles of immigrants be than the profiles of natives, and do they merely rise to about the level of the native born or do they cross over? Chiswick (1978) was the first to directly estimate the model shown in Figure 4.1. Using a cross-section analysis of the 1970 U.S. census, Chiswick showed that, overall, immigrant adult men earned about 1% less than similar natives on average; holding constant human capital variables of education and experience and demographic variables such

as location and marital status, there was no significant difference. Upon
arrival, immigrants earned about 16% less than comparable natives, but
their earnings increased at a rate of 1.5% for each year of residence in
the destination, at a declining rate. The regressions also showed that
there was indeed a significant crossover, at about 13 years.

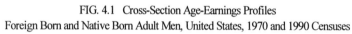

FIG. 4.1   Cross-Section Age-Earnings Profiles
Foreign Born and Native Born Adult Men, United States, 1970 and 1990 Censuses

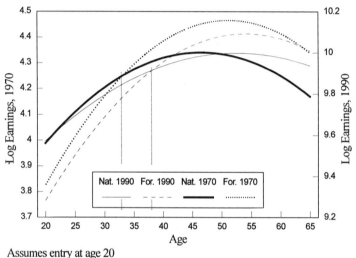

Assumes entry at age 20
Evaluated at means of foreign born

Figure 4.1 shows the profiles from Table 2, Col. 3 of Chiswick
(1978), assuming an immigrant enters at age 20 (this is identical to the
graph in Borjas (1994), except that Borjas' calculations show log
earnings on the left axis ranging from 8.4 to 9.1). These profiles were
calculated after holding constant education, potential experience,
weeks worked, rural residence, southern residence, and marital status.
In 1970 the immigrant profile crosses the native profile at age 33 (13
years after arrival). For comparison, the profiles from an identical
regression using the 1990 census is included, with 1990 earnings scaled
on the right axis. The crossover for 1990 occurs later, at about age 38.

The slope is actually steeper in 1990 (about 2.1% per year duration), but immigrants earn about 29% less than natives upon arrival, vs.16% in 1970.

The Chiswick (1978) analysis also showed that immigrants received less return for a year of schooling (5.7%) than natives (7.2%) ceteris paribus. The cause was hypothesized as self-selection, i.e. those with less schooling who make the investment of migration may come from the upper tail of the distribution of innate ability, while those with high levels of schooling who migrate may be more widely dispersed in terms of innate ability.

However, the earnings return for education is higher for immigrants from English-speaking developed countries. This could indicate that the lower returns to education for immigrants is partly because such education is not perfectly transferable. The steeper profiles and crossovers are also robust across country of origin although immigrants from some countries (Mexico, Cuba, Asia/Africa) earned significantly less than immigrants from the British Isles. Duration in the origin is less equalizing for immigrants from English-speaking countries, because their labor market experience is more transferable upon arrival—they are more equal to begin with. All of the results of this analysis support the assimilation and self-selection hypotheses.

Subsequent studies found these results to be robust for other periods and for other countries. For example, convergence and overtaking of native wage levels was found for Northern and Western European immigrants at the turn of the century, while other groups did not achieve parity (Blau, 1979). A BLS sample of Iowa immigrants from 1894 showed a slightly greater rate of convergence for immigrants who arrived without skills than for those who were skilled upon arrival, although not enough to overcome a large initial disadvantage (Eichengreen, 1986). Ferrie (1995, 1997) found upward occupational mobility for immigrants between 1850 and 1860, although at a lower rate than between 1970 and 1980, with variation in mobility depending on skill level; Hatton (1997) also found rapid increases in earnings for pre-1890 immigrants. Chiswick (1979) found consistency across most ethnic groups—only Chinese immigrants showed no crossover. Similar patterns were noted in Canada (Tandon, 1973; Swan, 1991); Israel (Chiswick, 1979); and Australia (Chiswick, 1992). In Great Britain duration in the destination seemed to have no significant effect, possibly because most recent immigrants were from countries in the British commonwealth countries or others with strong English influence; education provided a lower return for immigrants to Britain (Chiswick, 1980). Bell (1997), on the other hand, found rapid assimilation for a disadvantaged group of black immigrants with significant foreign work experience. Carliner (1980) found lower earnings, ceteris paribus, for recent immigrants than earlier immigrants, and for earlier immigrants and 3rd generation immigrants than 2nd generation immigrants, consistent across several ethnic groups; returns to schooling were higher for natives than for earlier immigrants, who had higher returns than recent immigrants.

These results are not without controversy. They depend upon the comparison ethnic and age groups, are sensitive to controls for human capital variables, and may change over time. For example, Chiswick (1979), using the 1970 census, showed a crossover for Mexican immigrants compared to natives of Mexican ancestry at about 15 years. Borjas (1994), using the 1990 census, found no such crossover for Mexican immigrants, while there remained a significant crossover for white immigrants compared to white native-born workers. Assimilation also does not seem to work the same for women: in a replication of the 1979 Chiswick analysis, immigrant women were shown to earn more than native women upon arrival, but there was negative convergence with duration in the destination (Long, 1980).

The main challenge to the assimilation/self-selection hypothesis comes from the cohort-quality hypothesis of Borjas, described above. Borjas' original paper (Borjas, 1985) departed from the usual cross-section tests, which he specified as the main source of upward bias in the estimation of earnings assimilation of immigrants. Decomposing the growth in earnings (absolute and relative to natives) of separate cohorts of immigrants using both the 1970 and 1980 censuses, Borjas estimated that the within-cohort growth in earnings was less than the across-cohort growth for more recent cohorts, and that this effect was most pronounced for certain groups such as Mexican immigrants. Borjas attributed the results to a decline in quality of more recent immigrants.

Responses to Borjas' hypothesis were of two types. Chiswick (1986a), for example, tested directly for changes in cohort quality and found that despite the recent shift in the ethnic composition of immigrants, the trend in cohort quality is not absolutely negative, with the trend for Mexicans either up or down depending on the comparison group, the trend for recent Cuban refugees down, the trend for Asians up. Other papers directly challenge Borjas's specifications. For example, Jasso and Rosensweig (1990) questioned the exclusion of certain groups of immigrants and remigrants; Yeungert (1991) included the self-employed, which Borjas excluded.

A substantial literature has developed around the cohort quality/assimilation debate. Many studies have found little or no support for the cohort quality hypothesis (LaLonde and Topel, 1991, 1992; Yeungert, 1994; Funkhouser and Trejo, 1995; Duleep and Regets, 1996a, 1996b). Smith (1992) found evidence in support of the hypothesis, as did Borjas in several subsequent papers.

Since this book only provides a very indirect test of the cohort quality hypothesis, it will not delve into details of the debate. Most of the emphasis, and most of the information about immigrant adjustment in the past, was based upon tests of earnings. As LaLonde and Topel point out, however, the overall lower level of education of immigrants would result in declining earnings over time because of declines in relative prices for low skilled occupations in the U.S., even if there were no change in cohort quality. Less emphasis has been placed on the employment and unemployment experience of immigrants. Borjas (1992) estimated that the changing national origin mix caused a 1-2 percentage point increase in the unemployment rate, but does not address immigrant adjustments over time. Until recently, Chiswick (1982) provided the only comprehensive study of immigrant assimilation in employment and unemployment. Using 1970 Census data, the study showed that white foreign-born men worked about one week less per year than native-born white men, but after holding constant socioeconomic variables such as schooling, experience, and marital status, immigrants in the U.S. for less than 5 years worked 2.9 weeks less, between 5 and 9 years 1.1 weeks less, with no significant difference after 9 years. Using a different data set for 1976, the convergence was most rapid in the first 5 years (11.36 weeks for persons immigrating in 1975, to 2.1 weeks less for persons immigrating in 1971), and there was virtually no significant difference between native-born workers and longer-tenured immigrants. These results verified the assimilation hypothesis for weeks worked.

More recent studies show that these results are robust over time. A new study (Chiswick and Hurst, 1998a), using data from the 1990 Census, shows that the patterns are the same, except that convergence of weeks worked between immigrants and native-born workers occurs during the 10-14 year period following immigration rather than the 5-9 year period in the previous study. An interesting contrast between Chiswick (1982) and Chiswick and Hurst (1997) is that citizenship status was significantly positive in the latter study (not significant in the former), and in fact for citizen immigrants who speak English only or speak it very well the number of weeks worked not only converges, but exceeds that of native-born workers (naturalization was found to contribute to increases in earnings in a study by Nasar [1997]). Unemployment rates for foreign-born men were on average lower than for native-born men, after holding constant a vector of demographic variables, but a disaggregation by time in the destination showed that the differential was positive in the first three years in an OLS regression, not significant in a logistic regression. A study using the same CPS data as in part of the data set in this book finds that employment rates of immigrants converge to those of native-born workers after only 1-2 years, and that the effects of cyclical downturns are more severe for immigrants (Chiswick, Cohen, and Zach, 1997). A smaller study using 1982 CPS data shows that immigrants in their first two years in the U.S. worked a shorter year than earlier cohorts of immigrants, and had higher unemployment rates and longer duration of unemployment (Sehgal, 1985). No covariates were controlled for in the Sehgal study.

4.2   UNEMPLOYMENT AND LABOR MARKET TURNOVER

The question of what causes unemployment is one of the most widely investigated subjects in labor economics. The literature is massive. This chapter is not intended as a thorough review of all of the empirical literature on unemployment and turnover. Rather, it is a brief summary of the empirical test of key components of turnover theory, particularly centered around search theory, as described in Chapter 3. Many of the articles discussed in this chapter are summarized from several good reviews by Lippman and McCall (1976), Parsons (1977), Mortensen (1986), and Devine and Kiefer (1991) and will be indicated as such. Others articles are reviewed directly.

Directly testing the validity of search theory is difficult, both because of data constraints, and because of the lack of a well-focused model that does not overlap with competing hypotheses, such as those describing firm behavior. In fact, Devine and Kiefer suggest that " . . . search theory itself is never tested. The models we can write down precisely enough to be subject to test are patently false. The question is whether one can write down models that are simple enough to be useful, yet not disastrously at odds with labor market data." (p. 8). Some of the empirical work has tried to test structural models that focus on a particular specification of a search model, testing that specification against alternatives. A large (perhaps a majority) of the studies measure specific parameters or effects that validate small parts of the theory, such as the effects of unemployment insurance benefits on duration. Similarly, many studies measure differences in behaviors between demographic groups such as women, youths, and minorities. A separate line of the literature addresses firm behavior through efficiency wages and implicit contracts.

A. Demographic Groups

A large number of studies, over a long history, have drawn inferences about turnover hypotheses from the differences in outcomes between various demographic groups. Most of the models focus on two characteristics that differ between groups—search costs, and firm-specific human capital. For instance, women are expected to have more career interruptions than men, lower firm-specific human capital, and lower search costs because of both lower market wages and a higher value of non-market labor. Thus women would be expected to have higher quit and layoff rates than men. The same is expected for youths, because of lower firm-specific human capital and higher discount rates. Similarly, minorities tend to have lower firm-specific as well as general human capital. Thus differences in such rates between demographic groups have applications to search theory, efficiency wage hypotheses, reservation wage models, and possibly insider-outsider hypotheses. Furthermore, if these perceptions are false, they could result in statistical discrimination, of the type described by Aigner and Cain (1977).

The studies of demographic groups are important for this book for two reasons. First, the analysis does not directly test turnover hypotheses, but draws indirect inferences from differences between two demographic groups—immigrants and native-born workers. Second, although this book focuses on adult men, and many immigrants are non-minorities, immigrants have much in common with the groups studied previously, particularly low levels of firm-specific human capital. Thus, much of this analysis is guided by previous research on demographic groups.

B. Unemployment Rates

Ehrenberg (1980) reports simple but illustrative frequencies about unemployment rates of demographic groups in 1977. The figures are classic: lowest rates for white males, slightly higher for white females, higher for black males, and highest for black females. In all groups the unemployment rate declined with age until retirement, but the drop was most dramatic for young blacks—at age 45-54 the unemployment rate of non-white women was 5.6% and of non-white men 5.2%, compared to white females of 5.0% and white males of 3.0%; but at age 16-17 the numbers were 44.7%, 38.7%, 18.2%, and 17.6% respectively. Probabilities of labor force entrants finding jobs in the first month after entry were also significantly lower for non-white teens than for white teens. Information was also provided on probabilities of transitions between labor force states.

C. Separation Rates

One of the most widely studied demographic groups is black youths. Several important pieces were published in a book called The Black Youth Unemployment Crisis (Freeman and Holzer, ed., 1986). Ballen and Freeman (1986), for example, focus on inner city blacks, and find, in contrast to Ehrenberg's results, " . . . sluggish improvement in the employment position of blacks as they age . . . " (p.84). Yet this is only true for the transition between nonemployment and employment whereas the probability of moving from employment to nonemployment declines from 5.0% at age 16-19 to 3.3% at age 20-24. The movement into unemployment is highest for blacks and the movement into employment is lowest for blacks and the duration of employment and nonemployment, rather than frequency of spells, is the greatest contributing factor in the different unemployment rates between white and black youth. Harry J. Holzer's analysis suggests that reservation wages of black youth are higher than optimal, based upon aspirations similar to those of whites in their community, which are not as easily attainable for blacks, which contributes to longer durations of nonemployment and shorter duration of employment in specific low-skilled jobs. Peter Jackson and Edward Montgomery show that the largest cause of the difference between the unemployment rates of white and black young men is due to job losers and labor force entrants, rather than job leavers. Similar to Ballen and Yellen's results, these differentials do not improve with age.

D. Quit Rates

Early tests of quit rates by demographic group used data aggregated at the industry level. Burton and Parker (1969) found that a 1% increase in the percent female in an industry in 1960 increased the quit rate by about 0.5% (t = 3.3), evaluated at the mean quit rate, while a 1% increase in percent nonwhite increased the quit rate by about 1% (t = 3.0). A somewhat different specification using the same data (variable percentages for 49 industries from published BLS sources). Pencavel (1970) found a smaller elasticity for females (about 0.1), with no significant difference for blacks. Stoikov and Ramon (1968) found no significant effect for either group. Weiss (1984) found that the probability of quitting was higher for whites than non-whites, and decreased in age, but was not significantly different for males.

Blau and Kahn (1981) found that young women and blacks do have somewhat higher quit rates than young men and whites respectively, but the quit functions of each group predicted lower propensities to quit given personal and job characteristics, and the personal characteristics also predicted lower quit rates if the job characteristics were held constant. These tests were done only on persons aged 14-24 in 1971, however. Current cohorts of women are hypothesized to have stronger labor force attachment than their earlier cohorts. Contradicting the expectation is one proportional hazard study, wherein women born in 1944-46 had a lower quit probability than men, consistent across tenure and race, while those born in 1950-52 had a higher probability (Light and Ureta, 1990a). Yet in a subsequent paper (Light and Ureta, 1990b), the authors found that women were more likely than men to quit for "unobserved" reasons, but less likely to quit because of observed differences. Furthermore, the unobserved differentials were nonexistent for a more recent cohort of women, indicating that employers had no more risk in identifying female nonquitters than male nonquitters for more recent cohorts of women (and are therefore not justified in statistically discriminating against women). Meitzen (1986) found that, for younger cohorts, women's quit propensities increased with greater tenure, just the opposite of men, a result that was not confirmed by Light and Ureta.

E. Labor Force Movement of Youth

Two articles have particular salience for this study of the labor market adjustments of immigrants, although they do not address immigrants directly, but focus on youth (of all races). There are important differences between immigrants and native-born youth, primarily that immigrants arrive at all ages (although migration diminishes with age) and thus the level of schooling and potential experience of immigrants may be greater than for native-born youth. However, such schooling and experience often has a low degree of transferability to the U.S. labor market. Thus there are enough similarities between youth and immigrants that these studies provide a historical benchmark that, while indirect, can provide insights about what we might expect in the immigrant adjustment process.

In both studies, a key difference from other studies is the importance of movements in and out of the labor force, rather than movements in and out of employment. Topel and Ward (1992) examine a panel study that follows a large sample of young men through the first 15 years of their labor market experience starting at age 18. They do not have information on demographic characteristics such as schooling, hours worked, or marital status. But their results are significant. Job change is a strong adjustment factor for young men— by the tenth year after entry, over half of workers had held 6 or more jobs, over a third 8 or more jobs. But in the early years the movement is not necessarily job to job—in the first year after entry, half of total labor market experience is nonemployment experience, and 3 of every 4 job endings is into nonemployment. No information is available about whether these nonemployment spells are unemployment or out of the labor force. Topel and Ward show that within-job wage growth is a random walk process, but more than a third of early wage growth can be attributed to job changes, and wage changes due to transitions are a much greater proportion of wage growth early and decline in importance as cumulative experience grows. Wage gains are lower with duration in the previous job, but higher (initial wages) with duration in the new job—in other words, the longer the duration in a job, the more likely that the job is a good match, and the lower the gain from future job transitions. This implies a natural tendency toward more frequent job changes early and more duration in employment as experience increases.

Summers and Clark (1990b) examine gross change data calculated by the BLS using CPS matched samples in 1976. Their results provide strong evidence of the relative importance of flows in and out of the labor force for youth. Of all flows into employment for males ages 16-19, 65.5% are from not-in-labor-force (NILF) status; over 71% of flows out of employment are into NILF. Similar NILF proportions of flows into and out of unemployment are 63% and 53% respectively. These flows are strongly influenced by school status, yet 52% of flows out of employment are to NILF even for young men who are out of school. Average employment for these men is 9.8 months for those out of school, 4.9 months for those in school, while average job duration is 4.3 months and 2.1 months respectively. Time spent looking for work is 1.4 months for those in school, 2.0 months for those out of school, while time spent NILF is 5.8 months and 2.9 months respectively. The conclusions drawn by Clark and Summers are: 1) job search for teenagers is a passive process, in which they enter the labor force only when a job is immediately available; 2) teenage unemployment is a voluntary occurrence; and 3) functionally the distinction between NILF status and unemployment is usually overstated, i.e. there is little substantial difference for teenagers. Clark and Summers also demonstrate the high cyclical sensitivity of youth unemployment, showing that high unemployment rates during expansionary economic periods can be explained by increases in labor force participation. Their overall conclusion is that improvements in the unemployment situation of youths must come from expansionary employment policy rather than structural policies such as job training.

F. Efficiency Wages and Firm Specific Human Capital

Tests of efficiency wage hypotheses are difficult because the decision variable is at the firm level, and firm-level data are limited. Many studies therefore make inferences by measuring the wages of individuals and controlling for variables that proxy for levels of firm-specific human capital. Parsons (1977) used the National Longitudinal Survey (NLS) of 1966 to estimate a wage equation controlling for job tenure within occupational groups for a sample of males age 45-59 (this is a test of his human capital model, but also applies to efficiency wages). The results show that Managers and Proprietors (expected to have the highest level of firm-specific human capital) had the highest tenure-wage elasticity (.107), while Farm Laborers and Sales workers coefficients were not significantly different from 0. The results for other professions, however, were not as consistent with the hypothesis. Four other studies reviewed by Parsons in the same paper measured the effects of various dimensions of skill in industry cross-sectional studies of quit rates, and the four studies tend to support the efficiency wage (or the specific-human capital form of search theory)—where the signs of the parameters were wrong they were not statistically significant from zero, except for one study which found that the percent of workers who were production workers (a negative measure of skills) significantly increased the quit rate. Similar results were generally found for income, which was negatively correlated with quit rates.

The articles reviewed above were specifically attempting to test hypotheses about firm-specific human capital, although they can also be interpreted as tests of the efficiency wage hypothesis, which came later. More recent reviews have found similar results. Two such studies (Kreuger and Summers, 1987; Dickens and Katz, 1987) estimated wage equations holding personal characteristics constant. Whether regressing the resulting predicted wages against a wide number of industry characteristics (Dickens and Katz), or comparing inter-industry wage differentials against other time periods or countries (Kreuger and Summers), the conclusions were that efficiency wage theories had some support, although weak in some cases. In contrast, one study (Leonard, 1987) used firm level data to test monitoring intensity and found little significant correlation between workers wages and supervisory intensity, or between supervisors/worker wage ratio and the supervisor/worker quantity.

One of the most extensive tests of efficiency wage hypotheses (Campbell, 1993) used a rich data set on firm behavior from the Employment Opportunity Pilot Project (EOPP). Turnover costs were measured directly by screening and training expenses; screening costs had a direct positive effect on the starting wage of a job, while training costs had a direct positive effect on the top wage. The wage equation results were then used as an instrument for an "alternate wage" in a quit equation, which used a proportional hazards model of employment duration. The top wage was found to negatively impact quit rates, as expected, while the alternate wage had a positive coefficient, as expected, but was not significant. Overall Campbell's results supported the efficiency wage hypothesis, although not as strongly as he expected.

CHAPTER 5

The Theory of Immigrant Unemployment and Turnover, and Hypotheses

In Chapters 2 and 3 the theoretical models of immigration and labor turnover were discussed. This chapter will apply the concepts regarding the flow variables of unemployment established in Chapter 3 to the process of assimilation described in Chapter 2. The theoretical behavior of immigrants during the adjustment period will be expressed within the context of the turnover models described in Chapter 3. The hypotheses for the empirical analysis will be defined. This chapter draws heavily on Chiswick (1982).

The discussion of assimilation and self-selection above centered on the *result* of the adjustment process—as immigrants acquire the necessary labor market-specific and firm-specific skills, the differentials with native-born workers in earnings and other labor market outcomes diminish or even disappear.

How the process of adjustment affects unemployment is a slightly different question. Even if they make lower wages because of lower productivity, immigrants need not necessarily have higher unemployment rates or fewer weeks worked—if they will accept, and if employers can pay, wages less than or equal to their marginal product, and if information was perfect, they should not have higher rates of unemployment. The basic assimilation theory says, however, that unemployment develops as a result of the process of labor market adjustments made by immigrants.

The unemployment rate of immigrants is higher than the unemployment rate of native-born workers—in March 1990, the average rate for adult foreign-born men was 6.18%, compared to 4.85% for native-born workers (1990 U.S. Census, PUMS files). This result can occur from three basic processes (holding constant entry into and exit from the labor force as in equation 3.5 above): 1) a higher rate of quits for the foreign born, holding the job finding rate constant; 2) a higher rate of involuntary separations, holding the job finding rate constant; or 3) a lower rate of job finding, holding quit and separation rates constant. A fourth cause can be attributed to flows into or out of the labor force, as discussed in Chapter 3 above—unemployment can increase if either flows from outside the labor force into unemployment exceed flows out of the labor force from unemployment, or from flows out of the labor force from employment exceeding flows into employment from outside the labor force. Many studies either ignore labor force flows, or assume that the flows in the two directions are equal.

In reality, unemployment is likely to be generated from combinations of all four processes described above. Here the immigrant effects for each will be analyzed separately. In each hypothesis below, separations from employment are into nonemployment only, in other words, we ignore quits or layoffs that result in reemployment without an intervening period of nonemployment.

Hypothesis Number 1. *Recent immigrants will have a higher rate of voluntary job quitting than the native born,* ceteris paribus. *Over time this differential will diminish and converge to the rates of the native born.*

There are several theoretical explanations for higher quit rates for immigrants. First, except for periods spent in formal schooling, the acquisition of labor market specific capital is an "experience good"—knowledge of the job and skill requirements and non-pecuniary conditions is usually obtained after hire. But the job matching model and the efficient turnover model say that if the employer/employee match does not fit, the employer will reduce the worker's wages, inducing a quit. The job match is likely to be worse for recent immigrants because of the lower transferability of skills; in addition, if job finding rates are *higher* for immigrants, as we argue below, the probability of a poor match may increase as a result (Blaustein, 1993).

Second, search models suggest that a person will quit and search if the expected benefits of searching while unemployed minus (unemployed) search costs exceed those of searching while employed minus (employed) search costs. If wages are lower for immigrants, opportunity costs (lost wages) of search will be lower for immigrants while unemployed. While employed, however, opportunity cost is the loss of nonemployment time, such as in home production, as long as such search does not result in a loss of wages. Nonemployment time may be valued at the rate of wages, in which case the incentive to quit is indeterminate. If however, circumstances such as a multiple concurrent jobs, underground labor, or otherwise high values of home production result in a higher value of nonemployment time for immigrants, then this plus lower costs of search while unemployed should increase the incentive to quit.

In addition, search theory says that a person will quit if the expected wage, which depends on the distribution of job offers, is higher than the person's reservation wage. This can occur for immigrants simply because the reservation wage starts out at a low enough level. Or as the immigrant acquires labor market-specific skills, the distribution of wage offers, hence the level of possible wage offers, will increase. In the efficient turnover model, as modified above, this will lead to more efficient job matches.

These effects will diminish over time as immigrant workers acquire firm-specific skills. Recent immigrants have strong incentives to invest in general skills (e.g. truck driving), but not firm-specific skills; employers will provide general training if and only if they can pay wages far enough below the marginal product to cover the cost of the training. As more general skills are acquired, and as information about the worker to firms, and about job requirements to the worker, becomes easier to obtain, incentives increase for both the worker and the employer to invest in firm-specific training. As the proportion of the immigrant's skills that is firm-specific increases, the benefit from quitting diminishes, as expressed in Becker's and Parson's models.

Hypothesis Number 2. *Recent immigrants will have a higher rate of involuntary job loss than the native born,* ceteris paribus. *Over time this differential will diminish and converge to the rates of the native born.*

If a job match is poor, the employer has an incentive to terminate the employment "contract"; the job matching model suggests the employer will lower the worker's wage. If the worker refuses the wage cut, a layoff will result, and in the efficient turnover model this results in a more efficient allocation of labor. Even if a worker was willing to accept a wage cut, however, this may not be viable. The implicit contract model suggests that layoffs are the common solution in many cases (this is an example of why some have claimed that the distinction between layoffs and quits is not as distinct as we might think (McLaughlin, 1991).

As explained in Chapter 3, layoffs (as well as quits) are inversely related to the amount of firm-specific human capital possessed by the worker. As expressed in Hypothesis 1, recent immigrants have less incentive to invest in firm-specific human capital, and their employers also have less incentive to make these investments. Thus higher layoff rates for recent immigrants are consistent with human capital models. Implicit contract hypotheses suggest that layoffs are the result of worker and firm preferences for layoffs over wage cuts, and that workers tend to be laid off in reverse order of their seniority with the firm. Since recent immigrants by definition would have less seniority, they would be subject to higher rates of layoffs.

Human capital and implicit contract hypotheses imply that immigrant unemployment will be more sensitive to cyclical fluctuations; for the same reason, immigrants should also be more vulnerable to seasonal cutbacks, although on the aggregate the net effect depends on the proportion of immigrants in typically seasonal industries or occupations. In addition, immigrants should be more vulnerable to random events, such as firm closures. This latter effect could be exacerbated by the type of firm that employs immigrants—if they employ greater proportions of less skilled workers, it is possible that many firms employing high proportions of immigrants are less capitalized and less stable. In addition, the employment of illegal aliens subjects employers to government sanctions and increases the degree of risk. There is some evidence, however, that illegal aliens are *not* more likely to work in new, independently owned, or "underground" establishments (Chiswick, 1988).

Hypothesis Number 3. *Recent immigrants will have a higher ratio of quits to layoffs than the native born,* ceteris paribus. *Over time this differential will diminish and converge to the rates of the native born.*

Assimilation theory suggests that voluntary quit rates and involuntary layoff rates should both be higher for immigrants than for native-born workers: quit rates because experiencing many employers is a primary means available for recent immigrants to acquire labor market-specific skills; layoff rates because marginal productivity lags behind wage rates more for recent immigrants, and other reasons as expressed above.

Assimilation theory does not directly suggest which of the differentials in rates should be higher. However, the distinction is potentially important. Verification of Hypothesis 3 would provide support to the voluntary hypothesis of immigrant assimilation, implying that most of the unemployment of immigrants is due to many short spells rather than a few persons with long spells, and would suggest that turnover would lead to increasing wages over time (since wage rates are positively related to quit rates and negatively to layoff rates). Refutation of Hypothesis 3 would suggest that the unemployment of immigrants may be due to longer spells of unemployment for smaller groups, supporting the view of Clark and Summers expressed previously.

Hypothesis Number 4. *Recent immigrants will have a lower duration of unemployment than the native born, ceteris paribus. The duration of unemployment should be higher for layoff unemployment than for quit unemployment. Over time these differentials will diminish and converge to the rates of native born workers.*

Among the three potential causes of relatively higher unemployment for immigrants at the beginning of this chapter was a lower rate of job finding, or higher duration of unemployment. Neither immigration theory nor turnover theories clearly predict, *ex ante*, what sign unemployment duration should assume for immigrants compared to native-born workers. Several factors should work in the immigrant's favor, reducing unemployment duration. Probably the most important is a lower reservation wage. The lower earnings of immigrants compared to native workers, *ceteris paribus*, is well documented, as described above. Much of this difference could probably be described, although not easily measured, as differences in reservation wages. If wage offers are lower on average for recent immigrants because of lower productivity, and if knowledge were perfect, immigrants would arrive at the destination country with the expectation of wages lower than the native population—it is the difference with wages in the origin country, as in equation 2.1, that determines the decision to migrate. Lower reservation wages are rational, since they increase the size of the wage offer distribution, increasing the probability of finding a match, ρ, thereby increasing the *expected* wage, defined as above as ρW_X. On the other hand, the same reasoning should lead to a limit to the downward flexibility of reservation wages of immigrants—below a certain point the differential in equation 2.1 would be too small to justify migration or might lead to migration back to the country of origin.

Several factors other than lower reservation wages might lead to lower unemployment duration for immigrants. One is a possibly greater motivation or proclivity to work (the self-selection hypothesis). Another is the lower rate of claiming unemployment insurance. It has been shown (Atkinson and Micklewright, 1991; Ehrenberg, 1976; Feldstein, 1973) that higher unemployment insurance replacement rates increase the duration of unemployment, primarily because they reduce the costs of search. Immigrants are not usually eligible for benefits during their first year in the U.S. because of income and job duration requirements in state systems. Illegal immigrants are technically not eligible for UI benefits because they are not legally eligible, therefore available, to work (North and Houstoun, 1976). Recent immigrants also may be fearful that applying for benefits might have an adverse impact on their immigration status.

On the other hand, some important characteristics might lead to higher unemployment duration for immigrants. Primary among these characteristics is the lower levels of labor market-specific human capital, which reduces the size of the job offer distribution. Less information about employers, less knowledge of the labor market process, and fewer resources may make the search effort less efficient. The insider/outsider model suggests that recent immigrants, outsiders almost by definition, should have fewer job opportunities. Other models of wage rigidity, such as efficiency wages, might make the actual wage higher than the immigrant's productivity, diminishing the comparative advantage of lower reservation wages.

Which of these effects dominates, and what is the net effect on unemployment, is not clear. The assimilation model, however, which proposes substantial "job hopping" by recent immigrants, would seem to lean toward lower duration. If immigrants are acquiring skills by experiencing many employers, the optimization of this process should call for a relatively quick reentrance into employment. In addition, if job finding rates were the same or lower than for native-born workers, the combination with the relatively unambiguous higher separation rates for immigrants should lead to substantially higher rates of unemployment and fewer weeks worked. Unemployment is higher for recent immigrants, but not drastically so. Higher unemployment rates would be consistent with lower unemployment duration than for the native born if the duration was not *as much* lower as the job separation rate was higher. Again, however, as immigrants gain market skills, reservation wages should rise, UI eligibility should increase, and unemployment duration should converge to the rates of native-born workers.

Hypothesis Number 5. *Recent immigrants will have greater flows into and out of the labor force than native born workers, ceteris paribus, implying a higher probability of being a labor force entrant (new entrant or reentrant), and a higher probability of being not in the labor force (NILF), overall and compared to the probabilities of being job leavers or losers or employed. Over time these differentials will diminish and converge to the rates of native born workers.*

Newly arrived immigrants are likely to have higher probabilities of being labor force entrants for several reasons. First, if they are newly arrived and looking for work (unemployed), they theoretically should be labor force entrants by definition. The definition of labor force entrant is somewhat ambiguous in the case of immigrants, however. The key question is "Why did you start looking for work?" (see Appendix D). If a man was either working or looking for work in his country of origin, had a short migration period, then immediately began looking for work upon arrival, he may answer that question as "quit job" or "lost job". According to analysts at the Census Bureau, there are no instructions in the field manuals that help an interviewer interpret the answers, so they may be recorded as is. Except for the period of migration itself, these answers are technically correct from the individual's point of view, but for our purposes the correct answer would be "other," making him a labor force entrant (technically a new entrant, but the distinction is not made in this analysis), since his arrival in the U.S. labor market has a different impact on the employment rate and on the job loser or leaver rates than if he had quit or lost a U.S. job. If we accept that all new immigrants who are unemployed should be labor force entrants, then the actual number is probably underestimated. However, for most immigrants, the higher probability of being out of the labor force in the origin country and the probable long length of time in transition between countries would probably result in a specification of entrant.

Recent immigrants are likely to be less eligible for unemployment compensation benefits than native-born workers, because of work history requirements in state laws (Chiswick and Hurst, 1997). They would therefore have less incentive to report themselves as looking for work. Recent immigrants may also have higher participation rates in the informal or "underground" labor market, or have otherwise higher values of non-market production. Therefore, recent immigrants would have a higher probability of dropping out of the labor force after a quit or layoff, and a higher probability of remaining out of the labor force rather than accept a low paying job.

Finally, it was suggested earlier that the labor market characteristics of recent immigrants have many similarities to those of native-born youth. Youth were shown to have a low attachment to the labor force, which increases with increasing experience and wages. Some of the same factors may apply to recent immigrants as well. In fact, non-market time may be actually more productive for immigrants than for youth in acquiring market specific (not firm-specific) skills, such as through language classes or training workshops. Thus search activity may be more passive for recent immigrants, and spells of nonemployment may be combinations of quit or layoff unemployment, followed by periods out of the labor force, followed by periods of entrant unemployment.

Which of the two labor market outcomes (entrant vs. NILF) is more pronounced for immigrants is theoretically ambiguous, thus an empirical question.

Hypothesis Number 6. *Recent immigrants will have higher rates of unemployment, and lower rates of employment, ceteris paribus, than native born workers. Over time these differentials will diminish and converge to the rates of native born workers.*

This hypothesis is simply a restatement of hypotheses in previous work (Chiswick, 1982; Chiswick, Cohen, and Zach, 1997; Chiswick and Hurst, 1997). It is simply derived from Hypotheses 1, 2, and 5, and the logic derives from those hypotheses.

CHAPTER 6

Data Sources

The primary sources of data for the empirical analysis of this book are seven samples of the Current Population Survey (CPS) plus the Survey of Income and Education conducted in 1976. Section 6.1 describes the CPS survey, section 6.2 describes the SIE survey, section 6.3 describes the method used to combine the data sets, and Section 6.4 is a description of problems with key variables and some of the adjustments made.

6.1 CURRENT POPULATION SURVEY

The CPS is a monthly survey conducted by the Bureau of the Census, Department of Commerce, for the Bureau of Labor Statistics of the Department of Labor. The CPS is designed to gather detailed information on the employment and labor force status of residents of the United States. Each month about 71,000 households are assigned to the survey, and approximately 57,000-60,000 participate in a comprehensive interview, resulting in about 170,000 records, about 120,000 age 14 and above. Each household is surveyed for four months, then again during the same four months in the following year. The samples are staggered, so that about one fourth of each sample is made up of a new group of households entering the rotation, and one fourth in their last rotation. The supplements in this analysis are spaced so that the probability of a household being in the sample twice is close to zero.

The CPS supplements information from the decennial U.S. Census of Population and Housing; while considerably smaller than the census, the CPS is the only comprehensive source of monthly labor market data, and serves as the source of official government statistics on employment and unemployment. While the census asks many more questions about demographic data, particularly about housing and family information, the CPS asks more detailed questions about labor market activities.

A. Basic Survey Questions

The CPS asks several important demographic questions, such as age, sex, race, marital status, educational attainment, veteran status, and family structure. The bulk of the survey focuses on the labor market activities of the adult (age 15 and above) members of the household. Information is received for each person on his or her labor market status (employed, unemployed, out of the labor force) as of the week prior to the survey. For each labor market state, other more detailed information is received. For example, for a person who is identified as unemployed, additional questions include the length of unemployment, what the person has been doing to look for work, and the reason for separation from the last job (or entry into the work force). Employed persons are asked about the hours normally worked, full time/part time status, whether any time was taken off the previous week and the reasons, union affiliation of the job, and hourly and weekly earnings data. Persons not in the labor force are asked about the reasons for not looking for work, if they want full time or part time work, and the time since they last worked full time. Detailed information is collected on occupation, industry, and class (government, private), as well as geographic information down to the level of Metropolitan Statistical Area (MSA).

B. Supplements

Frequently the CPS includes supplements to the basic survey to obtain more detailed information on special topics of interest to researchers, such as womens' fertility and birth expectations, persons in the armed forces, and special studies of workers displaced from their jobs because of plant closings, position elimination, or layoffs without recall. Of special interest to this book are the supplements providing information on the foreign born. Prior to 1994 the Census Bureau produced 6 such supplements: November 1979, April 1983, June 1986, June 1988, November 1989, and June 1991. All of these supplements are incorporated in this book. In addition, since January 1994 questions about the foreign born are being asked in all CPS surveys; this book includes the February 1994 supplement.

The foreign born supplements include questions about country of birth of each member of the household, year of immigration, citizenship status, and country of birth and year of immigration of the parents of the adult members of the household. In addition to the foreign born supplements, some of the surveys include other supplements as well. The 1979 supplement includes questions about speaking English or another language at home. The 1986 and 1988 supplements include questions about fertility and birth expectations, while 1983 includes questions about fertility only. The 1988 and 1991 surveys include questions about the potential for emigration—whether the interviewee had relatives living in a foreign country, if they had previously lived in the United States, if they are or were citizens, among other questions. The 1994 survey asks questions about displacement from a previous job—while there have been displacement supplements every two years since 1981, the February 1994 supplement is the only one to include questions on the foreign born.

6.2 SURVEY OF INCOME AND EDUCATION

The SIE was conducted during the months April-June 1976 by the Bureau of the Census, and was intended as a special supplement to CPS information with much greater detail about items such as education levels, income sources, language, poverty, and the need for bilingual education. The purpose of the SIE was to estimate poverty rates by state and identify characteristics of the population in poverty. 151,170 households were interviewed, encompassing about 320,000 adults.

The SIE contains a wide variety of information about education and income, as well as labor market outcomes, making it a valuable source of information for researchers, especially considering the relatively large size. However, the SIE is valuable for this book for a different reason. The questionnaire was designed by the Bureau of the Census, which also produces the CPS, and the questions on labor market status and foreign born status (except parental nativity) asked on the SIE are virtually identical to those asked on the CPS. This allows us to include the SIE as an additional "copy" of the CPS for 1976—all of the same questions will be added to the data set.

6.3   THE COMBINED DATABASE

The seven CPS surveys are combined with the SIE survey into one pooled data set comprising information from 1976 to 1994. Each survey is flagged with a dummy variable and all analyses will be run against 1976 as the benchmark. This is basically the same data set used in other studies (Chiswick, Cohen, and Zach, 1995; Funkhouser and Trejo, 1995), except much larger and covering a longer time period. The combination produces a database of about 1.1 million records of persons 14 and above, of which those younger than 18 are deleted. In addition, this analysis is limited to men between the ages of 25 and 64, so the final data set used in this analysis contains 328,233 observations.

There are several advantages to pooling these data sets into one. The most obvious is that the larger sample size improves accuracy and yields more robust results. Also important is the increase in information, providing period effects to ascertain if parameters are changing over time. In addition, the questions asked in the surveys in this book are mostly based on a labor force state at one point in time, a certain key week. This can result in significant error when trying to generalize about the overall labor market situation. With multiple data sets, we have 8 periods, which span 18 years and run across several seasonal periods.

6.4   DATA LIMITATIONS

Several problems arise from the composition of the data set used in this book. Some stem from the surveys themselves. Some stem from the pooling procedure.

There are important geographic limitations. The CPS and SIE are both stratified random samples, the CPS based upon 729 sample areas in 1,943 counties and independent cities in all states in the U.S. The sampling frame for the CPS is chosen to be representative on a national level, and the technical documentation warns that local area data are not as reliable as national level data (U.S. Department of Commerce, 1991). The SIE was developed with a higher priority of providing information about states, and employed a somewhat different sampling framework (Survey of Income and Education technical documentation, 1976). Thus caution is called for when using geographic areas as units of analysis or explanatory variables. This is not expected to be a major problem in this analysis, for two reasons. First, the only time local areas are used directly is in the unemployment rate. Since the rate used here is the average rate for the area in which a person lives computed from the sample by survey, it is not necessary that the areas be directly comparable across surveys.

Second, both the CPS and the SIE provide sampling weights derived from known distributions specifically to make the weighted observations sum to the population in each area. All persons in a sampling area get the same basic weight, which is then adjusted according to known distributions of sex, race, age, and rural/non-rural or metropolitan/non-metropolitan residence. Any differences in sampling framework should be mitigated by the sample weights. All calculations done in this book, including the means and frequencies reported in various tables, are weighted (see the comment on weights in the footnotes).

CHAPTER 7

The Model, Estimating Equations, and Methodology

This chapter will define the conceptual model for estimating the hypotheses of Chapter 5. The estimating equations will then be specified.

This data used in this book, as defined in Chapter 6, is primarily cross-section data, although several periods are combined in a pooled cross-section/time series framework. Because of the cross-sectional nature, it is not possible to test for actual flows into or out of various unemployment or labor force states, as can be done with longitudinal data. This book will make inferences about flows from comparing the conditional probabilities of being in specified states. "Probability" as used here is defined simply as a dummy variable, 1 if a person is in the state, 0 otherwise. The states of interest are: 1 = currently employed; 2 = having quit the previous job; 3 = having involuntarily lost the previous job; 4 = being a new entrant or reentrant to the labor force; and 0 = being out of the labor force. These variables are specified so that every individual must be in one of the 5 states.

7.1   FUNCTIONAL FORM AND DEPENDENT VARIABLES

The functional form of the main model is as follows. Let P_{ji} stand for the probability that individual i is currently in state j. The hypotheses for this book suggest that P_{ji} is function of a vector, X, of independent, fixed, nonstochastic exogenous variables, which we represent in a stochastic process as:

$$P_{ij} = X\beta + \varepsilon_{ij}. \qquad 7.1$$

The specification of the X vector follows later in this chapter. This is a linear probability model, and can be estimated with ordinary least squares (OLS) techniques. However, assumptions of linearity in equation 7.1 create a number of problems, as noted by several authors (Summers and Clark, 1990c; Pindyck and Rubinfeld, 1991; Greene, 1993). Most obvious is that the error terms will be heteroscedastic in a way that depends on β. In addition, there is no natural scale to measure the effect of being in one state as opposed to another. Perhaps most serious is the fact that while the values of the dependent variable are either 0 or 1, we cannot constrain Xβ to the same interval, so the predictions can be greater than 1 or less than 0. Finally extreme values of X can bias some of the parameter estimates.

To get around the problems with OLS, we modify the functional form as follows: This is typically called the multinomial logit, or

$$P_{ij} = \frac{e^{\beta_j x_i}}{1 + \sum\limits_{k=0}^{4} e^{\beta_k x_i}}. \qquad 7.2$$

multiple logit model (Greene, 1993; Schmidt and Strauss, 1975). The restriction that β = 0 is commonly imposed as a normalization, so that all of the probabilities add up to 1. Differentiating Equation 7.2 yields the partial effects of the regressors on the probabilities:

$$\frac{\partial P_j}{\partial x_i} = P_j [\beta_j - \sum_k P_k \beta_k] \qquad 7.3$$

Standard errors cannot be computed on the probabilities in equation 7.2. The standard errors can be computed for the partial effects in equation 7.3, but without some strong simplifying assumptions, only with some difficulty (see Greene, 1995). In this book the probabilities from equation 7.2 will be calculated, but not the partial effects. Taking logs of both sides of equation 7.2 and normalizing on a particular category k gives the estimating equation:

$$\ln \left\lfloor \frac{P_{ij}}{P_{ik}} \right\rfloor = X_i (\beta_j - \beta_k) \qquad 7.4$$

The log function in equation 7.4 is the odds ratio, which is the probability of each state relative to the probabilities of the other states. For example, (dropping the i subscript for convenience), ln (P_1/P_0) is the log of the odds that a person is employed instead of being out of the labor force. If we interpret the states as choices between flows, we can say that ln (P_1/P_0) is the log of the odds that a person chooses to work rather than drop out of the labor force. Ln (P_2/P_3) gives the log of the odds that a person who is unemployed had quit their job instead of being laid off. Thus, this form can test the hypotheses in Chapter 5 jointly.

Equation 7.4 is the major estimating equation for the probability calculations. A second model considers the job finding rate as a negative function of the duration of unemployment—a higher duration of unemployment for an individual implies a lower probability of finding a job, *ceteris paribus*. The CPS asks how long an unemployed person has been looking for work. It would be convenient to simply regress this duration variable against X, and a negative coefficient on a "foreign-born" variable would imply that foreign-born men have a higher job finding rate. There are two problems with the data, however. First, no information is given on how long a person was unemployed if they currently hold a job or if they are out of the labor force—so the data on duration is only applicable to the subpopulation that is still unemployed. Second, the subpopulation of unemployed is censored, that is, they have not completed their spells of unemployment, so we do not know their actual duration.

One appropriate approach for modeling censored duration data is to model the duration of unemployment for individual i in time t as a hazard rate, $h_i(t)$, such as in a proportional hazards model. This is not possible in this analysis, however, because such an approach requires data on the uncensored spells of unemployment, i.e., it requires failures. This problem is discussed more thoroughly in Chapter 10. In this book, however, flows into the various states described above are the desired variables of interest, and we are attempting to estimate them using information about state probabilities. Since an accurate estimate of the job finding rate is not the variable of interest, percentage differentials between such rates for various groups will suffice. The unemployment duration variable itself will be used to proxy for percentage differentials in the probability of exiting unemployment. The derivation is discussed further in Chapter 10.

7.2 EXPLANATORY VARIABLES

The variables used as independent, or explanatory, variables in this book will be mostly fairly standard variables used in previous studies of immigrant adjustment (Chiswick and Hurst, 1997; Chiswick, 1982; Chiswick, 1979), selected both because of their potential effect on turnover, and/or because they have been found in other studies to differ in their effects between native-born men and foreign-born men. To summarize, it is expected that the probability for foreign-born men of quitting, being laid off, finding a job, and the other labor force dependent variables as defined above, would depend upon the initial transferability of skills, postmigration investment in labor market skills, the distribution of wages, the cost of job search, local labor market characteristics, other regional characteristics, the individual's value of non-market work, other measurable individual characteristics, and other unmeasurable group characteristics. In addition, because the use of several surveys over time provides a time series, period effects, or cyclical effects, can be tested. Each of these determinants will be described in turn.

A. Postmigration Acquisition of Labor Market Skills

Two variables, **schooling** and **experience** (estimated as age-schooling-5) are used as measures of investments in skills. It is difficult to separate such investments into premigration and postmigration portions. Hashmi (1987) found that premigration education was significantly positively related to postmigration education. In the data sets used here, only the 1976 SIE includes questions on premigration education, so premigration education is not differentiated from postmigration schooling in this book. The assimilation hypothesis predicts rapid accumulation of country-specific skills over time in the destination, so the primary variable to assess postmigration investment in skills is duration in the destination, or **years since migration**. This variable is included in two forms—as a continuous variable, added quadratically to a **foreign-born dummy** variable, and as increments of duration categorical variables.

B. Wage Distribution, and the Cost of Search

Search theory, as discussed in Chapter 3, predicts that the **expected wage**, which is a function of the distribution of wage offers, is an important determinant of the probability of quits, layoffs, and job finding. According to search theory, as discussed in Chapter 3, higher expected wages should generally increase both search costs and benefits. Once unemployed, higher costs and benefits should both work to shorten search time. On the other hand, despite the shorter time unemployed, higher expected wages could increase the unemployment rate. Higher expected wages could be expected to increase the probability of a person quitting, because of the greater likelihood that wages in other jobs might exceed wages in the current job; offsetting this effect is the possibility that higher expected wages might indicate higher efficiency wages.

Higher expected wages could have an ambiguous effect on layoffs. On the one hand they could be a sign of wages in that occupation being higher than marginal productivity, increasing layoffs; on the other hand, they might also increase the expected costs of replacing laid off workers. Clearly, however, higher expected wages should induce movement into the labor force, which would tend to push up the unemployment rate if the movement was not into employment.

Another important wage effect is the **variance of expected wages**. In most cases, the variance should work in the opposite direction from the average. A higher variance would increase the probability that a current job offer is lower than future offers, increasing the potential return from additional search if unemployed. A higher variance would serve to reduce information about expected wages, increasing risk. Thus a higher variance should reduce movement into the labor force, and reduce the probability of quitting a job, ceteris paribus. In addition, a higher variance would improve the accuracy of job matches, reducing the incentives for layoffs.

No completely accurate estimate of the distribution of wages to an individual is possible, because the true distribution includes the individuals' personal characteristics. McLaughlin (1991) estimated an individual's expected wage with a wage equation, based upon the individual's characteristics, then included the estimate as an instrument in an equation with lags of the same characteristics. The collinearity between such an instrument and the lagged variables (over .9 correlation in each case for McLaughlin) is problematic. This book uses two simple computations as proxies for expected wages. The first is the **average wage in the individual's major occupation group**. The second is the **wage variance in the individual's major occupation group**. It must be noted that these variables might be collinear with the schooling variable, to the extent that schooling affects occupational choice in a way that affects wages, and might be expected to reduce the effect of the schooling variable.[1]

C. Local Labor Market Conditions

Quit rates are procyclical, layoff rates countercyclical; we can expect that this effect is important at the local labor market area as well as in business cycles. The **average unemployment rate for the SMSA/State** of the residence of the immigrant is used to proxy for the local labor market effects, partly cyclical effects, partly structural differences across geographical areas. These rates are calculated from the samples.

D. Other Regional Effects

Holding constant the unemployment rate, other unmeasurable regional or areal level effects may differ between **foreign-born** men and native-born workers. It has been shown (Chiswick, 1982, who used the rural/urban distinction rather than metropolitan/nonmetropolitan) that living in a **metropolitan area** can increase the number of weeks worked for both native-born and **foreign-born** workers, and that living in the **South** has a depressing effect on weeks worked for **foreign-born** but not native-born workers. These variables are entered. To separate out the part of these effects that affect only agriculture workers, a dichotomous variable is also entered for employment in the **agricultural** wage and salary sector. Since occupation information is not available for 3/4 of men out of the labor force, the agriculture variable will tend to overestimate employment in agriculture relative to NILF status, and thus will be a poorer predictor of the NILF dependent variable. But it provides interesting information for the different categories of unemployment in Chapter 9.

E. Individual Value of Non-market Work

Marital status is important for determining attachment to the labor force and stability of employment. Being married with spouse present has been shown to reduce the probability of quits (Weiss, 1984), separations in general (McLaughlin, 1991); and duration of unemployment (Nickell, 1979). A dummy variable for **married, spouse present**, is added. Other variables are available to measure other nonmarket effects, such as family income, but are often not consistent across the various surveys or have incomplete information.

F. Period Effects

Each survey is given a dichotomous identifier, and the changes in the effects of the exogenous variables over time can be controlled. Three types of period effects can show up in the parameter estimates of the period dummy variables. First is a business cycle effect—the unemployment rate in 1979 was 5.8% compared to 7.7% in 1976. Second is a seasonal effect—even though the average yearly unemployment rate was slightly lower in 1994 (6.1%) than in 1991 (6.7%), unemployment in the transportation and material moving occupation in the 1994 survey (February) was 10.2%, compared to 7.2% in the 1991 survey (June). Third is a trend effect, such as an increase in the percentage of the work force that is foreign born, an overall decline in the "quality" of **foreign-born** men, or a change in the structural/frictional unemployment composition over time.

Separating the three effects can be difficult. This book controls for the three effects as follows. The **average area unemployment rate** in the particular survey, as mentioned above, will partially control for the business cycle effects, as well as regional differences in unemployment. The unemployment rate is calculated within the samples by survey year, so it will account for differences across surveys (cyclical and seasonal effects) as well as across areas, but holding constant variables to measure seasonality and cyclical effects, the area unemployment rate will be interpreted primarily as a geographical control. The areas used are SMSAs, on the assumption that SMSAs would be the closest approximation to "labor markets" which people would consider in assessing unemployment rates. If a person had a code of "outside SMSA" or if the rate couldn't be calculated, the rate assigned is the average rate for the state.

By itself, the area unemployment rate would be heavily influenced by the month of the survey. To partially account for seasonal effects, a **seasonal adjustment factor** is added for the month of the specific survey, computed for each individual's major occupation group, calculated with the Census X-11 program on not-seasonally-adjusted rates published by the BLS. The seasonal adjustment factor is also a partial control for occupation effects as well as the survey month. As such, it might be expected to be collinear with other variables that are collinear with occupation, particularly schooling, but the correlation between the variables was very small, and adding the adjustment factor to the equation had almost no effect on schooling. This variable can also provide information about different sensitivities to seasonal factors between **foreign-born** men and native-born men. Finally, the **survey year** dummy variable, holding constant area unemployment rates and seasonal factors, accounts for trend effects and other unmeasured effects that are correlated with the particular survey, after controlling for cyclical and seasonal effects..

G. Other Individual Level Effects

Other effects not mentioned above may be associated with the individual. **Race**, or ethnic group, is the most important. Wage distributions, as well as responses to changes in such distributions, seasonal and cyclical effects, area unemployment rates, schooling and experience, and responses to the other demographic variables mentioned above may all differ by race, and it has been shown that rates and duration of unemployment and labor force participation are different by race (Hoffman, 1991; Holzer, 1986; Ehrenberg, 1980; Parsons, 1972). Four racial groups are considered here: non-Hispanic white (White), Hispanic white (Hispanic), black, and other minorities (which are primarily Asian). Hispanics that are coded in other races are considered as being from those races.

Other variables were tested during the course of the analysis but are not necessarily included in the reported models. Union status of the person and union contract status of the person's job can be tested—the presence of a union and/or a contract should increase layoffs and reduce quits. No reasonable hypothesis exists for veteran status (possibly veterans may have a higher job finding rate), so that variable is not tested. Part-time employment would be expected to increase job turnover and shorten search time. Family income beyond a person's individual income should have a pure income effect, increasing job search times and inducing greater turnover. However, the family income variable in this dataset is provided for every male, but it cannot be separated from the individual man's income, which is available for only 1/4 of the men, so would have a tendency to measure both family income effects and the individual's income effect. The data set includes persons reporting themselves as self-employed. We might expect that self-employed persons have a different attachment to the labor force (self-employment may be a substitute for unemployment or dropping out of the labor force), have lower search costs and therefore spend less time unemployed, and have lower risk from both quits and layoffs when not self-employed.

The variable names, definitions, and expected signs for the partial effects on each of the dependent variables described above are provided in Table 7.1. Appendix A provides details on the definitions of the dependent variables.

Table 7.2 shows the means and standard deviations of the independent and dependent variables for native-born men, foreign-born men, and the full pooled sample of men ages 25-64.

Foreign-born men average about 41 years of age, about 1 year younger than native-born men. The level of schooling, 11.8 years, is also 1 year less than that of native-born men, so they have about the same level of experience on average. Native-born men and foreign-born men differ little in their marital status (about 74% married), but foreign-born men are much more likely to live in metropolitan areas, outside the South, and to work in the agricultural wage and salary sector. The area unemployment rate is slightly higher on average for foreign-born men, 6.9% compared to 6.5% for native-born men, as is the seasonal adjustment factor (99.2 compared to 98.0), indicating that foreign-born men are slightly more likely to live in higher unemployment areas and to work in occupations with more seasonality, or (less likely) are more strongly represented in the high seasonal factor survey years.

Foreign-born mens' average occupational wage was about 92% of the average occupational wage for native-born men. The average variance of occupational wages for foreign-born men was about 83% of the wage variance for native-born men. So while the occupations of foreign-born men are compensated at about the same rate as the occupations of native-born men, foreign-born men cluster more in occupations with less wage variance. Foreign-born men represent about 6.9% of the sample unweighted, and about 8.0% weighted.[2] Their average years since migration is about 16.4 years.

Means for the dependent variables are shown at the bottom of Table 7.2. Foreign-born men have about the same employment ratio (84.1%, of population) as native-born men (84.6%), with a slightly greater probability of being job losers, job leavers, or labor force entrants, and a slightly lower probability of being out of the labor

Table 7.1. Independent Variables : Names, Descriptions, and Expected Signs of Partial Effects

VARIABLES	Variable Description	Emp.	NILF	Un-emp.	Loser	Leavr	En-trant	Dura-tion
				Expected Signs of Partial Effects on Dependent Variables				
Schooling	Highest level of schooling completed	+	-	-	-	-	+	-
Potential Experience	Age minus schooling minus 5	+	+/-	-	-	-	-	-
Married (Sp. Pres)	1 if married, spouse present; 0 otherwise	+	-	-	-	-	+	-
Metrop. Area	1 if metropolitan residence; 0 otherwise	+	-	-	-	+	+	-
South	1 if living in Southern states; 0 otherwise	?	?	?	?	?	?	?
Agriculture	1 if agric. wage/salary sector, 0 otherwise	+	+	-	-	+	+	-
November 1979	1 if November 1979 survey; 0 otherwise	+	+	-	-	+	+	-
April 1983	1 if April 1983 survey; 0 otherwise	-	+	+	+	-	-	+
June 1986	1 if June 1986; 0 otherwise	+	+	-	-	+	+	-
June 1988	1 if June 1988; 0 otherwise	+	+	-	-	+	+	-
November 1989	1 if November 1989 survey; 0 otherwise	+	+	-	-	+	+	-
June 1991	1 if June 1991; 0 otherwise	+	+	-	-	+	+	-
February 1994	1 if February 1994 survey; 0 otherwise	+	+	-	-	+	+	-
Area Unemp. Rate	Unemployment rate in SMSA or state	-	+/-	+	+	-	-	+
Seas/Occ Adj. Fact.	Seasonal factor within major occ. group	-	-	+	+	-	-	-
Average Occ. Wages	Average hourly wage within occ. group	+	-	-	+	-	+	-
Var., Occ. Wages	Variance of hourly wage within occ. group	-	+	+	-	+	-	+
Foreign Born	1 if foreign born; 0 otherwise; YSM=0	-	-	+	+	+	+	-
Yrs. Since Mig.	Number of years since migration to U.S.	+	+	-	-	-	-	+

Table 7.1 (continued)

		Expected Signs of Partial Effects on Dependent Variables						
VARIABLES		Emp.	NILF	Un-emp.	Loser	Leavr	En-trant	Dura-tion
YSM 25 Years +	Immigrated 25+ years before survey date	0	0	0	0	0	0	0
YSM 20-24 Years	Immigrated 20-24 years before survey date	0	0	0	0	0	0	0
YSM 15-19 Years	Immigrated 15-19 years before survey date	0	0	0	0	0	0	0
YSM 10-14 Years	Immigrated 10-14 before survey date	?	?	?	?	?	?	?
YSM 7-9 Years	Immigrated 7-9 years before survey date	?	?	?	?	?	?	?
YSM 5-6 Years	Immigrated 5-6 years before survey date	?	?	?	?	?	?	?
YSM 3-4 Years	Immigrated 3-4 years before survey date	-	+	+	+	+	+	-
YSM 2 Years or Less	Immigrated within 2 years of survey date	-	+	+	+	+	+	-

Table 7.2. Means and Standard Deviations of Independent and Dependent Variables 1976-94, Native Born, Foreign Born, and Pooled, Men Ages 25-64

VARIABLES	Native Born		Foreign Born		Pooled	
	Means	Std. Dev.	Means	Std. Dev.	Means	Std. Dev.
Age	41.8	11.3	40.8	11.8	41.7	11.4
Schooling	12.8	3.2	11.8	5.1	12.7	3.4
Potential Experience	23.9	12.4	24.0	13.2	23.9	12.5
Married, Spouse Present	0.744	0.434	0.740	0.473	0.743	0.437
Metropolitan Residence	0.705	0.454	0.923	0.287	0.722	0.448
South	0.343	0.472	0.219	0.446	0.333	0.472
Agriculture	0.025	0.156	0.045	0.223	0.027	0.161
Area Unemp. Rate %	6.5	2.8	6.9	3.0	6.6	2.8
Seas. Adjusment Factor	98.0	8.1	99.2	10.2	98.1	8.3
Average, Occ. Wages	6.91	3.30	6.39	3.34	6.87	3.30
Variance, Occ. Wages	29.63	16.53	24.48	19.98	29.22	16.84
Foreign Born					0.08	0.27
Duration in U.S. (FB)			16.4	13.7		
YSM 25 Years or More			0.214	0.442		
YSM 20-24 Years			0.126	0.357		
YSM 15-19 Years			0.099	0.322		
YSM 10-14 Years			0.171	0.406		
YSM 7-9 Years			0.136	0.370		
YSM 5-6 Years			0.078	0.289		

Table 7.2 (continued)

VARIABLES	Native Born		Foreign Born		Pooled	
	Means	Std. Dev.	Means	Std. Dev.	Means	Std. Dev.
YSM 3-4 Years			0.068	0.271		
YSM 2 Years or Less			0.082	0.297		
White	0.857	0.348	0.379	0.523	0.819	0.385
Hispanic	0.030	0.170	0.358	0.517	0.056	0.231
Black	0.102	0.301	0.066	0.269	0.099	0.299
Other Minority	0.011	0.103	0.196	0.428	0.026	0.159
Job Loser	0.032	0.176	0.042	0.216	0.033	0.179
Job Leaver	0.004	0.065	0.005	0.074	0.004	0.066
Labor Force Entrant	0.008	0.086	0.012	0.117	0.008	0.089
Not in Labor Force	0.109	0.310	0.099	0.322	0.108	0.311
Employed	0.846	0.359	0.841	0.394	0.846	0.361
Weeks Unemployed	21.71	25.47	20.04	25.43	21.53	25.47
Sample Size	305,548		22,685		328,233	

Sources: Current Population Survey, various supplements, 1979-94; Survey of Income and Education, 1976.

force. Unemployed foreign-born men have been looking for work about 1.7 fewer weeks than unemployed native-born men on average.

Table 7.3 reports the means disaggregated by racial group. First, the difference in percent foreign born within race is most striking. In Table 7.2, whites made up 85.7% of native-born men (weighted) but only 38.0% of foreign-born men, while Hispanics comprised only 3.0% of native-born men but 35.8% of foreign-born men; other minorities account for only 1.1% of native-born men but 19.6% of foreign-born men. In Table 7.3 we see that foreign-born men are only about 4% of white men and 5% of black men, but 51% of Hispanic men and 61% of other minority men.

The other variables in Table 7.3 are consistent with means reported in other work. The lowest average education is among Hispanics (10.2 years) and the highest is among other minorities (13.5 years). Blacks have a significantly lower married rate (57%) and are much more likely to live in the South than other groups; whites are about 10 percentage points more likely to live in non-metropolitan areas (which probably include suburbs) and have a higher wage variance; Hispanics are almost 3 times more likely than the other racial groups to work in agriculture. Among the dependent variables, blacks have the lowest employment ratio (about 75%) and the highest probability of being lob losers or leavers or labor force entrants. The number of job leavers is very small in this sample, and never gets as high as 1% of the population for any group.

Finally, Table 7.4 shows the means of the same explanatory variables within the various labor force dependent variables. Men out of the labor force are the oldest, at about 50 years on average, which is explained by higher rates of disability or retirement. About 77% of employed men are married, while only half of lob leavers are married. Job losers are more likely than the other categories to live in high unemployment areas. The highest average occupational wages and wage variances are for employed persons, the lowest for those out of the labor force. The foreign-born percent of employed men is about 8.0%, the same as for the population as a whole from Table 7.2, but 10% of job losers are foreign born, 9% of job leavers. While only 7% of those out of the labor force are foreign born, foreign-born men make up 12% of labor force entrants. Years since migration is about 15-16 years on average, but 18 years for those out of the labor force and 14 years for labor force entrants.

Table 7.3. Means and Standard Deviations of Independent and Dependent Variables 1979-91, Pooled, Men Ages 25-64, by Racial Group

VARIABLES	White Means	White Std. Dev.	Black Means	Black Std. Dev.	Hispanic Means	Hispanic Std. Dev.	Other Minority Means	Other Minority Std. Dev.
Age	42.1	11.3	40.9	12.7	38.9	12.1	40.1	9.3
Schooling	13.0	3.1	11.4	3.9	10.2	4.9	13.5	3.6
Potential Experience	24.0	12.3	24.5	14.6	23.6	13.8	21.5	10.6
Married, Spouse Present	0.768	0.416	0.571	0.561	0.710	0.519	0.710	0.400
Metropolitan Residence	0.698	0.452	0.807	0.447	0.878	0.374	0.834	0.329
South	0.313	0.456	0.538	0.565	0.337	0.540	0.180	0.339
Agriculture	0.025	0.152	0.022	0.167	0.067	0.287	0.023	0.132
Area Unemp. Rate %	6.5	2.8	6.6	3.2	6.8	3.0	6.6	2.3
Seas. Adjustment Factor	98.1	7.9	97.7	9.7	98.7	12.0	99.3	7.6
Average, Occ. Wages	6.95	3.67	6.62	2.91	6.41	3.00	6.17	2.82
Variance, Occ. Wages	29.91	16.46	27.06	19.46	29.01	18.53	26.95	15.59
Foreign Born	0.04	0.19	0.05	0.26	0.51	0.57	0.61	0.43
Duration in U.S. (FB)	21.5	14.8	12.5	11.6	14.4	12.6	11.3	9.5
YSM 25 Years or More	0.369	0.497	0.097	0.338	0.144	0.415	0.084	0.277
YSM 20-24 Years	0.167	0.384	0.092	0.330	0.118	0.382	0.072	0.258
YSM 15-19 Years	0.075	0.272	0.119	0.370	0.120	0.385	0.097	0.297
YSM 10-14 Years	0.114	0.327	0.196	0.453	0.206	0.479	0.210	0.407
YSM 7-9 Years	0.091	0.297	0.164	0.422	0.159	0.433	0.173	0.378
YSM 5-6 Years	0.045	0.213	0.108	0.354	0.089	0.338	0.111	0.314

Table 7.3 (continued)

VARIABLES	White Means	White Std. Dev.	Black Means	Black Std. Dev.	Hispanic Means	Hispanic Std. Dev.	Other Minority Means	Other Minority Std. Dev.
YSM 3-4 Years	0.048	0.221	0.082	0.313	0.068	0.297	0.100	0.301
YSM 2 Years or Less	0.067	0.258	0.098	0.339	0.067	0.295	0.136	0.343
Job Loser	0.028	0.164	0.062	0.273	0.053	0.257	0.031	0.152
Job Leaver	0.004	0.063	0.006	0.086	0.005	0.080	0.007	0.073
Labor Force Entrant	0.006	0.077	0.019	0.153	0.012	0.124	0.016	0.110
Not in Labor Force	0.102	0.298	0.163	0.418	0.095	0.335	0.130	0.296
Employed	0.860	0.342	0.747	0.493	0.833	0.427	0.814	0.343
Weeks Unemployed	21.53	24.63	23.93	31.3	17.32	24.92	18.92	17.43
Sample Size (Total)	277,797		25,339		14,189		10,908	
Sample Size (For. Born)	9,432		1,347		6,726		5,180	

Sources: Current Population Survey, various supplements, 1979-94; Survey of Income and Education, 1976.

Table 7.4. Means and Standard Deviations of Independent and Dependent Variables 1976–94, Pooled, Men Ages 25–64, by Labor Force/Employment Status

VARIABLES	Job Losers Means	Job Losers Std. Dev.	Job Leavers Means	Job Leavers Std. Dev.	Lab. Force Entrants Means	Lab. Force Entrants Std. Dev.	Not in Labor Force Means	Not in Labor Force Std. Dev.	Employed Means	Employed Std. Dev.
Age	39.0	11.2	36.1	10.0	38.8	11.8	49.8	12.9	40.9	10.8
Schooling	11.6	3.0	12.5	2.8	12.0	3.4	10.9	4.0	13.0	3.3
Pot. Experience	22.4	12.1	18.5	10.5	21.8	12.9	33.8	14.2	22.8	11.7
Married, Sp. Present	0.600	0.508	0.501	0.501	0.511	0.501	0.633	0.489	0.766	0.422
Metro. Residence	0.732	0.459	0.711	0.454	0.745	0.437	0.683	0.472	0.727	0.445
South	0.286	0.469	0.353	0.479	0.315	0.466	0.378	0.492	0.329	0.469
Agriculture	0.027	0.169	0.031	0.173	0.044	0.206	0.004	0.060	0.029	0.169
Area Unemp. Rate %	8.1	3.7	6.9	2.8	7.4	2.9	6.7	2.9	6.5	2.8
Seas. Adj. Factor	99.4	10.8	98.0	8.9	98.1	11.5	95.9	8.2	98.4	8.1
Avg., Occ. Wages	6.80	2.71	6.64	3.08	6.33	3.07	5.77	2.40	7.01	3.39
Var., Occ. Wages	25.41	16.67	27.16	17.70	25.12	17.96	22.29	12.39	30.30	17.09
Foreign Born	0.10	0.31	0.09	0.28	0.12	0.33	0.07	0.26	0.08	0.27
Duration in U.S. (FB)	15.4	12.8	16.3	12.6	13.7	14.3	18.0	16.6	16.3	13.3
YSM 25 Years +	0.176	0.422	0.252	0.480	0.168	0.403	0.295	0.486	0.207	0.437
YSM 20-24 Years	0.139	0.383	0.114	0.351	0.093	0.313	0.092	0.308	0.129	0.362
YSM 15-19 Years	0.088	0.313	0.099	0.330	0.070	0.275	0.071	0.274	0.103	0.328
YSM 10-14 Years	0.200	0.443	0.188	0.432	0.148	0.382	0.104	0.326	0.178	0.412

Table 7.4 (continued)

VARIABLES	Job Losers		Job Leavers		Lab. Force Entrants		Not in Labor Force		Employed	
	Means	Std. Dev.	Means	Std. Dev.	Means	Std. Dev.	Means	Std. Dev.	Means	Std. Dev.
YSM 7-9 Years	0.137	0.381	0.142	0.385	0.135	0.368	0.118	0.344	0.138	0.372
YSM 5-6 Years	0.108	0.343	0.034	0.201	0.090	0.309	0.073	0.277	0.077	0.288
YSM 3-4 Years	0.072	0.286	0.049	0.240	0.073	0.280	0.076	0.282	0.067	0.269
YSM 2 Years or Less	0.053	0.249	0.087	0.312	0.209	0.438	0.150	0.381	0.074	0.283
White	0.702	0.474	0.764	0.425	0.631	0.484	0.771	0.426	0.832	0.373
Hispanic	0.091	0.298	0.064	0.245	0.084	0.279	0.049	0.220	0.055	0.228
Black	0.184	0.402	0.131	0.338	0.233	0.424	0.149	0.361	0.087	0.282
Other Minority	0.024	0.158	0.041	0.199	0.052	0.222	0.031	0.176	0.025	0.155
Weeks Unemployed	22.15	25.54	18.01	23.04	22.04	26.62	0.00	0.00	0.00	0.00
Sample Size	10,161		1,427		2,584		34,576		279,236	

Sources: Current Population Survey, various supplements, 1979-94; Survey of Income and Education, 1976.

Employment, Unemployment, Out of the Labor Force

Chapter 8 begins the empirical analysis of employment, unemployment, and labor force participation probabilities. While Chapter 9 focuses on the unemployment states of job leaver, job loser, or labor force entrant, Chapter 8 combines these three states into the state of unemployment, and analyzes the joint probabilities with the NILF and employment states. Thus all adult men are part of the analysis in this chapter. As discussed in Chapter 6, the analysis uses a subsample of the main data set, comprising 103,393 men of ages 25-64.

8.1   BASIC MODEL VARIABLES, COEFFICIENTS

Tables 8.1, 8.2, and 8.3 display the results of the analysis of the basic model variables for native-born men and foreign-born men separately, not controlling for years since migration. Table 8.1 presents the coefficients and asymptotic t-statistics estimated from the multinomial logit model using equation 7.4. Column 1 of each section within each table presents the coefficients for the odds of being unemployed versus being employed; column 2 shows the odds of being out of the labor force versus employed; and column 3 shows the odds of being unemployed versus being out of the labor force. The coefficients are not marginal effects, and the magnitudes are meaningless in this context. The signs and significance levels of the coefficients are important information, however, particularly because of the detail they provide on pairwise comparisons.

The marginal effects can best be considered by examining the probabilities calculated in Table 8.2, and the associated differentials in Table 8.3, using equation 7.2. For these probability calculations, the reference person has the mean values of the continuous variables, shown at the bottom of Table 8.2, and is in the modal population for each of the dichotomous categorical variables. Thus the reference person is married, lives in a metropolitan area in the non-South, does not work in agricultural wage and salary employment, and was surveyed in 1976.

It appears from Table 8.1 that most of the explanatory variables have similar effects on the employment, unemployment, and NILF odds for both native-born and foreign-born men, as the signs are similar in most cases. More of the coefficients in the foreign-born model are statistically insignificant, probably reflecting the smaller sample size (the sample size at the bottom of the table reflect only the raw numbers used in the analysis, but each person was weighted to reflect their overall proportion in the population, as shown in Table 7.2). It also appears that overall the variables together explain about the same amount of the overall variance in the probabilities. A native-born reference man has an overall probability of 91.8% of being employed, 3.5% of being unemployed, and 4.7% of being out of the labor force For a foreign-born reference man the probabilities are 91.5%, 4.5%, and 4.0% respectively. In both the foreign-born and native-born samples the control variables add about 7 percentage points to the probability of being employed (compared to the raw means from Table 7.2), with about 6 of those points coming from persons out of the labor force and about 1 point coming from unemployed persons. Thus our first test indicates that the control variables account more for the odds of being out of the labor force than for unemployment.

Schooling has the clear effect of increasing employment odds versus both unemployment and NILF, consistent with human capital theory, and reducing unemployment odds versus both employment and NILF. NILF odds increase relative to unemployment and decrease relative to employment. Table 8.2 shows the effects of increasing schooling. When choosing values to set for comparisons of the continuous variables, the rule generally followed was to pick a rounded value that was reasonably close to 1 standard deviation from the mean values in the pooled sample. Thus we compare probabilities at the mean schooling level of 12.8 years for native-born men and 11.8 years

Table 8.1. Multinomial Logit Coefficients of Employment, Unemployment, and NILF States Native Born and Foreign Born Adult Men, All Races

VARIABLES	NATIVE BORN			FOREIGN BORN		
	Unemployed vs. Employed	NILF vs. Employed	Unemployed vs. NILF	Unemployed vs. Employed	NILF vs. Employed	Unemployed vs. NILF
Schooling	-0.1398	-0.0422	-0.0977	-0.0552	-0.0175	-0.0377
	(-41.12)	(-17.73)	(-25.05)	(-8.21)	(-3.15)	(-4.51)
Potential Experience	-0.0224	-0.0577	0.0353	-0.0170	-0.1120	0.0950
	(-6.73)	(-23.84)	(9.03)	(-1.75)	(-16.57)	(8.48)
Experience Squared	0.0002	0.0023	-0.0021	0.0002	0.0027	-0.0025
	(3.17)	(53.81)	(-28.61)	(1.19)	(22.80)	(-12.40)
Married (Spouse Present)	-0.8754	-0.9253	0.0500	-0.2915	-0.4760	0.1845
	(-45.12)	(-62.52)	(2.16)	(-4.89)	(-9.66)	(2.50)
Metropolitan Area	-0.0362	-0.0803	0.0442	0.1277	-0.1848	0.3125
	(-1.74)	(-5.43)	(1.81)	(1.17)	(-2.24)	(2.38)
South	-0.1379	0.1506	-0.2885	-0.0081	-0.1561	0.1479
	(-6.79)	(10.68)	(-12.22)	(-0.12)	(-2.81)	(1.78)
Agriculture	-0.3531	-3.5142	3.1611	-0.1037	-3.2265	3.1228
	(-6.28)	(-34.42)	(27.58)	(-0.90)	(-11.17)	(10.18)
November 1979	-0.6596	-0.7133	0.0537	-0.2067	0.2912	-0.4980
	(-14.46)	(-23.54)	(1.02)	(-1.42)	(2.72)	(-2.86)

Table 8.1 (continued)

	NATIVE BORN			FOREIGN BORN		
VARIABLES	Unemployed vs. Employed	NILF vs. Employed	Unemployed vs. NILF	Unemployed vs. Employed	NILF vs. Employed	Unemployed vs. NILF
April 1983	-0.1019	-0.6145	0.5126	0.2973	-0.0617	0.3591
	(-2.67)	(-20.76)	(11.22)	(2.83)	(-0.62)	(2.60)
June 1986	-0.1187	-0.4037	0.2850	0.1595	0.1462	0.0133
	(-3.22)	(-15.41)	(6.63)	(1.39)	(1.57)	(0.09)
June 1988	-0.1598	-0.2625	0.1027	-0.0606	0.2332	-0.2938
	(-3.87)	(-9.69)	(2.17)	(-0.45)	(2.38)	(-1.84)
November 1989	-0.1807	-0.1885	0.0078	0.2035	0.0083	0.1952
	(-4.40)	(-7.09)	(0.17)	(1.63)	(0.09)	(1.28)
June 1991	-0.0468	-0.1006	0.0538	0.2947	0.2385	0.0562
	(-1.25)	(-3.81)	(1.23)	(2.87)	(2.79)	(0.44)
February 1994	-0.2716	0.4392	-0.7109	0.1851	1.2549	-1.0698
	(-5.97)	(13.73)	(-13.34)	(1.73)	(15.16)	(-8.27)
Area Unemp. Rate	0.1264	0.0365	0.0899	0.1229	0.0336	0.0893
	(37.96)	(12.67)	(21.82)	(10.97)	(3.20)	(6.20)
Seas/Occ Adjust. Fact.	0.0081	-0.0288	0.0369	0.0005	-0.0557	0.0562
	(5.98)	(-28.24)	(22.92)	(0.16)	(-16.98)	(12.71)
Average, Occ. Wages	0.0590	-0.0335	0.0925	0.0225	-0.1075	0.1300
	(12.80)	(-9.74)	(16.70)	(1.55)	(-10.64)	(7.65)

Table 8.1 (continued)

VARIABLES	NATIVE BORN			FOREIGN BORN		
	Unemployed vs. Employed	NILF vs. Employed	Unemployed vs. NILF	Unemployed vs. Employed	NILF vs. Employed	Unemployed vs. NILF
Variance, Occ. Wages	-0.0283	-0.0375	0.0093	-0.0180	0.0112	-0.0292
	(-29.79)	(-52.30)	(8.11)	(-6.87)	(8.18)	(-10.14)
Constant	-1.3318	2.5762	-3.9080	-2.5043	4.5821	-7.0864
	(-9.45)	(25.71)	(-23.96)	(-6.43)	(13.32)	(-14.26)
Sample Size	80,738			22,655		

Sources: Current Population Survey, various supplements, 1979-94; Survey of Income and Education, 1976.

Notes: asymptotic t-ratios in parentheses.

Table 8.2. Estimated Probabilities for Changes in Explanatory Variables Native Born and Foreign Born Adult Men, All Races

VARIABLES	NATIVE BORN			FOREIGN BORN		
	NILF	Unemp.	Employed	NILF	Unemp.	Employed
Reference Person	0.047	0.035	0.918	0.040	0.045	0.915
Schooling = 16 Yrs	0.042	0.023	0.936	0.038	0.036	0.926
Schooling = 9 Yrs	0.053	0.058	0.889	0.042	0.052	0.906
Potential Exper. = 36	0.112	0.029	0.859	0.070	0.041	0.888
Potential Exper. = 12	0.035	0.042	0.922	0.047	0.050	0.903
Unmarried	0.105	0.075	0.820	0.062	0.058	0.880
Non-Metropolitan Res.	0.050	0.036	0.913	0.048	0.040	0.913
South	0.054	0.030	0.915	0.034	0.045	0.921
Agriculture	0.001	0.026	0.972	0.002	0.042	0.956
November 1979	0.024	0.019	0.957	0.053	0.036	0.910
April 1983	0.026	0.033	0.942	0.037	0.060	0.903
June 1986	0.032	0.032	0.936	0.046	0.052	0.902
June 1988	0.037	0.030	0.933	0.050	0.042	0.908
November 1989	0.039	0.030	0.931	0.040	0.055	0.906
June 1991	0.043	0.034	0.924	0.049	0.059	0.892
February 1994	0.071	0.026	0.902	0.126	0.049	0.825
Area Unemp. Rate=11.5%	0.054	0.063	0.883	0.045	0.077	0.879
Seas. Adjust. = 113%	0.031	0.040	0.929	0.019	0.046	0.935

Table 8.2 (continued)

	NATIVE BORN			FOREIGN BORN		
	NILF	Unemp.	Employed	NILF	Unemp.	Employed
Avg. Occ. Wages = $12	0.039	0.047	0.914	0.022	0.052	0.926
Var. Occ. Wages x 2	0.016	0.016	0.968	0.053	0.029	0.918

Means for Reference Person:	Mean	Std Dev.	Mean	Std Dev.
Schooling	12.8	6.2	11.8	5.1
Potential Experience	24.0	24.1	24.0	12.1
Area Unemp. Rate (%)	6.54	5.44	6.85	2.94
Seas/Occ Adjust. Fact.	98.03	15.87	99.21	10.24
Average, Occ. Wages	6.91	6.38	6.39	3.34
Variance, Occ. Wages	29.58	32.04	24.49	19.97
YSM for For. Born	(a)	(a)	16.38	13.60

Notes: (a)—variable not entered

Table 8.3. Differentials in Estimated Probabilities for Changes in Explanatory Variables Native Born and Foreign Born Adult Men, All Races

NUMERIC DIFFERENTIALS: VARIABLES:	NATIVE BORN			FOREIGN BORN		
	NILF	Unemp.	Employed	NILF	Unemp.	Employed
Reference Person	0.000	0.000	0.000	0.000	0.000	0.000
Schooling = 16 Yrs	-0.005	-0.012	0.017	-0.002	-0.009	0.011
Schooling = 9 Yrs	0.006	0.023	-0.029	0.002	0.007	-0.009
Potential Exper. = 36	0.065	-0.006	-0.059	0.030	-0.004	-0.027
Potential Exper. = 12	-0.011	0.007	0.004	0.007	0.005	-0.012
Unmarried	0.058	0.040	-0.099	0.022	0.013	-0.035
Non-Metropolitan Res.	0.004	0.001	-0.005	0.008	-0.006	-0.002
South	0.007	-0.005	-0.003	-0.006	0.000	0.006
Agriculture	-0.045	-0.009	0.054	-0.038	-0.003	0.041
November 1979	-0.023	-0.016	0.039	0.013	-0.009	-0.005
April 1983	-0.021	-0.003	0.023	-0.003	0.015	-0.012
June 1986	-0.015	-0.003	0.018	0.006	0.007	-0.013
June 1988	-0.010	-0.005	0.015	0.010	-0.003	-0.007
November 1989	-0.007	-0.005	0.013	0.000	0.010	-0.010
June 1991	-0.004	-0.001	0.006	0.009	0.014	-0.023
February 1994	0.025	-0.009	-0.016	0.086	0.004	-0.090
Area Unemp. Rate=11.5%	0.007	0.028	-0.035	0.005	0.032	-0.036
Seas. Adjust. = 113%	-0.016	0.005	0.011	-0.021	0.001	0.020
Avg. Occ. Wages = $12	-0.008	0.012	-0.005	-0.018	0.007	0.011
Var. Occ. Wages x 2	-0.030	-0.019	0.050	0.013	-0.016	0.003

Table 8.3 (continued)

PERCENT DIFFERENTIALS:	NATIVE BORN			FOREIGN BORN		
VARIABLES:	NILF	Unemp.	Employed	NILF	Unemp.	Employed
Reference Person	0.0	0.0	0.0	0.0	0.0	0.0
Schooling = 16 Yrs	-11.0	-35.0	1.9	-5.9	-19.7	1.2
Schooling = 9 Yrs	13.6	64.3	-3.2	4.0	15.6	-0.9
Potential Exper. = 36	138.6	-17.4	-6.4	75.7	-8.0	-2.9
Potential Exper. = 12	-24.3	20.5	0.5	18.4	10.5	-1.3
Unmarried	125.2	114.2	-10.7	54.8	28.7	-3.8
Non-Metropolitan Res.	7.8	3.1	-0.5	20.0	-12.2	-0.3
South	15.9	-13.1	-0.3	-13.9	-0.2	0.6
Agriculture	-96.8	-25.6	5.9	-95.9	-5.8	4.5
November 1979	-48.9	-46.1	4.3	33.1	-19.1	-0.5
April 1983	-44.5	-7.4	2.5	-7.2	32.9	-1.3
June 1986	-31.9	-9.4	2.0	14.1	15.7	-1.4
June 1988	-21.8	-13.4	1.6	25.3	-6.6	-0.8
November 1989	-16.0	-15.4	1.4	-0.2	21.3	-1.0
June 1991	-9.0	-4.0	0.6	23.7	30.8	-2.6
February 1994	52.5	-25.1	-1.7	216.2	8.5	-9.8
Area Unemp. Rate=11.5%	15.2	80.0	-3.8	12.3	70.0	-4.0
Seas. Adjust. = 113%	-34.2	14.2	1.2	-52.6	2.9	2.2
Avg. Occ. Wages = $12	-16.1	34.4	-0.5	-44.6	14.8	1.2
Var. Occ. Wages x 2	-65.2	-54.4	5.4	32.0	-35.4	0.3

for foreign-born men with those at 16 years and 9 years of schooling, mean experience (about 24 years) to 36 years and 12 years of experience, a seasonal adjustment factor (on average about 98-99) of 113, an area unemployment rate of 11.5% (compared to an average of about 6.5%), average occupational wages of $12 per hour (compare to an average of $6-7) and occupational wage variances twice the average variance for each group.

For native-born men, an increase in completed schooling from the mean of 12.8 years to 16 years increases employment probabilities by about 2 percentage points, reducing both unemployment (to 4.2%) and labor force nonparticipation (to 2.3%); the unemployment probability for persons with only 9 years of schooling would be about 5.8%. For foreign-born men, schooling has a much smaller impact. A foreign-born man at 16 years of education has an employment probability only 1 percentage point greater than at the mean level of schooling (even though the increase in schooling is a year greater than for native-born men), which is almost entirely drawn from a reduction in unemployment. Thus the "return" to schooling, in terms of labor force participation and employment/unemployment rates is smaller for foreign-born men, reflecting the lower transferability of skills acquired prior to immigration. This result is consistent with earlier studies (Chiswick, 1982; Chiswick and Hurst, 1987; Chiswick, Cohen, and Zach, 1997).

More years of potential experience clearly increase the employment odds for both native-born and foreign-born men compared to both unemployment and NILF status, but the total effect on unemployment is unclear, since higher levels of experience tend to increase the odds that a person will be unemployed rather than out of the labor force. The experience effect is clearly quadratic, having less effect over time. Also, the odds of being unemployed versus employed, although having the same sign as for native-born men, is not significant for foreign-born men.

Table 8.2 shows a clearer picture of the effect of experience on labor force odds, and shows that the effects are not the same at different points of labor force experience. It seems apparent that in the early years labor force participation increases with experience, as workers acquire more general and, as time progresses, more firm-specific human capital. As workers get older, however, they are more likely to become disabled or to retire. For example, the average level of experience in both the native-born and foreign-born samples is 24 years. Thus increasing experience to 36 years or reducing it to 12 years would be the same numerical change in experience. Yet for native-born men, increasing experience from 12 years to 24 years reduces labor force participation by 1 percentage point, while an additional 12 years reduces labor force participation by 6.5 percentage points. Unemployment probabilities, on the other hand, only decline from 4.2% to 2.9% over the whole range of 24 years. These effects are smaller for foreign-born men.

The nonlinear effect of experience on labor force participation and employment ratios, and the linear effect on unemployment probabilities, is somewhat difficult to spot from Tables 8.1 or 8.2. Figure 8.1 shows the effects of potential labor force experience on the probabilities of being in each of the various labor force for native-born men.

Figure 8.1. Effect of Experience on Labor Force Probabilities
Pooled Sample of Native-Born and Foreign-Born Men, Ceteris Paribus

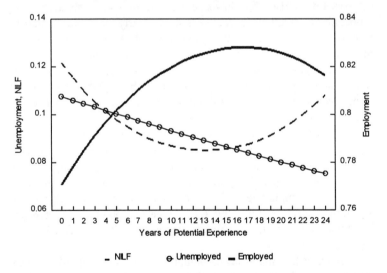

At 0 years of experience, the NILF probability is 5.2%, falls to its nadir of 3.5% between 13 and 14 years, then rises thereafter; at 36 years of experience, 11.2% of adult native-born men are out of the labor force. A similar pattern works in the opposite direction for employment probabilities, which rise from 89.5% at 0 years of experience to peak at 92.4% between 15 and 19 years, and decline thereafter; at 36 years experience the employment rate is 85.9% for native-born men. Unemployment probabilities actually decline continuously with experience—in later years persons not working tend to drop out of the labor force rather than continue to look for work.

For foreign-born men the patterns are similar, but the effect of potential experience is again slower than for native-born men. The NILF probability starts at 11.3% at 0 years experience, bottoms out at 3.9% at 19-23 years, and rises thereafter, and is 7.0% at 36 years experience. Similarly, employment probabilities rise from 83.2% at 0 years to 91.5% at 20-25 years, then decline to 88.8% at 36 years.

The effect of marriage is to increase the odds of being in the labor force and of being employed, judging by the significance levels as indicated by the t-ratios in Table 8.1, all consistent with labor economics theory. The effect of marriage on the odds of being unemployed are not clear from Table 8.1, as unemployment is higher compared to NILF, but lower compared to employment, but the probability calculations in Table 8.2 show clearly that being unmarried increases the probability of being unemployed. We see similar patterns for marriage as we do for schooling—for native-born men, being unmarried (alternatively, married but spouse absent) increases the NILF and unemployment probabilities by 123% and 114% respectively, while for foreign-born men the effects are smaller, as the respective increases are 55% and 29%.

A metropolitan residence likewise increases employment and labor force participation odds, while the effect on unemployment odds is unclear, higher compared to NILF, lower compared to employment. Table 8.3 shows that living in a nonmetropolitan area has very little effect on unemployment for native-born men, but reduces the unemployment probability by 0.6 percentage points, and increases labor force nonparticipation by 0.8 percentage points, for foreign-born men.

Living in the South has ambiguous effects. For native-born men, employment odds increase relative to unemployment for Southern residence, but native-born men in the South are more likely to be out of the labor force than their counterparts in the non-South, compared to either employment or unemployment. Changes in the probabilities due to living in the South is less than a percentage point either way for any of the labor force states. Southern residence has just the opposite effect on foreign-born men, who are more likely to be employed and less likely to be out of the labor force, with no effect on unemployment. The "Southern" effect is even smaller for foreign-born men than for native-born men, perhaps because of the small percentage living in the South (see Table 7.2).

Working in the agricultural wage and salary sector increases employment odds and labor force participation odds for both native-born and foreign-born men. This result for foreign-born men is different from that of Chiswick and Hurst (1997) who found weeks worked lower and unemployment rates higher for agricultural foreign-born workers compared to other foreign-born workers. Chiswick and Hurst were using data from the 1990 Census, however, and considered persons who had both and agricultural industry and occupation, working or not. This analysis uses a dichotomous variable assigned by the Census Bureau to wage and salary workers in the agricultural industry. The variable will overestimate the proportion employed compared to out of the labor force, because only about 25% of persons who are out of the labor force at the time of the survey are asked questions about their previous employment; thus, of all persons listed as agricultural wage and salary workers, the CPS captures the employed and unemployed but only one fourth of those out of the labor force. Thus the variable is useful as a control, but has less value as an explanatory variable for employment and labor force participation.

The dummy variables for survey year, as described above, show primarily either trend effects, or unmeasured differences between the surveys, since we have controlled for the area unemployment rate (a partial control for cyclical patterns) and for the effects of seasonality. As such, it appears, not totally consistently, that for native-born men the trend over time (compared to the benchmark of 1976) is for greater odds of being employed or in the labor force, with the net effect on unemployment unclear because of higher odds compared to being out of the labor force, but lower odds compared to being unemployed. These results are fairly consistent with published national statistics.

The trend effects are clearer when we review the calculated probabilities in Table 8.2 and 8.3. Even after holding constant the area unemployment rate and the occupational seasonal adjustment factors, we see that, for native-born men, unemployment probabilities decline from 3.5% in the benchmark recession year 1976 to 1.9% in the low-unemployment year of 1979, and are about the same in the recession years 1983 and 1991; in all other years the unemployment rate is lower than in 1976. It is possible that the cyclical effects are not completely smoothed by the area unemployment rate variable. But the trends for NILF and employment rates, which are less collinear with area unemployment rates, are clear. The employment probability is significantly higher (95.7%) in 1979 than in 1976 (91.8%), but declines continuously through 1994; although declining continuously through the 1980s, the employment probability is still higher than in 1976, until 1994, when the probability is actually lower (90.2%). The NILF probability progresses in the opposite direction, declining to 2.4% in 1979 from 4.7% in 1976, but then increasing until the NILF probability in 1994 is 7.1%.

For foreign-born men, the pattern is different. The probability of being out of the labor force is about the same or higher than in 1976 for every year except 1983. In 1994 the NILF probability is 12.6% for foreign-born men. For both native-born and foreign-born men the high NILF probability in 1994 is in large part due to the 1994 survey's high seasonal factor and thus suffers from collinearity with the seasonal adjustment factor. However, the much larger effect and the overall high NILF probability for foreign-born men is also partly the result of a growing percentage of that population which has recently migrated, which we will see has a higher NILF probability.

The effect of the local area unemployment rate is unambiguous and just what we would expect—the higher the unemployment rate in an area, the lower the odds that a person will be employed, and the higher the odds of unemployment. An increase to 11.5% from the mean of 6.5% would increase unemployment probabilities from 3.5% to 6.3% for native-born men, and from 4.5% to 7.7% for foreign-born men, and reduce employment and labor force participation probabilities for both groups. Of course, this variable is effective mostly as a control; the endogeneity of the variable, since it is calculated in-sample, reduces its value as an explanatory variable. The area unemployment rate is more interesting when comparing the voluntary/involuntary types of unemployment in Chapter 9.

The seasonal/occupational adjustment factor is more difficult variable to interpret. In Table 8.1, for native-born men, the effect of a higher seasonal/occupation factor on labor force participation is ambiguous, increasing labor force participation relative to employment but decreasing it relative to unemployment. But the odds of being employed appear to be higher, and the odds of being unemployed are unambiguously higher. Raising the seasonal adjustment factor from the mean level (98.0 in the native-born sample) to 113 increases employment probabilities, but also increases unemployment probabilities, as labor force participation increases as well. For foreign-born men, a higher seasonal/occupation factor decreases labor force nonparticipation more (52.5%) than for native-born men (34.0%), and the unemployment rate is virtually unchanged for foreign-born men.

Thus, persons in more highly seasonal occupations (or higher seasonal periods) are more likely to be employed but also more likely to be unemployed because they are more likely to stay in the labor force when unemployed, and this trend is stronger for foreign-born men. It is possible that persons in highly seasonal occupations have a more consistent attachment to the labor force because they have expectations of future work when unemployed, are eligible for unemployment benefits, and/or because of compensating differentials. Recently arrived foreign-born men, however, are generally less eligible for unemployment compensation benefits, and probably have lower compensating differentials. We can conclude, therefore, that there is a higher seasonal sensitivity for foreign-born men. The adjustment factor variable is also performing as intended, as a control on the seasonal effect of the various surveys. When entered separately, the major effect is to increase the magnitude of the intercept, and to reduce the magnitudes and significance levels of a few of the survey year dummy variables, particularly February 1994, the highest seasonal period.

Average occupational wages generally have the effects hypothesized in Chapter 7, and most of the effects are highly significant. Higher average occupational wages have their strongest impact on increasing labor force participation for both nativity groups, but more for foreign-born men—the NILF probability declines from 4.0% to 2.2%, compared to a decline from 4.7% to 3.9% for native-born men. It seems reasonable to conclude from this result that higher average wages induce entry into the labor force. Unemployment clearly increases with higher average wages, although this effect is much smaller for foreign-born men and is not significant for the latter group compared to being employed. So as more people are induced into the labor force because of higher wages, employment increases, but so does unemployment. It is also possible that higher wages induce higher layoff rates, which we will test in Chapter 9.

Occupational wage variances, by contrast, do not consistently work in the opposite direction from wage averages as hypothesized, and the effects are dramatically different for foreign-born men from native-born men.[3] A higher wage variance reduces unemployment for both native-born and foreign-born men, but has a stronger effect on native-born men. For native-born men this could be because of a lower quit rate or because a higher variance implies that occupational wages are more accurately matched in occupations with more heterogeneous workers. However, the determinants of such lower unemployment rates are different between the two groups. Higher wage variances increase labor force participation and employment for native-born men, but have just the opposite effect on foreign-born men.

There are several possible reasons that higher wage variances have opposite effects on foreign-born men and native-born men. Perhaps there is a difference in information between the two groups. Foreign-born men may also be more homogeneous in their skill types, as seen by their lower average wage variance. Higher wage variances may cause foreign-born men to be more passive in their job search. Higher occupational wage variances in general indicate less wage rigidity and greater economic efficiency, but this may be more true for native-born men than for foreign-born men, about whom employers have less information. Finally, it may simply be the case that foreign-born men are more risk averse than native-born men. At any rate, for foreign-born men the lower probability of unemployment is a more a result of lower labor force participation than because of higher employment.

Table 8.3 presents the same information as Table 8.2, but instead of the raw probabilities, it shows the differentials, numeric in the top table and percentage in the bottom table, between the probability calculated by the "change" variable and the reference probability. For example, increasing schooling to 16 years from the mean reduces the NILF probability by about 0.5 percentage points for native-born men, or by about 11.0 percent.

While the information is the same as in Table 8.2, some overall patterns are easier to see in Table 8.3. First, except for the survey dummy variables, most of the differentials for foreign-born men have the same sign as the differentials for native-born men—only 6 of the 36 possible comparisons have different signs. Thus the effects of changes in demographic, geographic, or wage characteristics are similar for native-born men, at least in their direction. The notable exceptions are: low levels of experience, which appear to show that the effect of experience is more linear for native-born men; Southern residence, which increases labor force participation by 14% for foreign-born men and decreases it by 16% for native-born men; and occupational wage variance, which reduces labor force participation for foreign-born men and increases it for native-born men.

Second, while the signs are mostly the same, the magnitudes are not. In all but 4 of the 30 possible comparisons (except for the survey year dummy variables) where the signs are the same, the absolute value—the magnitude of the differential—is smaller for foreign-born men. Thus, while the basic model controls work in the same direction, they have less effect on foreign-born men. This is an example of the lower transferability of skills for the human capital variables, such as education and experience. It may also indicate that foreign-born men have other characteristics which we have not identified which have more of an impact on their labor market transitions than they would for native-born men. The three notable exceptions are the greater effect of nonmetropolitan residence on reducing labor force participation of foreign-born men, the greater impact of seasonality in increasing labor force participation, and the greater impact of higher average wages on increasing labor force participation.

Finally, Table 8.3 shows more clearly the differences in trend effects between native-born and foreign-born men. Although the patterns are not perfectly consistent, generally native-born men had higher probabilities of labor force participation and employment, and lower probabilities of unemployment, while the trends were just the opposite for foreign-born men, although of generally smaller magnitude. This may be an indication that labor force outcomes are worse for more recent cohorts of foreign-born men, but the many insignificant coefficients cast some doubt on that conclusion.

8.2   THE FOREIGN-BORN VARIABLES

Up to this point the focus has been on what are essentially control variables, although they have a great deal of information in themselves about differences between native-born men and foreign-born men. The point of the book, however, is to examine differentials between foreign-born men and native-born men, after controlling for demographic, geographic, period, and wage effects. It is an underlying assumption here that, after controlling for schooling, area of residence, seasonality factors, expected wages, etc., inclusion of a foreign-born dummy variable and variables to specify years since migration will display fundamental innate differences between native-born men and foreign-born men that can't be explained by differences in their means or differences in their responses.

Tests for the "foreign-born" effect and for duration in the U.S. are displayed in four basic models. First, we consider two specifications to account for years since migration. One adds a dichotomous variable to the basic model to account for simple foreign-born status, plus a continuous variable to account for YSM (years since migration), plus a variable to account for quadratic nonlinearity in the YSM variable. A second specification dispenses with the foreign-born dummy variable and replaces the continuous duration variables with incremental variables to measure discontinuities in the effects of duration in the U.S.

Each of these two specifications is then run on two separate samples—a pooled sample of both native-born and foreign-born men, and a foreign-born sample. The foreign-born sample measures the actual effects of duration in the U.S. for foreign-born men using the foreign-born characteristics and behavioral effects to estimate the equation. Thus the foreign-born sample is measuring differences between foreign-born persons at different lengths of duration. Given that there are differences in mean characteristics and behavioral effects, however, the pooled sample measures differences between foreign-born men and native-born men, holding constant differences in the mean characteristics or behavioral effects of the basic model variables.

Table 8.4 shows the coefficients and associated probabilities for each of the four models described in the previous paragraph. Only the foreign-born and years since migration variables are shown in Table 8.4, although the models control for the same "basic model" variables as in Tables 8.1 and 8.2. The basic model coefficients and probabilities are virtually identical to those in Tables 8.1 and 8.2, so are not repeated here. Instead, the complete tables are included for reference in Hurst (1997).

The dummy variable for "Foreign-born", in the upper part of the table for the pooled model, indicates the differential, ceteris paribus, between a native-born man and a foreign-born man, in the odds of being in each of the states; the associated probabilities are shown in the lower part of the table. This would be at the time of arrival for

Table 8.4. Multinomial Logit Coefficients and Probabilities of Labor Force States, Foreign Born and Years Since Migration Variables

COEFFICIENTS:	POOLED			FOREIGN BORN		
	Unemployed vs. Employed	NILF vs. Employed	Unemployed vs. NILF	Unemployed vs. Employed	NILF vs. Employed	Unemployed vs. NILF
VARIABLES:	(b)	(b)	(b)	(b)	(b)	(b)
Schooling, Exper., ...				(a)	(a)	(a)
Foreign Born	-0.1321	0.4470	-0.5791			
	(-2.07)	(9.16)	(-7.65)			
Years Since Mig. (YSM)	0.0033	-0.0819	0.0852	-0.0061	-0.0742	0.0681
	(0.46)	(-15.00)	(10.06)	(-0.86)	(-13.90)	(8.07)
YSM Squared	0.0001	0.0015	-0.0014	0.0001	0.0014	-0.0013
	(0.40)	(13.04)	(-7.65)	(0.75)	(13.21)	(-7.31)
Schooling, Exper., ...	(b)	(b)	(b)	(b)	(b)	(b)
YSM 25 Years or More	0.1051	-0.3605	0.4656	0.0705	-0.0558	0.1263
	(1.63)	(-7.92)	(6.24)	(0.71)	(-0.72)	(1.05)
YSM 20-24 Years	0.0124	-0.6958	0.7082	0.1327	-0.3974	0.5301
	(0.16)	(-9.25)	(6.93)	(1.29)	(-4.24)	(3.96)
YSM 15-19 Years	-0.1526	-0.5631	0.4105	-0.1112	-0.4094	0.2981
	(-1.63)	(-6.74)	(3.42)	(-0.97)	(-4.10)	(2.03)
YSM 10-14 Years	-0.0634	-0.6031	0.5397	0.0743	-0.4234	0.4977
	(-0.99)	(-8.83)	(6.02)	(0.81)	(-4.83)	(4.08)

Table 8.4 (continued)

VARIABLES	POOLED			FOREIGN BORN		
	Unemployed vs. Employed	NILF vs. Employed	Unemployed vs. NILF	Unemployed vs. Employed	NILF vs. Employed	Unemployed vs. NILF
YSM 7-9 Years	-0.2175	-0.1144	-0.1031	(a)	(a)	(a)
	(-2.90)	(-1.74)	(-1.08)			
YSM 5-6 Years	-0.0239	-0.1188	0.0949	0.2052	0.0222	0.1830
	(-0.27)	(-1.41)	(0.82)	(1.88)	(0.22)	(1.29)
YSM 3-4 Years	-0.2611	0.1190	-0.3801	-0.0607	0.2356	-0.2963
	(-2.53)	(1.43)	(-3.04)	(-0.50)	(2.37)	(-1.97)
YSM 2 Years or Less	0.0533	0.8622	-0.8089	0.2694	0.9003	-0.6309
	(0.57)	(13.64)	(-7.69)	(2.37)	(10.65)	(-4.68)
Sample Size	103,393			22,655		

Table 8.4 (continued)

PROBABILITIES:	POOLED			FOREIGN BORN		
	NILF	Unemp.	Employed	NILF	Unemp.	Employed
Reference Person	0.045	0.036	0.919	0.071	0.046	0.883
Schooling, Exper., . . .	(b)	(b)	(b)	(b)	(b)	(b)
Foreign Born at Entry				(a)	(a)	(a)
YSM = mean	0.028	0.034	0.938	0.032	0.045	0.923
YSM = mean + 10	0.023	0.036	0.940	0.028	0.045	0.927
Reference Person	0.045	0.036	0.919	0.041	0.041	0.917
Schooling, Exper., . . .	(b)	(b)	(b)	(b)	(b)	(b)
YSM 25 Years or More	0.032	0.040	0.928	0.039	0.044	0.917
YSM 20-24 Years	0.023	0.037	0.940	0.028	0.048	0.924
YSM 15-19 Years	0.026	0.031	0.942	0.028	0.038	0.934
YSM 10-14 Years	0.025	0.034	0.940	0.027	0.045	0.928
YSM 7-9 Years	0.041	0.029	0.930	(a)	(a)	(a)
YSM 5-6 Years	0.040	0.035	0.925	0.042	0.050	0.908
YSM 3-4 Years	0.051	0.028	0.921	0.052	0.039	0.910
YSM 2 Years or Less	0.101	0.035	0.864	0.095	0.051	0.855

Sources: Current Population Survey, various supplements, 1979-94; Survey of Income and Education, 1976.

Notes: asymptotic t-ratios in parentheses; (a)—variable not entered; (b) shown in Appendix A.

foreign-born men. In the foreign-born model, the foreign-born dummy variable is not entered, so the reference person is a foreign-born man at arrival, and the years since migration variables measure the effects of duration directly for foreign-born men.

In the second specification, the incremental variables (YSM 2 Years or Less, YSM 3-4 Years, etc.) measure the differentials in the odds or probabilities of being in the various labor force states between foreign-born men in the increments and native-born men (in the pooled model) or between foreign-born men in the increments and foreign-born men at the benchmark duration of 7-9 years (in the foreign-born model).

For either model, the coefficients for the "basic model" are not much different than in the models without the foreign-born or duration variables in Tables 8.1 and 8.2. For the foreign-born equation, this indicates that there is little collinearity between duration in the U.S. and the other demographic or control variables, in other words, the means of the characteristics of the basic model variables may change with longer duration in the U.S., but not the slope coefficients. We expect more differences in the coefficients between the pooled model and the native-born model, since there were some large differences in means in some cases (South, for example; see Table 7.2).

Foreign-born men at arrival are clearly more likely to be out of the labor force than native-born men, compared to either being employed or unemployed. The higher NILF odds decline over time in the destination, and do so quadratically. All coefficients are statistically significant. We have hypothesized that foreign-born men when they first arrive would have a higher probability than native-born men of being out of the labor force, and this is substantiated by the probability calculations, with a foreign-born man at arrival having a 7.0% probability of being out of the labor force compared to 4.5% for a native-born man. This probability also declines with duration in the U.S., and drops below the native-born probability after about 7 years after arrival.

We have also hypothesized that foreign-born men would have a lower employment ratio at arrival than native-born men. The coefficients in Table 8.4 do not provide clear information, however, as the odds of being employed compared to NILF are lower, but compared to unemployment they are higher; in addition, any differentials in the unemployed/employed odds do not change with duration in the U.S. The probability calculations, however, show an employment probability of 90.0% for foreign-born men at arrival compared to 91.9% for native-born men. The employment probability also progresses as predicted, increasing with duration in the U.S., surpassing the native-born employment probability about 5-6 years after arrival.

Our hypotheses, however, also center upon greater turnover for foreign-born men, and thus predict a higher rate of unemployment at arrival, decreasing to converge to the native-born norm over time. In fact, neither the coefficients for the odds nor the probabilities estimated in Table 8.4 consistently support these hypotheses. The odds of being unemployed compared to being out of the labor force or to being employed are lower for foreign-born men; compared to NILF, the unemployed odds increase quadratically with duration in the U.S., but there is no change with duration in the U.S. in the odds of being unemployed compared to being employed. This pattern is the same in the foreign-born sample, wherein duration in the U.S. acts to decrease the odds of being out of the labor force, but has no effect on unemployment versus employment.

In the probability calculations, foreign-born men at arrival are not substantially different in terms of unemployment, with a probability of 3.1% of being unemployed, ceteris paribus, compared to a probability of 3.6% for native-born men. Unemployment probabilities then increase over time in the destination, but slowly, crossing the native-born unemployment probability at about 17-18 years. Thus, if we superficially accepted these unemployment probabilities as entry rates, we would conclude that rates of turnover into unemployment are either the same or lower for foreign-born men upon arrival at the destination than for native-born men. We challenge this assumption later. But for now it appears that the lower employment ratio that we observe for foreign-born men is due to much lower rates of labor force participation, not higher rates of unemployment, and do not support that particular part of Hypothesis Number 6.

Other configurations show similar results. The foreign-born model in Table 8.4 actually predicts higher unemployment (4.6%) probabilities at arrival than the pooled model, with about the same probabilities of being out of the labor force (7.1%), and slightly lower employment probabilities (88.3%). The unemployment probability does not change with duration in the U.S. in the foreign-born model. This model cannot be compared directly to the pooled model, because it is estimated around the characteristics mean values of foreign-born men only, where the pooled model estimates the coefficients around the values of native-born and foreign-born men combined. But the conclusions are roughly the same—foreign-born men have lower rates of employment than native-born men upon arrival at the destination, but this result is mostly a consequence of the higher probabilities of being out of the labor force.

To this point we have been estimating the effects of years in the destination as a smooth curvilinear process, estimating the crossover points by applying the coefficients of YSM and YSM squared directly to specified years. It has been shown in previous work, however, that the adjustment process is not smooth, and has turning points at various increments of duration in the destination. The second specification, also shown in Table 8.4, replaces the foreign-born dummy variable and continuous duration variables with increments of duration, beginning with 2 years or less and rising to 25 years or more. For the pooled model, each increment refers to the difference between foreign-born men in that increment of years since migration and the benchmark native-born men; for the foreign-born model, the increment 7-9 years was chosen as the benchmark

In the pooled model, foreign-born men in the U.S. less than 5 years have significantly higher odds of being out of the labor force than native-born men. There is no significant difference between 5 and 10 years, but after about 5 years the signs reverse and somewhere after 9 years the coefficients become significant, so that foreign-born with long duration in the U.S. have lower odds than native-born men of being out of the labor force. The probability calculations show that this convergence is strongest in the first few years—the probability of being out of the labor force is 10.1% for newly arrived foreign-born men (compared to 4.5% for native-born men), dropping to 5.1% in the 3-4 year increment of duration in the U.S., and dropping as low as 2.3% after about 20 years, before rising again as older foreign-born men become more likely to be disabled or to retire. In the foreign-born model, foreign-born men have significantly higher odds of being out of the labor force during their first 4 years after arrival than at 7-9 years, and significantly lower odds after 10-14 years. The NILF probability in the foreign-born model is 9.5% in the first two years (compared to 4.1% for the benchmark foreign-born man at 7-9 years in the U.S.), dropping to about 2.7% after about 10 years in the U.S.

The trends for unemployment and employment odds again are not clear from the incremental portion of Table 8.4. In both the pooled and foreign-born models, coefficients on the unemployment/employment odds are not generally significant, except for lower unemployment odds in the 3-4 and 7-9 year increments in the pooled model and a higher odds in the 2 years or less category in the foreign-born model.[4] Compared to NILF, unemployment odds are significantly lower during the first 4 years then generally higher after about 10 years, while employment odds compared to NILF are lower in the first 2 years in the pooled model, for the first 4 years in the foreign-born model, then higher after about 10 years. The probability calculations in the pooled model show that employment probabilities for foreign-born men in the first 2 years are about 5.5 percentage points lower, ceteris paribus, than for native-born men, but rise rapidly to exceed the native-born norm after just a few years, rising to 94.2% after 15 years (compared to the native-born probability of 91.9%). Similarly, in the first 2 years foreign-born men have a 6.5 point lower probability of being unemployed than their counterparts who have been in the U.S. 7-9 years, but after 10 years the probabilities are higher. In both the pooled and the foreign-born model, the years since migration effect on unemployment probabilities is not clear, rising and falling over duration in the U.S. with no consistent pattern. One interesting result is a 1 percentage point *higher* probability of unemployment in the first 2 years in the foreign-born model, but the significance of this result is doubtful because of conflicting odds estimates.

The differences between the continuous calculations and the incremental calculations are displayed graphically in Figures 8.2, 8.3, and 8.4, which portray the probabilities from the pooled sample from Table 8.4 (these figures are also reproduced in Chiswick and Hurst, 1998b). Figure 8.2 shows how there is a huge drop in the NILF probabilities in the incremental model after the first couple of years, then the continuous model traces out the pattern over time fairly well after that. Figure 8.3 shows the wild fluctuations around the unemployment probabilities in the incremental model. These fluctuations can be traced to the large number of insignificant coefficients in Table 8.3. There are three main sources for this impreciseness. First is the small sample size—the number of unemployed foreign-born men in the sample is only about 1,330. Second is measurement error of the variables themselves. The CPS changes its increment reporting scheme from sample to sample, with only the 1983 sample having actual years reported continuously. Not only are the increments overly general, but the blocks themselves are

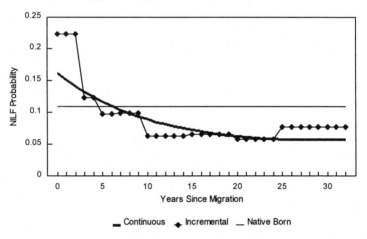

Figure 8.2. Probabilities of Being Out of the Labor Force
Adult Foreign-Born Men (Native Benchmark) -- Continuous and Incremental YSM

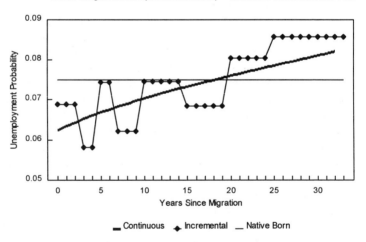

Figure 8.3. Probabilities of Being Unemployed
Adult Foreign-Born Men (Native Benchmark) -- Continuous and Incremental YSM

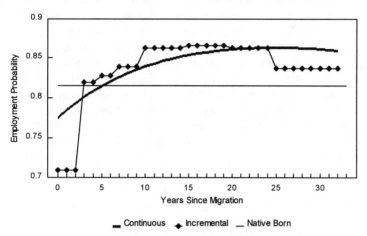

Figure 8.4. Probabilities of Being Employed, Over Time in U.S.
Adult Foreign-Born Men (Native Benchmark) -- Continuous and Incremental YSM

inconsistent, necessitating an adjustment that artificially forced men in some increments into inaccurate categories in some years. The continuous YSM variable was calculated as the midpoint of the increments, so has its own measurement error, but at least it is reasonably consistent across surveys. Finally, the unemployment dependent variable is more collinear, than are employment and NILF, with explanatory variables such as the area unemployment rate and the seasonal adjustment factor, so it is harder to estimate with the inclusion of those variables in the model.

Figure 8.4 shows the employment probabilities. As with NILF probabilities, the continuous curve traces out the incremental model results fairly well after the initial jump at 2 years. In interpreting the results of our analysis regarding the effects of duration in the U.S., it might be worthwhile to consider both specifications to get a complete picture. The continuous variable might actually be more accurate over most of the range, but the maximum likelihood process does not account for the "outliers" at the first couple of years, thus overly smoothes out the important initial adjustment. So in considering the adjustment process in the first two years, the incremental model would be preferred; after that the continuous model might be preferred.

8.3   DISAGGREGATION BY RACIAL/ETHNIC GROUP

Before examining unemployment in more detail in Chapter 9, It would be interesting to test if the odds and probabilities of the various labor force states differ by ethnic group. In this section tests are run separately for the 4 major racial/ethnic groups—non-Hispanic whites, Hispanic whites, blacks, and other minorities. The coefficients and standard deviations are reported in Table 8.5, except for the coefficients for the incremental YSM variables which are included in Hurst (1997), and the probabilities are reported in Table 8.6.

This section will focus primarily on the computed probabilities, referring to the odds estimates when probability effects are not clear. In addition, the number of foreign-born who are unemployed or out of the labor force is small enough so that separate models for the foreign-born by racial/ethnic group would not be robust. Therefore, the discussion in this section focuses only on pooled native-born/foreign-born samples.

It is clear that there are major differences in the labor force/employment probabilities by race. First, for the reference native-born man at the group means, whites have the highest employment probability, 93.1%, and the lowest unemployment probabilities, 2.7%, and NILF probabilities, 4.1% (except that other minorities are have an NILF probability of only 3.2%). In contrast, black native-born reference men have the lowest employment probabilities and highest probabilities of unemployment and of being out of the labor force. Hispanic native-born reference men have high unemployment probabilities (8.4%) but low probabilities of being out of the labor force (4.8%), while other minority native-born reference men are similar to whites, except for a higher unemployment probability, 5.0%.

Increasing the schooling level from the means to 16 years has the strongest impact on reducing unemployment probabilities for blacks, by about 40%, and for whites, by about 30%, and less of an reduction for Hispanics (23%) other minorities (18%). This would be consistent with our findings for foreign-born men, namely a lower return to higher levels of schooling, as the smaller effect for Hispanics and other minorities is correlated with their much greater percent foreign-born (Table 7.3). A level of 16 years of schooling also reduces labor force nonparticipation the most for blacks, by about 36% compared to 5-16% for the other groups.

Table 8.5. Multinomial Logit Estimates of Employment, Unemployment, and NILF States, Pooled Sample of Native Born and Foreign Born Adult Men, by Racial Group

VARIABLES	WHITE			BLACK		
	Unemployed vs. Employed	NILF vs. Employed	Unemployed vs. NILF	Unemployed vs. Employed	NILF vs. Employed	Unemployed vs. NILF
Schooling	-0.1270 (-33.07)	-0.0190 (-7.20)	-0.1080 (-24.38)	-0.1241 (-14.77)	-0.1067 (-16.70)	-0.0174 (-1.81)
Potential Experience	-0.0310 (-8.27)	-0.0785 (-29.85)	0.0475 (10.89)	-0.0079 (-1.02)	-0.0024 (-0.39)	-0.0055 (-0.60)
Exper. Squared	0.0005 (6.97)	0.0027 (58.91)	-0.0022 (-27.75)	-0.0005 (-3.15)	0.0008 (8.12)	-0.0013 (-7.75)
Married (Sp Pres.)	-0.8836 (-39.62)	-0.8648 (-52.10)	-0.0188 (-0.71)	-0.6284 (-14.55)	-0.9691 (-26.99)	0.3407 (6.50)
Metrop. Area	-0.1473 (-6.35)	-0.1119 (-6.99)	-0.0354 (-1.31)	0.0482 (0.79)	-0.0194 (-0.40)	0.0676 (0.93)
South	-0.1862 (-7.73)	0.2328 (14.92)	-0.4190 (-15.18)	-0.3131 (-6.69)	-0.2608 (-6.69)	-0.0522 (-0.92)
Agriculture	-0.5808 (-8.18)	-3.3922 (-30.48)	2.8114 (21.61)	-0.3334 (-2.50)	-3.9748 (-14.05)	3.6414 (11.90)
November 1979	-0.5275 (-10.47)	-0.7772 (-23.77)	0.2497 (4.32)	-0.6796 (-6.33)	0.3073 (3.78)	-0.9869 (-7.82)

Table 8.5 (continued)

VARIABLES	WHITE			BLACK		
	Unemployed vs. Employed	NILF vs. Employed	Unemployed vs. NILF	Unemployed vs. Employed	NILF vs. Employed	Unemployed vs. NILF
April 1983	0.0339	-0.6086	0.6425	-0.1009	-0.0276	-0.0733
	(0.78)	(-18.90)	(12.55)	(-1.22)	(-0.36)	(-0.72)
June 1986	-0.1283	-0.3935	0.2652	-0.0412	0.1970	-0.2382
	(-2.96)	(-13.76)	(5.34)	(-0.52)	(2.88)	(-2.47)
June 1988	-0.1026	-0.2779	0.1753	-0.1907	0.3909	-0.5816
	(-2.13)	(-9.29)	(3.22)	(-2.08)	(5.56)	(-5.41)
November 1989	-0.1514	-0.2103	0.0590	0.0460	0.6268	-0.5808
	(-3.15)	(-7.18)	(1.09)	(0.53)	(9.06)	(-5.60)
June 1991	0.0685	-0.1710	0.2396	-0.0204	0.5515	-0.5719
	(1.61)	(-5.82)	(4.84)	(-0.26)	(8.12)	(-5.88)
February 1994	-0.2207	0.3533	-0.5740	0.0017	1.4948	-1.4931
	(-4.24)	(10.18)	(-9.53)	(0.02)	(18.50)	(-12.76)
Area Unemp. Rate	0.1215	0.0375	0.0840	0.1404	0.0521	0.0883
	(32.84)	(12.02)	(18.46)	(17.40)	(6.71)	(8.83)
Seas/Occ Adjust. Fact.	0.0073	-0.0290	0.0363	-0.0025	-0.0397	0.0372
	(4.59)	(-25.66)	(19.52)	(-0.82)	(-15.45)	(10.19)
Average, Occ. Wages	0.0628	-0.0121	0.0749	0.0069	-0.2106	0.2175
	(12.01)	(-3.23)	(12.04)	(0.62)	(-21.32)	(15.54)

Table 8.5 (continued)

VARIABLES	WHITE			BLACK		
	Unemployed vs. Employed	NILF vs. Employed	Unemployed vs. NILF	Unemployed vs. Employed	NILF vs. Employed	Unemployed vs. NILF
Variance, Occ. Wages	-0.0274	-0.0393	0.0119	-0.0242	-0.0125	-0.0117
	(-25.14)	(-49.50)	(9.15)	(-12.87)	(-8.06)	(-5.09)
Foreign Born	0.1435	0.7147	-0.5712	-0.3400	0.1819	-0.5219
	(1.15)	(8.34)	(-4.01)	(-1.73)	(1.12)	(-2.21)
Years Since Mig. (YSM)	-0.0179	-0.0959	0.0780	0.0095	-0.0967	0.1062
	(-1.46)	(-11.36)	(5.57)	(0.37)	(-4.50)	(3.41)
YSM Squared	0.0004	0.0016	-0.0013	0.0002	0.0020	-0.0019
	(1.48)	(9.94)	(-4.50)	(0.24)	(4.13)	(-2.53)
Constant	-1.5062	2.2831	-3.7893	0.1105	4.3508	-4.2402
	(-9.18)	(20.68)	(-20.16)	(0.35)	(16.61)	(-11.41)
Sample Size	80,147			25,180		

Table 8.5 (continued)

VARIABLES	HISPANIC			OTHER MINORITY		
	Unemployed vs. Employed	NILF vs. Employed	Unemployed vs. NILF	Unemployed vs. Employed	NILF vs. Employed	Unemployed vs. NILF
Schooling	-0.0477	-0.0296	-0.0181	-0.0775	-0.0727	-0.0048
	(-5.36)	(-3.63)	(-1.57)	(-5.27)	(-7.28)	(-0.29)
Potential Experience	-0.0113	-0.0535	0.0422	0.0237	-0.0922	0.1159
	(-1.04)	(-6.00)	(3.15)	(1.30)	(-8.31)	(5.71)
Exper. Squared	-0.0001	0.0019	-0.0019	-0.0006	0.0024	-0.0031
	(-0.35)	(12.40)	(-8.07)	(-1.75)	(11.85)	(-7.82)
Married (Sp Pres.)	-0.2304	-0.6766	0.4462	-0.3474	-0.5823	0.2349
	(-3.61)	(-11.39)	(5.37)	(-3.15)	(-7.47)	(1.84)
Metrop. Area	0.0776	-0.2070	0.2845	-0.5801	-0.6868	0.1067
	(0.82)	(-2.48)	(2.36)	(-4.48)	(-7.11)	(0.70)
South	-0.0890	-0.2634	0.1745	-0.0660	-0.1451	0.0791
	(-1.41)	(-4.43)	(2.10)	(-0.49)	(-1.52)	(0.50)
Agriculture	0.0744	-2.4117	2.4861	0.0618	-3.6707	3.7324
	(0.66)	(-12.36)	(11.31)	(0.24)	(-6.74)	(6.34)
November 1979	-0.3934	0.4315	-0.8249	-0.4301	0.2929	-0.7231
	(-2.47)	(3.12)	(-4.07)	(-1.56)	(1.59)	(-2.28)

Table 8.5 (continued)

VARIABLES	HISPANIC			OTHER MINORITY		
	Unemployed vs. Employed	NILF vs. Employed	Unemployed vs. NILF	Unemployed vs. Employed	NILF vs. Employed	Unemployed vs. NILF
April 1983	-0.0615	-0.1133	0.0518	-0.0797	0.3849	-0.4646
	(-0.51)	(-0.89)	(0.31)	(-0.39)	(2.35)	(-1.88)
June 1986	-0.0701	0.0251	-0.0952	0.1728	0.3642	-0.1914
	(-0.61)	(0.23)	(-0.63)	(0.86)	(2.30)	(-0.80)
June 1988	-0.1907	0.1550	-0.3457	-0.0203	0.7517	-0.7720
	(-1.51)	(1.41)	(-2.16)	(-0.09)	(4.83)	(-2.91)
November 1989	-0.1593	0.1888	-0.3480	0.0488	0.6035	-0.5547
	(-1.30)	(1.73)	(-2.21)	(0.21)	(3.89)	(-2.11)
June 1991	-0.1322	0.2826	-0.4148	0.0549	0.6073	-0.5524
	(-1.18)	(2.73)	(-2.84)	(0.28)	(4.17)	(-2.37)
February 1994	-0.1015	1.3822	-1.4837	-0.0381	1.1682	-1.2063
	(-0.80)	(12.17)	(-9.16)	(-0.19)	(8.02)	(-5.12)
Area Unemp. Rate	0.1067	0.0374	0.0694	0.1436	0.0318	0.1118
	(9.12)	(2.97)	(4.28)	(6.71)	(1.85)	(4.35)
Seas/Occ Adjust. Fact.	0.0053	-0.0456	0.0509	-0.0011	-0.0400	0.0389
	(1.54)	(-12.29)	(10.54)	(-0.17)	(-7.43)	(4.94)
Average, Occ. Wages	0.0283	-0.1801	0.2084	0.0334	-0.0178	0.0512
	(1.76)	(-12.68)	(10.07)	(1.34)	(-1.06)	(1.78)

Table 8.5 (continued)

VARIABLES	HISPANIC			OTHER MINORITY		
	Unemployed vs. Employed	NILF vs. Employed	Unemployed vs. NILF	Unemployed vs. Employed	NILF vs. Employed	Unemployed vs. NILF
Variance, Occ. Wages	-0.0170	0.0060	-0.0229	-0.0208	-0.0047	-0.0161
	(-5.72)	(2.74)	(-6.45)	(-4.46)	(-1.78)	(-3.11)
Foreign Born	-0.4045	-0.6367	0.2323	0.2567	1.2203	-0.9637
	(-3.59)	(-5.62)	(1.51)	(1.57)	(11.33)	(-5.20)
Years Since Mig. (YSM)	0.0143	0.0029	0.0114	-0.0579	-0.1474	0.0895
	(1.27)	(0.27)	(0.77)	(-2.87)	(-11.08)	(3.89)
YSM Squared	0.0000	0.0002	-0.0002	0.0012	0.0027	-0.0015
	(-0.04)	(0.77)	(-0.55)	(2.41)	(8.55)	(-2.62)
Constant	-2.4059	3.7814	-6.1873	-1.6588	3.7447	-5.4035
	(-5.90)	(9.55)	(-11.43)	(-2.30)	(6.61)	(-6.25)
Sample Size	14,189			10,862		

Sources: Current Population Survey, various supplements, 1979-94; Survey of Income and Education, 1976.

Notes: asymptotic t-ratios in parentheses.

Table 8.6. Estimated Probabilities for Changes in Explanatory Variables—by Racial Group

VARIABLES	WHITE			BLACK		
	NILF	Unemp.	Employed	NILF	Unemp.	Employed
Reference Person	0.041	0.027	0.931	0.059	0.087	0.854
Schooling = 16 Yrs	0.039	0.019	0.942	0.038	0.052	0.909
Schooling = 9 Yrs	0.043	0.045	0.912	0.072	0.112	0.816
Potential Exper. = 36	0.105	0.025	0.870	0.102	0.057	0.842
Potential Exper. = 12	0.033	0.032	0.935	0.041	0.118	0.842
Unmarried	0.089	0.061	0.850	0.132	0.140	0.728
Non-Metropolitan Res.	0.046	0.032	0.923	0.060	0.083	0.856
South	0.052	0.023	0.926	0.047	0.066	0.887
Agriculture	0.001	0.016	0.982	0.001	0.068	0.931
November 1979	0.020	0.017	0.964	0.082	0.045	0.873
April 1983	0.023	0.029	0.948	0.058	0.080	0.862
June 1986	0.028	0.025	0.947	0.071	0.083	0.846
June 1988	0.032	0.025	0.943	0.086	0.071	0.843
November 1989	0.034	0.024	0.942	0.104	0.087	0.809
June 1991	0.035	0.030	0.936	0.098	0.082	0.820
February 1994	0.058	0.022	0.920	0.218	0.073	0.709
Area Unemp. Rate=11.5%	0.048	0.049	0.903	0.069	0.158	0.774
Seas. Adjust. = 113%	0.027	0.031	0.942	0.033	0.087	0.880
Avg. Occ. Wages = $12	0.038	0.037	0.924	0.020	0.094	0.886
Var. Occ. Wages x 2	0.013	0.013	0.974	0.045	0.048	0.907
Foreign Born at Entry	0.080	0.030	0.890	0.072	0.063	0.865

Table 8.6 (continued)

VARIABLES	WHITE			BLACK		
	NILF	Unemp.	Employed	NILF	Unemp.	Employed
YSM = mean	0.023	0.026	0.951	0.030	0.075	0.895
YSM = mean + 10	0.021	0.027	0.952	0.023	0.087	0.890
Reference Person	0.041	0.027	0.931	0.058	0.087	0.855
Schooling, Exper.,....	(b)	(b)	(b)	(b)	(b)	(b)
YSM 25 Years or More	0.030	0.029	0.941	0.035	0.135	0.830
YSM 20-24 Years	0.018	0.027	0.955	0.022	0.065	0.913
YSM 15-19 Years	0.026	0.024	0.950	0.021	0.050	0.929
YSM 10-14 Years	0.021	0.022	0.957	0.026	0.091	0.883
YSM 7-9 Years	0.038	0.032	0.930	0.061	0.060	0.879
YSM 5-6 Years	0.040	0.020	0.940	0.033	0.084	0.884
YSM 3-4 Years	0.069	0.024	0.907	0.066	0.099	0.835
YSM 2 Years or Less	0.115	0.037	0.848	0.094	0.049	0.857

Means for Ref. Person:	WHITE		BLACK	
	Mean	Std Dev.	Mean	Std Dev.
Schooling	13.0	5.8	11.4	3.9
Potential Experience	24.0	22.7	24.5	14.5
Area Unemp. Rate (%)	6.54	5.19	6.59	3.22
Seas/Occ Adjust. Fact.	98.100	14.840	97.740	9.650
Average, Occ. Wages	6.95	6.22	6.62	2.91
Variance, Occ. Wages	29.87	30.51	27.06	19.46
YSM for For. Born	21.54	14.77	12.47	11.59

Table 8.6 (continued)

VARIABLES	HISPANIC			OTHER MINORITY		
	NILF	Unemp.	Employed	NILF	Unemp.	Employed
Reference Person	0.048	0.084	0.868	0.032	0.050	0.919
Schooling = 16 Yrs	0.042	0.065	0.893	0.027	0.041	0.932
Schooling = 9 Yrs	0.049	0.088	0.862	0.043	0.068	0.889
Potential Exper. = 36	0.095	0.067	0.839	0.062	0.040	0.898
Potential Exper. = 12	0.041	0.097	0.861	0.035	0.048	0.916
Unmarried	0.088	0.099	0.813	0.055	0.067	0.878
Non-Metropolitan Res.	0.059	0.077	0.864	0.059	0.083	0.858
South	0.038	0.078	0.884	0.028	0.047	0.925
Agriculture	0.004	0.094	0.902	0.001	0.054	0.945
November 1979	0.074	0.057	0.869	0.043	0.032	0.925
April 1983	0.043	0.080	0.877	0.046	0.045	0.908
June 1986	0.049	0.078	0.872	0.045	0.058	0.898
June 1988	0.056	0.070	0.874	0.065	0.047	0.888
November 1989	0.058	0.072	0.870	0.057	0.051	0.893
June 1991	0.063	0.073	0.864	0.057	0.051	0.892
February 1994	0.169	0.067	0.765	0.096	0.045	0.859
Area Unemp. Rate=11.5%	0.054	0.130	0.816	0.035	0.094	0.870
Seas. Adjust. = 113%	0.025	0.092	0.883	0.019	0.049	0.932
Avg. Occ. Wages = $12	0.018	0.100	0.882	0.029	0.060	0.912
Var. Occ. Wages x 2	0.057	0.057	0.887	0.029	0.029	0.942
Foreign Born at Entry	0.027	0.059	0.914	0.099	0.059	0.842
YSM = mean	0.028	0.071	0.900	0.029	0.039	0.931

Table 8.6 (continued)

VARIABLES	HISPANIC			OTHER MINORITY		
	NILF	Unemp.	Employed	NILF	Unemp.	Employed
YSM = mean + 10	0.031	0.081	0.889	0.017	0.034	0.950
Reference Person	0.046	0.083	0.870	0.031	0.050	0.919
Schooling, Exper.,...	(b)	(b)	(b)	(b)	(b)	(b)
YSM 25 Years or More	0.035	0.091	0.874	0.024	0.039	0.937
YSM 20-24 Years	0.031	0.085	0.883	0.022	0.036	0.942
YSM 15-19 Years	0.030	0.069	0.902	0.018	0.038	0.944
YSM 10-14 Years	0.025	0.075	0.900	0.022	0.040	0.938
YSM 7-9 Years	0.033	0.054	0.912	0.037	0.037	0.926
YSM 5-6 Years	0.021	0.072	0.907	0.050	0.059	0.891
YSM 3-4 Years	0.020	0.059	0.921	0.053	0.030	0.917
YSM 2 Years or Less	0.043	0.065	0.893	0.102	0.067	0.831

Means for Ref. Person:	Mean	Std Dev.		Mean	Std Dev.
Schooling	10.2	4.9		13.5	3.6
Potential Experience	23.6	13.8		21.5	10.6
Area Unemp. Rate (%)	6.77	3.02		6.64	2.33
Seas/Occ Adjust. Fact.	98.720	11.999		99.250	7.600
Average, Occ. Wages	6.42	3.01		6.18	2.82
Variance, Occ. Wages	24.02	18.53		26.96	15.59
YSM for For. Born	14.40	12.58		11.33	9.47

Notes: (b)—not shown, other variables held constant are the same as above.

Living in a metropolitan area has a differential impact among the racial groups. For whites a non-metropolitan residence has a small negative effect on employment (about 0.8 percentage points), while increasing the NILF and unemployment probabilities by about a half a percentage point each. This pattern is even stronger for other minorities, reducing employment by about 6 points while increasing NILF and unemployment probabilities by about 3 points each. But there is little effect of non-metropolitan residence on blacks, and for Hispanics a non-metropolitan residence reduces labor force participation but also reduces unemployment probabilities.

For all groups, living in the South decreases the probability of unemployment, although this improvement is small. Living in the South increases employment and labor force participation for all groups except, curiously, for whites, where a Southern residence reduces employment and labor force participation. Working in the agricultural wage and salary sector has the effects mentioned above, greatly increasing employment rates and labor force participation rates, an artifact of the way the questions are asked. One interesting discrepancy is the effect on unemployment probabilities. The agricultural wage and salary sector reduces unemployment probabilities for whites and blacks, but increases them for Hispanics and other minorities, although the non-significant coefficients for the unemployed/employed odds cast doubt on the latter results.

The trend effects and the area unemployment rate seem to follow the pattern of the pooled sample fairly consistently for all racial groups. Likewise for the occupational seasonal adjustment, increasing employment, unemployment, and labor force participation. The average occupational wage has similar effects for the 4 racial groups, tending to increase the probabilities of employment, unemployment, and labor force participation, except the effect on other minorities is small and actually reduces the probability of employment slightly. The variance of occupational wages is similar across racial groups, increasing employment and labor force participation and reducing unemployment, except for reducing labor force participation for Hispanics.

The number of years of residence in the U.S. has somewhat different effects on labor force/employment probabilities depending upon race. For whites, the pattern generally follows that of the pooled sample above—a higher probability of being out of the labor force for the first 4 years, but declining in magnitude until the probability drops below that of native-born men somewhere between 5 and 6 years; a lower probability of being employed for the first 4 years, with a similar rise and crossover between 5 and 14 years, and an inconsistent pattern for the unemployment probability. For black foreign-born men the patterns on all of the dependent variables are similar as for whites, except for a higher probability of being out of the labor force at the 7-9 year increment.

These patterns are similar for Hispanics and other minorities, with two notable exceptions. Hispanic foreign-born men have lower NILF probabilities, ceteris paribus, and higher employment probabilities, than native-born Hispanic men, from arrival on. The differences for the first 2 years are not significant, and in the 3-6 year increments the probabilities of being out of the labor force for Hispanic foreign-born men are around 2%, lower than foreign-born or native-born men of any race, and only rising above 3.5% after 25 years residence in the U.S. One possible explanation for this result is return migration(if Mexican immigrants who are unemployed and unable to claim unemployment benefits return to Mexico they would not be counted in the survey as being out of the labor force, underestimating the NILF probability, and possibly the unemployment probability as well.

For other minorities, an important difference from other ethnic groups is that unemployment probabilities are consistently lower by a couple of percentage points for foreign-born other minorities after 6 years than for their native-born counterparts. We should maintain some skepticism about these results, however, as the coefficients are not statistically significant.

Despite some differences between races, in general one result is consistent: the overall pattern for the pooled sample—higher NILF probabilities and lower employment probabilities in the early years after arrival for foreign-born men, but then convergence and then a crossover after about 10 years in the U.S., with inconsistent patterns for unemployment—holds strongly *within* racial groups. Many comparisons of foreign-born men with native-born men in previous studies compare foreign-born men with white native-born persons, or with native-born persons of all races, which is practically the same thing. But foreign-born men are disproportionately represented by Hispanics and other minorities, and the adjustment pattern of immigrants within their own racial group is quite strong, even if this does not always appear in a pooled analysis. After an initial adjustment in the destination country, labor force patterns of foreign-born men may reflect racial/ethnic characteristics as much as nativity.

8.4 SUMMARY OF CHAPTER 8

Chapter 8 began the empirical analysis of employment, unemployment, and labor force participation probabilities. Separate sections focused first on the basic model variables and the differences between native-born men and foreign-born men in their return to human capital or their labor market responses to differences in their characteristics, then later focused on variables used to measure differences in labor market outcomes after controlling for the basic model variables. Coefficients for the log odds for changes in the probabilities and calculations of the probabilities themselves were shown.

The basic model variables showed both similarities and differences between foreign-born men and native-born men in changes in the probabilities of being in various labor market states because of their characteristics. Most of the explanatory variables had similar effects in terms of direction on the employment, unemployment, and NILF odds and probabilities for both native-born and foreign-born men, but the effects are generally weaker for foreign-born men. For example, increased levels of schooling increased employment and labor force participation and reduced unemployment for both groups, but the effects were smaller for foreign-born men. This result was generally similar for most of the other basic model explanatory variables, including experience, marriage, agricultural wage and salary sector employment, the area unemployment rate, the seasonal adjustment factor, and average occupational wages.

Notable exceptions in terms of direction included metropolitan residence, which decreased unemployment for foreign-born men but not native-born men, Southern residence, which increased labor force participation for foreign-born men but decreased it for native-born men, and a higher occupational wage variance, which increased labor force participation for native-born men but reduced it for foreign-born men. Notable exceptions to reduced magnitudes for foreign-born men included metropolitan residence, which had a stronger impact on reducing labor force participation for foreign-born men, and the seasonal adjustment factor and average occupational wages, which had a stronger effect of increasing labor force participation for foreign-born men.

One important difference between foreign-born men and native-born men is shown by the period effect dummy variables. The employment and labor force participation probabilities for native-born men were higher in the 1980s and 1990s compared to the benchmark of 1976, although the improvement was greatest in 1979 and diminished thereafter. For foreign-born men the trend was just the opposite, showing a worsening of the labor market conditions in the 1980s and 1990s, although many of the odds coefficients were not significant. At least part of this effect can be attributed to an increase in the proportion of foreign-born men who recently migrated. An additional factor may be the changing occupational structure, wherein immigrants are increasingly concentrated in low-skilled occupations, which have been in less demand in recent decades.

After controlling for the basic model variables, Chapter 8 showed that there clearly is a difference in labor market outcomes between foreign-born men shortly after arrival in the U.S. and native-born men, but that these differences diminish quickly and equalize with duration in the U.S. Employment probabilities and labor force participation probabilities were significantly lower for foreign-born men upon arrival, ceteris paribus, and were clearly lower for the first couple of years after arrival. After about 4 years, however, employment probabilities and labor force participation probabilities were either not significantly different for foreign-born men, or were higher. Unemployment probabilities were less predictable, possibly because of collinearity with area unemployment rate controls, and were smaller in some model specifications, higher in one case, but generally were characterized by insignificant coefficients for the odds ratios.

In conclusion, it appears that there is rapid assimilation of foreign-born men in the U.S. after arrival in terms of their labor market outcomes. They have lower returns from human capital or less response to non-human-capital characteristics. Their higher labor force nonparticipation and lower employment ratios shortly after arrival were predicted by the hypotheses of Chapter 7, but the predicted higher rate of unemployment was not substantiated. Further detail on unemployment will be provided in Chapter 9.

Job Losers, Job Leavers, Labor Force Entrants

Chapter 8 analyzed the full sample of native and foreign-born men, examining the differences in relation to the three common labor force categories of employment, unemployment, and labor force participation. The immigrant adjustment model, or assimilation hypothesis, however, makes inferences about the unemployment process—higher rates of job losing because of poor job matches, higher rates of job leaving due to "job shopping" or human capital acquisition, and, naturally, higher rates of labor force entry due to being out of the U.S. labor force prior to arrival in the U.S. In addition, while the assimilation hypothesis makes no direct predictions about whether unemployment among foreign-born men is more voluntary or involuntary, such questions normally arise around any discussion of unemployment.

These issues are not able to be addressed within the confines of the unemployment category as analyzed in Chapter 8. Chapter 9 takes a more detailed look at unemployment among foreign-born men. In this chapter the unemployment variable is disaggregated into job losers, job leavers, and labor force entrants. Labor force entrants, although aggregated here, can be either new entrants, never having worked a full time job more than 2 weeks, or reentrants, having worked full time previously but being out of the labor force prior to beginning the job search process. These three categories are analyzed in relation to each other. These persons all have one thing in common—they are not working, and they are able and available and looking for work.

The methodology is again a multinomial logit analysis, as the probability states are seen as choices that are made simultaneously. The leaver/loser log odds are similar to a ratio in that we can test whether there is a greater propensity for voluntary or involuntary job separations.

The voluntary/involuntary comparison is an underlying theme in this chapter. Keeping the terms in perspective is necessary, however. In this analysis, only job losers are considered "involuntarily" unemployed. Job leavers and labor force entrants are both "voluntarily" unemployed.. However, as we have noted previously, the line between voluntary and involuntary separations is not precise: quits may be due to involuntary changes in the job that substantially alter the terms of employment, or job losses may be due to a person declining to voluntarily accept changes, such as wage cuts. Labor force entrants might be seen as strictly voluntary (although the recent changes in welfare rules may alter that distinction). So these caveats must be kept in mind when calling unemployment states voluntary or involuntary.

9.1. THE BASIC MODEL

Tables 9.1 and 9.2 present the coefficients and probabilities for the basic model as in Chapter 8, modeled separately for native-born men and foreign-born men. This chapter will not examine every basic model variable as in Chapter 8. Because of the much smaller sample size, many of the coefficients, especially for foreign-born men, are not significant, so the impacts of many of the variables on odds or probabilities are difficult to assess. The focus will instead be on key variables such as schooling and experience that had the strongest impacts on unemployment states in Chapter 8, or else answer an important question about differences between foreign-born men and native-born men.

As in Chapter 8, the overall results for the reference men in Table 9.2 indicate that the basic model control variables do a good job of equalizing the overall probabilities of being in any of the states. Whereas the overall probability of being a job leaver was about 12% (of unemployed) for foreign-born men in Table 7.2, compared to 9% for native-born men, after controlling for the basic model variables the leaver probabilities are about 8% of unemployed men

Table 9.1. Multinomial Logit Coefficients of Unemployment States Native Born and Foreign Born Adult Men, All Races

VARIABLES	NATIVE BORN			FOREIGN BORN		
	Leaver vs. Entrant	Loser vs. Entrant	Leaver vs. Loser	Leaver vs. Entrant	Loser vs. Entrant	Leaver vs. Loser
Schooling	0.0132	-0.0714	0.0846	0.0760	-0.0253	0.1013
	(0.92)	(-7.43)	(6.77)	(2.43)	(-1.35)	(3.63)
Potential Experience	0.0418	0.0750	-0.0332	0.0968	0.1303	-0.0335
	(3.10)	(8.59)	(-2.77)	(2.40)	(5.52)	(-0.89)
Exper. Squared	-0.0014	-0.0016	0.0002	-0.0020	-0.0022	0.0001
	(-4.98)	(-9.52)	(0.91)	(-2.54)	(-5.11)	(0.18)
Married (Sp Pres.)	0.0355	0.2928	-0.2573	-0.0075	0.2860	-0.2935
	(0.48)	(5.82)	(-4.07)	(-0.03)	(1.97)	(-1.39)
Metrop. Area	-0.1393	0.0542	-0.1935	0.0760	-0.2176	0.2936
	(-1.76)	(0.99)	(-2.87)	(0.15)	(-0.74)	(0.63)
South	0.0912	-0.2515	0.3427	0.6080	0.4864	0.1216
	(1.21)	(-4.81)	(5.31)	(2.27)	(2.68)	(0.53)
Agriculture	-0.0959	-0.4588	0.3628	-1.5745	-0.2205	-1.3540
	(-0.48)	(-3.37)	(2.02)	(-1.91)	(-0.81)	(-1.68)
November 1979	0.4055	0.3540	0.0516	0.0849	-0.1913	0.2762
	(2.44)	(3.05)	(0.36)	(0.14)	(-0.49)	(0.54)

Table 9.1 (continued)

VARIABLES	NATIVE BORN			FOREIGN BORN		
	Leaver vs. Entrant	Loser vs. Entrant	Leaver vs. Loser	Leaver vs. Entrant	Loser vs. Entrant	Leaver vs. Loser
April 1983	0.3865	0.9478	-0.5613	0.6004	0.8971	-0.2968
	(2.57)	(9.63)	(-4.34)	(1.37)	(3.25)	(-0.77)
June 1986	0.4782	0.7960	-0.3177	-0.0392	-0.0679	0.0288
	(3.54)	(8.49)	(-2.78)	(-0.08)	(-0.25)	(0.07)
June 1988	0.3349	0.5638	-0.2288	0.6667	0.3596	0.3071
	(2.33)	(5.54)	(-1.86)	(1.25)	(1.01)	(0.66)
November 1989	0.4176	0.6743	-0.2567	0.9266	0.2694	0.6571
	(2.90)	(6.53)	(-2.12)	(1.98)	(0.83)	(1.62)
June 1991	0.2194	0.5570	-0.3376	-0.2462	-0.0990	-0.1472
	(1.66)	(6.18)	(-2.96)	(-0.58)	(-0.40)	(-0.38)
February 1994	0.0180	0.1296	-0.1116	-1.0810	0.1918	-1.2728
	(0.10)	(1.08)	(-0.73)	(-2.05)	(0.69)	(-2.60)
Area Unemp. Rate	-0.0493	0.0513	-0.1005	-0.0221	-0.0116	-0.0105
	(-3.18)	(5.17)	(-7.50)	(-0.52)	(-0.43)	(-0.27)
Seas/Occ Adjust. Fact.	0.0008	0.0097	-0.0088	0.0174	-0.0120	0.0294
	(0.17)	(2.90)	(-2.03)	(1.11)	(-1.61)	(1.97)

Table 9.1 (continued)

	NATIVE BORN			FOREIGN BORN		
VARIABLES	Leaver vs. Entrant	Loser vs. Entrant	Leaver vs. Loser	Leaver vs. Entrant	Loser vs. Entrant	Leaver vs. Loser
Average, Occ. Wages	0.0199	0.0778	-0.0579	0.1822	0.2428	-0.0606
	(1.20)	(6.71)	(-4.08)	(3.32)	(6.88)	(-1.20)
Variance, Occ. Wages	0.0091	0.0011	0.0080	-0.0211	-0.0296	0.0085
	(3.14)	(0.56)	(3.20)	(-2.19)	(-4.76)	(0.93)
Constant	-1.1030	-0.7696	-0.3334	-5.0558	0.2063	-5.2621
	(-2.12)	(-2.24)	(-0.72)	(-2.90)	(0.23)	(-3.21)
Sample Size	14,169			1,280		

Sources: Current Population Survey, various supplements, 1979-94; Survey of Income and Education, 1976.

Notes: asymptotic t-ratios in parentheses.

Table 9.2. Estimated Probabilities for Changes in Explanatory Variables Native Born and Foreign Born Adult Men, All Races

VARIABLES	NATIVE BORN			FOREIGN BORN		
	Leaver	Loser	Entrant	Leaver	Loser	Entrant
Reference Person	0.080	0.756	0.163	0.080	0.750	0.170
Schooling = 16 Yrs	0.105	0.694	0.201	0.127	0.693	0.180
Schooling = 9 Yrs	0.066	0.794	0.140	0.069	0.764	0.167
Potential Exper. = 36	0.059	0.741	0.200	0.060	0.767	0.173
Potential Exper. = 12	0.097	0.712	0.190	0.095	0.636	0.269
Unmarried	0.096	0.701	0.203	0.099	0.692	0.209
Non-Metropolitan Res.	0.095	0.737	0.168	0.063	0.793	0.145
South	0.105	0.701	0.194	0.095	0.794	0.111
Agriculture	0.102	0.669	0.229	0.021	0.763	0.216
November 1979	0.089	0.792	0.120	0.099	0.707	0.194
April 1983	0.053	0.874	0.073	0.067	0.854	0.079
June 1986	0.066	0.851	0.083	0.081	0.740	0.180
June 1988	0.070	0.828	0.102	0.111	0.768	0.122
November 1989	0.069	0.839	0.092	0.149	0.726	0.126
June 1991	0.063	0.834	0.103	0.068	0.745	0.187
February 1994	0.074	0.778	0.148	0.024	0.822	0.154
Area Unemp. Rate=11.5%	0.059	0.798	0.143	0.076	0.747	0.177
Seas. Adjust. = 110%	0.075	0.775	0.150	0.101	0.717	0.182

Table 9.2 (continued)

VARIABLES	NATIVE BORN			FOREIGN BORN		
	Leaver	Loser	Entrant	Leaver	Loser	Entrant
Avg. Occ. Wages = $10	0.070	0.796	0.134	0.071	0.854	0.075
Var. Occ. Wages x 2	0.098	0.746	0.156	0.082	0.654	0.264

Means for Ref. Person:	NATIVE BORN		FOREIGN BORN	
	Mean	Std Dev.	Mean	Std Dev.
Schooling	11.9	2.8	10.6	4.9
Potential Experience	21.7	12.0	23.8	13.0
Area Unemp. Rate (%)	7.89	3.45	7.88	3.49
Seas/Occ Adjust. Fact.	98.9	10.5	100.4	13.4
Average, Occ. Wages	6.77	2.80	6.07	2.90
Variance, Occ. Wages	26.24	17.03	19.39	15.45
YSM for For. Born	(a)	(a)	15.1	13.1

Notes: (a) - variable not entered

in both groups. Similarly, the probabilities of being a labor force entrant are reduced from 18% of unemployed native-born men to 16.3%, and from 20% to 17.0% for foreign-born men.

In Table 9.1, a higher level of schooling unambiguously reduces the odds of being a job loser, versus either job leaver or labor force entrant. This can be seen clearly in Table 9.2, where the probability of being a job loser in the native-born sample is reduced from 75.6% (of unemployed men) at the mean level of schooling to 69.4% at 16 years of schooling. In the foreign-born sample the similar reduction is from 75.0% to 69.3%. In a separate analysis the odds of being a job loser were significantly lower compared to being out of the labor force as well. On the surface it appears that schooling partly reduces the probability of being a job loser because more educated job losers drop out of the labor force at a higher rate than less educated job losers. More educated persons may have higher reservation wages, or may have greater values of non-market work, or greater opportunities outside of the market such as returning to school. But the overall probability of being a job loser is also lower for the more highly educated because of they are less susceptible to job loss. If the job loser percentage of the unemployed is multiplied by the probability of being unemployed in Table 8.2, the probability of being a job loser is 1.6% for a native-born reference man with 16 years of education, compared to 2.6% for a similar man at the mean level (11.9 years) of education.

For foreign-born men, higher levels of schooling increase the odds of being a job leaver, versus each of the other categories, and Table 9.2 shows that in the foreign-born sample a man with 16 years of education has a 12.7% (of unemployed) probability of being a job leaver compared to 8.0% for an unemployed foreign-born man with the mean level of education. This effect is similar but less strong for native-born men, partly because the odds of being a job leaver vs. a labor force entrant are not significantly different for native-born men (Table 9.1). More highly educated persons probably have more information about the job market, lowering search costs, and have greater potential benefits from leaving their job. If the leaver percentage of the unemployed is multiplied by the probability of being unemployed in Table 8.3, the probability of being a job leaver is 0.24% for a native-born man with 16 years of education, compared to 0.28% at the mean level of education, and 0.46% for a foreign-born man at 16 years, compared to 0.36% at the mean level of education.

Most interesting for the job leaver odds is that higher levels of schooling increase the odds of being a job leaver relative to being a job loser, in other words reducing the ratio of quits to layoffs, which is robust for both native-born and foreign-born men. The human capital model predicts that greater levels of firm-specific human capital reduce turnover. If schooling increases firm-specific human capital (there is some evidence that higher levels of schooling also increase post-schooling human capital investments (Altonji and Spletzer, 1991) then the effect should be to reduce both leaver and loser odds. The influence of schooling in increasing the voluntary proportion of separations would seem to refute that hypothesis. This result could be due to higher levels of schooling increasing the proportion of human capital that is general and transferable rather than firm-specific.

Finally for the schooling variable, one of the most interesting effects is on the probability of becoming a labor force entrant. For native-born men, the odds of being a labor force entrant vs. a job loser are significantly higher with increased schooling, with no significant difference for the leaver/entrant odds. For foreign-born men, on the other hand, the loser/entrant odds are not significant, and the odds of being an entrant vs. a job leaver are significantly lower. The net result shown in Table 9.2 is that increasing schooling from the mean to 16 years increases the probability of being a labor force entrant by 4 percentage points for native-born men but only 1 percentage point for foreign-born men. Since the sample is limited to men ages 25-64, more educated native-born men are more likely to be finishing their higher education and entering the labor force than less educated men who entered earlier; for foreign-born men however, their labor force entry odds are more influenced by their migration to the U.S., reducing the relative effect of education on labor force entry.

From Chapter 8 we know that greater levels of experience reduce the probabilities of being unemployed for both foreign-born and native-born men. In Table 9.1 we can see that this influence is not consistent across all unemployment categories. The odds of being a job loser are significantly higher with more experience, while the odds of being a job leaver are indeterminate—higher vs. entrants but lower vs. job losers. This last result indicates that younger workers (within the 25-64 age group) are more likely to be voluntarily unemployed, compared to involuntarily unemployed, than older workers. The big decrease in unemployment odds due to increased experience comes from lower odds of being a labor force entrant. For both native-born and foreign-born men, experience reduces the odds of being an entrant significantly, from 19% of unemployed native-born men with 12 years experience to 16.3% at 22 years, and from 26.9% of unemployed foreign-born men to 17.3% at 24 years. The decrease is quadratic for both groups, but for native-born men there is an increase in the probability between 22 and 36 years of experience, while for foreign-born men the probabilities are about the same at 24 and 36 years.

An interesting variable is agriculture. In Chapter 8 we noted that the agricultural wage and salary variable was problematic in dealing with NILF odds because of the way the labor market history questions were asked, but that should not be a problem within the overall category of unemployment. The agriculture sector has different effects on the relative category proportions of unemployment between native-born and foreign-born unemployed men. For example, the leaver/entrant odds are marginally significantly lower for foreign-born men in the agriculture sector compared to other sectors, but not for native-born men, while the loser/entrant odds are significantly lower for native-born men in the agriculture sector compared to other sectors, but not for foreign-born men. The leaver/loser odds are higher in the agriculture sector for native-born men and lower for foreign-born men (marginally significant). Consequently, 10.2% of unemployed agricultural native-born workers became unemployed by leaving their jobs and 67% by losing their jobs, compared to 2.1% and 76% for unemployed foreign-born agricultural workers. Thus agricultural sector unemployment appears to be more involuntary for foreign-born men than for native-born men.

There do not seem to be any major trends of note from the survey year dummy variables for foreign-born men as most of the odds coefficients are not significant. In Table 9.2 we can see that for native-born men increases in unemployment in the 1980s and 90s were largely attributable to involuntary unemployment—the job loser percentages of unemployment were substantially higher in each year after 1976 (even after controlling for area unemployment rates and seasonal factors), while job leaver probabilities and entrant probabilities declined. The clearest example is in 1983, where the job loser probability increased from 75.6% in 1976 to 87.4% in 1983, while the job leaver rates rose slightly and labor force entrant rates declined by 26%, substantiating that layoff rates are countercyclical. These results are not consistently the same for foreign-born men, however—the proportions change irregularly, and an examination of Table 9.1 shows that few of the coefficients on the survey year dummy variables are significant in the foreign-born model.

A higher area unemployment rate tends to increase the proportion of unemployed native-born men who are job losers, in the total probability and in the odds compared to the other states. Higher area unemployment rates increase the proportion of job separations that are involuntary (lower leaver/loser odds). The net result in terms of the proportion who are entrants is ambiguous in the odds coefficients, but an increase in the area unemployment rate from 7.9% to 11.5% reduces the probability of being a labor force entrant from 16.3% to 14.3%. Thus higher area unemployment rates reduce the probability of being in the labor force, and also of entering the labor force, consistent with what we would expect. But an interesting exception arises in the foreign-born model—area unemployment rates, which had little effect on the probabilities of employment, unemployment, or labor force participation, also have no significant effect on the categorical distribution within the unemployment variable. Thus foreign-born men seem to be less sensitive in their labor market adjustments to cyclical or geographical differences in unemployment.

In describing job search behavior, it was hypothesized that higher expected wages would encourage quits because the probability of finding a job with a higher wage would be greater for the employee, and encourage layoffs because a higher wage may signal wages higher than marginal productivity. In Chapter 8 it was noted that higher occupational wages produced increases in employment, but also in unemployment because of higher labor force participation. In Table 9.2 it appears that higher average wages do not induce quits, as the leaver proportion of unemployment declines from 8.0% at the mean wage of $6-7 to about 7.0% when the average occupational wage is $10, for both foreign-born and native-born men. And even though the NILF probability declines in Chapter 8, the entrant proportion of unemployment declines by about 3 percentage points for native-born men and by 9.5 percentage points for foreign-born men. In contrast, when the average occupational wage is increased to $10 per hour the job loser proportion of the unemployed increases by about 4 percentage points (to 79.6%), for native-born men, and by over 10 percentage points (to 85.4%) for foreign-born men. In addition, the leaver/loser odds decline significantly for native-born men (t-ratio = -4.08) with higher average occupational wages. So the hypothesis of higher expected wages encouraging quits is not supported here, while the hypothesis that higher wages encourages layoffs is supported. On the other hand, this latter result may be a case of men who are job losers staying in the labor force longer and looking for work longer, a suggestion that is verified in Chapter 10.

9.2   THE FOREIGN-BORN VARIABLES

Table 9.3 presents the coefficients and probability calculations for the foreign-born dummy variable, the continuous duration variables, and the incremental duration variables, in a similar fashion to Table 8.3. The full tables with the basic model coefficients and probabilities included can be found in Hurst (1997). As in Chapter 8, a pooled model compares foreign-born men at various levels of duration in the U.S. to native-born men, and a foreign-born only model compares foreign-born men at arrival to foreign-born men at the benchmark of 7-9 years or to the mean level of duration.

Probably the most interesting and important finding of this section involves the proportion of the unemployed who are labor force entrants. The odds of being a labor force entrant compared to being a job loser or leaver are significantly higher for foreign-born men at arrival. It can also be shown (from a separate analysis) that the entrant/NILF odds are significantly higher. These higher entrant odds decline quadratically with duration in the U.S. in the continuous models. The proportion of unemployed foreign-born men at arrival who are labor force entrants is 35.9% in the pooled model, compared to 16.2% for native-born unemployed men, and 29.3% for foreign-born men at arrival in the foreign-born model, compared to 12.8% for foreign-born men at the mean of 15 years since migration. The entrant proportions decline below the native-born proportions prior to reaching the mean duration in both the pooled and foreign-born models.

As strong as the results of the previous paragraph are, they mask an even stronger effect in the first two years (in Chapter 8 it was shown that the continuous model underestimates the large changes in the first two years for many outcomes). In the first two years after arrival in the U.S., 49.2% of foreign-born unemployed men in the pooled model are unemployed because of entering the labor force, compared to 16.2% of native-born men. In the foreign-born model 44.2% are labor force entrants in the first 2 years compared to 15.0% at 7-9 years of duration in the U.S. The entrant probabilities decline rapidly after

Table 9.3. Multinomial Logit Coefficients, and Probabilities, of Unemployment States, Foreign Born and Years Since Migration Variables

COEFFICIENTS	POOLED			FOREIGN BORN		
	Leaver vs. Entrant	Loser vs. Entrant	Leaver vs. Loser	Leaver vs. Entrant	Loser vs. Entrant	Leaver vs. Loser
VARIABLES:	(b)	(b)	(b)	(b)	(b)	(b)
Schooling, Exper., . . .						
Foreign Born	-1.2892	-1.0429	-0.2462	(a)	(a)	(a)
	(-4.93)	(-7.51)	(-0.99)			
Years Since Mig. (YSM)	0.1336	0.0997	0.0339	0.1322	0.0963	0.0359
	(4.51)	(6.08)	(1.24)	(4.41)	(5.63)	(1.30)
YSM Squared	-0.0025	-0.0019	-0.0006	-0.0024	-0.0020	-0.0005
	(-3.70)	(-5.34)	(-0.90)	(-3.58)	(-5.34)	(-0.73)
Schooling, Exper., . . .	(b)	(b)	(b)	(b)	(b)	(b)
YSM 25 Years or More	0.3711	-0.1074	0.4785	0.5508	-0.0601	0.6109
	(1.58)	(-0.66)	(2.34)	(1.44)	(-0.24)	(1.83)
YSM 20-24 Years	0.1709	0.1322	0.0387	0.2029	0.3145	-0.1116
	(0.51)	(0.63)	(0.13)	(0.46)	(1.13)	(-0.29)
YSM 15-19 Years	0.1358	-0.0872	0.2230	0.3502	0.1191	0.2311
	(0.37)	(-0.36)	(0.71)	(0.75)	(0.38)	(0.57)

Table 9.3 (continued)

COEFFICIENTS	POOLED			FOREIGN BORN		
	Leaver vs. Entrant	Loser vs. Entrant	Leaver vs. Loser	Leaver vs. Entrant	Loser vs. Entrant	Leaver vs. Loser
VARIABLES:						
YSM 10-14 Years	-0.0929 (-0.36)	-0.0338 (-0.20)	-0.0591 (-0.26)	0.0581 (0.15)	0.2355 (0.96)	-0.1774 (-0.54)
YSM 7-9 Years	-0.1876 (-0.64)	-0.3241 (-1.78)	0.1365 (0.52)	(a)	(a)	(a)
YSM 5-6 Years	-1.3017 (-2.47)	-0.1409 (-0.65)	-1.1608 (-2.31)	-1.2252 (-2.05)	0.1184 (0.42)	-1.3436 (-2.41)
YSM 3-4 Years	-0.6212 (-1.34)	-0.3165 (-1.27)	-0.3047 (-0.71)	-0.3858 (-0.71)	0.1097 (0.36)	-0.4955 (-1.00)
YSM 2 Years or Less	-1.2055 (-3.59)	-1.6763 (-8.81)	0.4708 (1.38)	-1.2086 (-2.77)	-1.5433 (-5.89)	0.3347 (0.80)
Sample Size	14,169			1,280		

PROBABILITIES	POOLED			FOREIGN BORN		
	Leaver	Loser	Entrant	Leaver	Loser	Entrant
VARIABLES:						
Reference Person	0.082	0.756	0.162	0.046	0.661	0.293
Schooling, Exper., . . .	(b)	(b)	(b)	(b)	(b)	(b)
Foreign Born at Entry	0.050	0.591	0.359	(a)	(a)	(a)
YSM = mean	0.093	0.751	0.156	0.085	0.787	0.128
YSM = mean + 10	0.107	0.767	0.126	0.102	0.790	0.109

Table 9.3 (continued)

PROBABILITIES VARIABLES	POOLED			FOREIGN BORN		
	Leaver	Loser	Entrant	Leaver	Loser	Entrant
Reference Person	0.082	0.757	0.161	0.082	0.769	0.150
Schooling, Exper., . . .	(b)	(b)	(b)	(b)	(b)	(b)
YSM 25 Years or More	0.124	0.708	0.168	0.139	0.713	0.147
YSM 20-24 Years	0.087	0.769	0.144	0.077	0.808	0.115
YSM 15-19 Years	0.099	0.731	0.170	0.102	0.765	0.132
YSM 10-14 Years	0.078	0.756	0.166	0.072	0.805	0.124
YSM 7-9 Years	0.088	0.705	0.207	(a)	(a)	(a)
YSM 5-6 Years	0.027	0.782	0.192	0.023	0.833	0.144
YSM 3-4 Years	0.058	0.729	0.213	0.052	0.807	0.141
YSM 2 Years or Less	0.075	0.432	0.492	0.072	0.486	0.442

Sources: Current Population Survey, various supplements, 1979-94; Survey of Income and Education, 1976.
Notes: asymptotic t-ratios in parentheses; (a)—variable not entered; (b) shown in Appendix B.

the first 2 years in the U.S. The probability calculations would seem to be inconsistent in showing fluctuating proportions after the first 2 years, tending to stay higher in the pooled sample, lower in the foreign-born sample. However, it is clear from the odds portion of Table 9.3 that these results are not statistically significant, so after 2 years we can say that the entrant proportions are the same for foreign-born men and native-born men. Thus it appears that the higher overall probability of being a labor force entrant in Table 7.2 can be attributed almost entirely to higher entry rates in the first 2 years.

There seems to be no significant reduction in the leaver/loser ratio with longer duration in the U.S.—job separations are slightly more likely to be involuntary for foreign-born men when they first arrive in the U.S., and this ratio converges over time to the native-born norm, but marginally. A comparison with Table 9.2 shows that these patterns of convergence over time hold perfectly when viewing the foreign-born sample alone.

Another important result of this chapter concerns the job loser and job leaver proportions of unemployment. Both are significantly lower for foreign-born men in their odds versus labor force entrants than for native-born men. In the pooled model the percentage of unemployed foreign-born men at arrival who are job losers is 59.1% compared to 75.7% for native-born men. If we multiply the percentage of unemployed men who are job losers by the probability of being unemployed from Table 8.3, we get a probability of being a job loser of 2.7% for native-born men, and 1.8% for foreign-born men at arrival, a -33% differential in the probability of being a job loser. Similarly, for the probability of being a job leaver, the native-born percentage is 8.2% (of unemployed native-born men) in the pooled model, compared to 5.0% for foreign-born men at arrival. In both cases the proportions rise over time and exceed the native-born proportions after about 10 years in the U.S.

The model in the lower part of Table 9.3 shows that the results in the preceding paragraph are robust when using increments to measure foreign-born effects rather than a foreign-born dummy and continuous YSM variables. The proportion of unemployed men who are job leavers is 7.5% for foreign-born men in the U.S. for 2 years or less, compared to the native-born proportion of 8.2%, and the proportion who are job losers is only 43.2%, compared to the native-born job loser proportion of 75.7%; these figures translate to a 0.3% probability of being a job leaver and a 1.5% probability of being a job loser for foreign-born men in the first 2 years, compared to 0.3% and 2.7% respectively for native-born men. These proportions equalize between foreign-born and native-born men after 2 years, as there is little significance in the odds coefficients after 2 years.

In Chapter 8 separate analyses were done for the four racial/ethnic groups. Similar analyses will not be discussed here, however, as the sample sizes are so small (there are only 12 foreign-born Hispanic job leavers, for example) that very few of the results are significant.

Table 9.4, shows a calculation of the probabilities of being a job loser, job leaver, or labor force entrant, computed by multiplying the proportions in Tables 9.2-9.3 by the estimated unemployment probabilities in Tables 8.2-8.3. The overall unemployment probabilities are repeated here for comparison. The probabilities in Table 9.4 are the actual probabilities of being in the states, rather than the proportion of those out of work. Table 9.5 converts the probabilities in Table 9.4 to percentage differentials from the probabilities for the reference person. The percentages are calculated from the complete numbers rather than the rounded values, so they will be more accurate than simple calculations made by hand from Table 9.4. For example, in Table 9.4 the probability of being a job loser with 16 years of education is 1.7% compared to 2.7% for the reference man with the mean level of education; this translates into a 37.6% lower probability of being a job loser for the more educated man. Table 9.6 provides percentage differentials between native-born men and all foreign-born men computed from the probabilities in Table 9.2.

One interesting observation is the effect of experience on the probability of being a labor force entrant. In Table 9.2 for native-born men and Table B.3 in Hurst (1997) for the pooled analysis it can be seen that the nonlinear effect of experience causes the labor force entry proportion of unemployment to decline at first, then rise to be greater at 36 years of experience than at 24 years. However, in Chapter 8 we showed that the probability of unemployment declined linearly; this linear decline in unemployment offsets the increasing proportion of labor force entrants. The net result in Table 9.5 is that the overall probability of being a labor force entrant is 41.8% greater at 12 years experience than at 24 years, but not really any different at 36 years, so the overall probability of labor force entry declines more or less to an asymptote.

Table 9.4. Estimated Total Probabilities of Unemployment, Tables 9.2 and 9.3 Applied to Unemployment in Tables 8.2 and 8.4, Pooled and Foreign Born Samples of Adult Men, All Races

VARIABLES	POOLED				FOREIGN BORN			
	Unemp.	Leaver	Loser	Entrant	Unemp.	Leaver	Loser	Entrant
Reference Person	0.036	0.003	0.027	0.006	0.046	0.002	0.030	0.013
Schooling = 16 Yrs	0.024	0.003	0.017	0.005	0.037	0.003	0.023	0.012
Schooling = 9 Yrs	0.055	0.004	0.043	0.008	0.053	0.002	0.036	0.015
Potential Exper. = 36	0.030	0.002	0.022	0.006	0.041	0.001	0.028	0.012
Potential Exper. = 12	0.043	0.004	0.030	0.008	0.050	0.003	0.027	0.021
Unmarried	0.073	0.007	0.051	0.015	0.058	0.003	0.035	0.020
Non-Metropolitan Res.	0.037	0.004	0.027	0.006	0.040	0.001	0.028	0.011
South	0.032	0.003	0.022	0.006	0.046	0.003	0.034	0.010
Agriculture	0.026	0.002	0.018	0.006	0.045	0.001	0.029	0.015
November 1979	0.020	0.002	0.016	0.003	0.037	0.002	0.022	0.013
April 1983	0.035	0.002	0.031	0.003	0.061	0.003	0.050	0.008
June 1986	0.034	0.002	0.028	0.003	0.053	0.003	0.034	0.016
June 1988	0.031	0.002	0.026	0.003	0.043	0.003	0.031	0.009
November 1989	0.032	0.002	0.026	0.003	0.056	0.005	0.038	0.013
June 1991	0.036	0.002	0.029	0.004	0.060	0.002	0.039	0.019
February 1994	0.028	0.002	0.022	0.004	0.046	0.001	0.033	0.013
Area Unemp. Rate=11.5%	0.063	0.004	0.050	0.009	0.078	0.003	0.050	0.024
Seas. Adjust. = 110%	0.040	0.003	0.031	0.006	0.048	0.003	0.030	0.015

Table 9.4 (continued)

VARIABLES	POOLED				FOREIGN BORN			
	Unemp.	Leaver	Loser	Entrant	Unemp.	Leaver	Loser	Entrant
Avg. Occ. Wages = $10	0.047	0.003	0.038	0.006	0.054	0.002	0.044	0.007
Var. Occ. Wages x 2	0.017	0.002	0.013	0.003	0.029	0.001	0.016	0.012
Foreign Born at Entry	0.031	0.002	0.018	0.011	(a)	(a)	(a)	(a)
YSM = mean	0.034	0.003	0.026	0.005	0.045	0.004	0.035	0.006
YSM = mean + 10	0.036	0.004	0.028	0.005	0.045	0.005	0.035	0.005
Reference Person	0.036	0.003	0.027	0.006	0.041	0.003	0.032	0.006
Schooling, Exper., . . .	(b)	(b)	(b)	(b)	(b)	(b)	(b)	(b)
YSM 25 Years or More	0.040	0.005	0.028	0.007	0.044	0.006	0.032	0.007
YSM 20-24 Years	0.037	0.003	0.028	0.005	0.048	0.004	0.039	0.005
YSM 15-19 Years	0.031	0.003	0.023	0.005	0.038	0.004	0.029	0.005
YSM 10-14 Years	0.034	0.003	0.026	0.006	0.045	0.003	0.036	0.006
YSM 7-9 Years	0.029	0.003	0.020	0.006	(a)	(a)	(a)	(a)
YSM 5-6 Years	0.035	0.001	0.027	0.007	0.050	0.001	0.042	0.007
YSM 3-4 Years	0.028	0.002	0.020	0.006	0.039	0.002	0.031	0.005
YSM 2 Years or Less	0.035	0.003	0.015	0.017	0.051	0.004	0.025	0.022

Notes: (a)—variable not entered; (b)—not shown, other variables held constant are the same as above.

Table 9.5. Estimated Percentage Differentials in Total Probabilities in Table 9.4, Pooled and Foreign Born Samples of Adult Men, All Races

VARIABLES	POOLED				FOREIGN BORN			
	Unemp.	Leaver	Loser	Entrant	Unemp.	Leaver	Loser	Entrant
Reference Person	0.0	0.0	0.0	0.0	0.0	0.0	0.0	0.0
Schooling = 16 Yrs	-32.0	-9.8	-37.6	-17.3	-19.3	22.6	-25.1	-12.9
Schooling = 9 Yrs	53.1	26.2	60.2	33.5	15.3	1.6	17.5	12.4
Potential Exper. = 36	-16.1	-38.5	-17.3	1.2	-10.1	-38.4	-9.0	-8.0
Potential Exper. = 12	19.5	44.3	12.1	41.8	9.5	32.5	-12.6	55.6
Unmarried	105.6	146.9	90.9	153.1	26.5	48.6	13.9	51.5
Non-Metropolitan Res.	3.3	21.0	0.7	6.6	-12.7	-34.8	-7.9	-19.9
South	-11.2	15.5	-16.8	1.0	0.1	28.3	11.0	-28.9
Agriculture	-27.2	-18.0	-34.0	0.1	-3.0	-74.0	-5.2	13.0
November 1979	-42.6	-37.9	-40.4	-54.7	-20.2	-10.5	-28.5	-3.1
April 1983	-1.2	-34.8	14.2	-56.2	33.4	30.8	65.1	-37.5
June 1986	-5.6	-22.8	5.3	-48.0	15.1	26.6	12.7	18.7
June 1988	-12.2	-22.7	-4.0	-44.9	-7.3	48.3	0.9	-34.6
November 1989	-11.5	-20.1	-2.7	-48.2	21.3	144.9	25.1	-6.5
June 1991	0.1	-22.2	9.4	-32.1	29.9	14.7	27.6	37.3
February 1994	-20.4	-36.5	-17.4	-26.2	0.9	-70.2	7.7	-3.4
Area Unemp. Rate=11.5%	77.9	33.1	86.8	58.7	69.0	55.9	66.2	77.5
Seas. Adjust. = 110%	11.7	7.4	13.5	5.5	4.7	32.5	-0.6	12.4

Table 9.5 (continued)

VARIABLES	POOLED				FOREIGN BORN			
	Unemp.	Leaver	Loser	Entrant	Unemp.	Leaver	Loser	Entrant
Avg. Occ. Wages = $10	32.7	16.2	41.1	2.2	16.4	17.5	43.8	-45.2
Var. Occ. Wages x 2	-51.6	-42.5	-52.9	-50.4	-36.1	-40.4	-48.5	-7.4
Foreign Born at Entry	-14.2	-47.6	-33.0	90.2	(a)	(a)	(a)	(a)
YSM = mean	-4.0	9.4	-4.7	-7.5	-2.4	80.4	16.2	-57.4
YSM = mean + 10	2.2	33.3	3.6	-20.3	-3.1	114.8	15.8	-64.0
Reference Person	0.0	0.0	0.0	0.0	0.0	0.0	0.0	0.0
Schooling, Exper., . . .	(b)	(b)	(b)	(b)	(b)	(b)	(b)	(b)
YSM 25 Years or More	12.2	69.4	5.0	16.9	7.2	83.2	-0.5	5.6
YSM 20-24 Years	3.5	9.5	5.3	-7.7	15.1	8.2	21.0	-11.7
YSM 15-19 Years	-12.0	6.2	-15.0	-7.2	-8.9	14.3	-9.3	-19.5
YSM 10-14 Years	-4.0	-9.6	-4.0	-0.7	8.9	-4.5	14.0	-9.9
YSM 7-9 Years	-18.6	-13.1	-24.2	4.9	(a)	(a)	(a)	(a)
YSM 5-6 Years	-1.8	-68.2	1.5	16.8	21.5	-65.7	31.7	17.0
YSM 3-4 Years	-22.8	-45.2	-25.6	2.0	-6.7	-40.3	-2.0	-12.2
YSM 2 Years or Less	-0.9	-9.3	-43.3	202.9	22.0	7.7	-22.9	260.8

Notes: (a) - variable not entered; (b) - not shown, other variables held constant are the same as above.

Table 9.6. Estimated Percentage Differentials in Total Probabilities in Table 9.2, Pooled and Foreign Born Samples of Adult Men, All Races

VARIABLES	NATIVE BORN				FOREIGN BORN			
	Unemp.	Leaver	Loser	Entrant	Unemp.	Leaver	Loser	Entrant
Reference Person	0.0	0.0	0.0	0.0	0.0	0.0	0.0	0.0
Schooling = 16 Yrs	-35.0	-15.5	-40.4	-20.0	-19.7	28.2	-25.9	-15.0
Schooling = 9 Yrs	64.3	35.2	72.5	40.5	15.6	0.3	17.8	13.2
Potential Exper. = 36	-17.4	-39.7	-19.0	1.2	-8.0	-30.7	-5.9	-6.5
Potential Exper. = 12	20.5	45.6	13.5	40.6	10.5	31.3	-6.2	74.6
Unmarried	114.2	156.8	98.5	166.0	28.7	59.4	18.8	58.2
Non-Metropolitan Res.	3.1	22.0	0.5	6.1	-12.2	-30.9	-7.3	-25.4
South	-13.1	13.3	-19.5	3.5	-0.2	19.3	5.6	-35.0
Agriculture	-25.6	-5.4	-34.2	4.2	-5.8	-75.3	-4.2	19.5
November 1979	-46.1	-40.6	-43.6	-60.4	-19.1	0.5	-23.8	-7.7
April 1983	-7.4	-39.0	7.0	-58.5	32.9	12.4	51.2	-38.3
June 1986	-9.4	-25.8	1.9	-54.0	15.7	17.4	14.0	22.0
June 1988	-13.4	-24.6	-5.2	-46.0	-6.6	29.9	-4.4	-33.3
November 1989	-15.4	-27.4	-6.1	-52.2	21.3	126.4	17.3	-10.4
June 1991	-4.0	-24.5	5.8	-39.4	30.8	12.2	30.0	43.5
February 1994	-25.1	-31.0	-22.9	-32.3	8.5	-66.7	18.8	-1.9
Area Unemp. Rate=11.5%	80.0	32.1	89.9	57.8	70.0	63.0	69.3	76.6
Seas. Adjust. = 110%	14.2	6.1	17.0	5.1	2.9	30.4	-1.7	10.3
Avg. Occ. Wages = $10	34.4	17.3	41.4	10.0	14.8	3.0	30.7	-49.7
Var. Occ. Wages x 2	-54.4	-44.5	-55.0	-56.3	-35.4	-33.6	-43.7	0.0

9.3   SUMMARY OF CHAPTER 9

Chapter 9 refocused the empirical analysis of labor market outcomes on unemployment, considering in detail the unemployment types of job loser, job leaver, and labor force entry. As in Chapter 8, the focus was first on the basic model variables and the differences between native-born men and foreign-born men in their return to human capital or their labor market responses to differences in their characteristics, then later on variables used to measure differences in labor market outcomes between native-born and foreign-born men after controlling for the basic model variables.

As in Chapter 8, the basic model variables seemed to have a smaller impact on changing the relative proportions of unemployment for foreign-born men than for native-born men, although normally working in the same direction. Increased levels of schooling significantly reduced the proportion of unemployed men who were job losers but increased the proportion who were labor force entrants, although the increase in the entrant probability was small for foreign-born men. One interesting difference is that while the job leaver proportion was higher with higher education for both nativity groups, the increase was smaller for native-born men; combined with the much lower unemployment probability for native-born men with higher education, the net result was an overall lower probability of being a job leaver, compared to a higher overall probability for foreign-born men.

There were two strong consistencies apparent in Chapter 9. First, the probability of being a labor force entrant was always significantly greater for foreign-born men in their first few years in the U.S., regardless of which model format was used or whether we were looking at the pooled sample or the foreign-born sample. While the actual *percentage point* differentials were small—usually no more than 1 percentage point—the *percentage* differentials between recently arrived foreign-born men and native-born men were quite large. So while they are more likely to be out of the labor force at any given time than native-born men, foreign-born men shortly after arrival are also more likely to *enter* the labor force.

Second, in most cases the differential between the newly arrived foreign-born and native-born men in the probability of being a job loser or job leaver is most often strongly negative, and except in a few inconsistent and insignificant cases, foreign-born men never have a greater probability of being job leavers or job losers. Thus if we accept the probabilities of being in the states of job loser or job leaver as indicative of the probabilities of entering those states, then Hypotheses 1 and 2 of Chapter 5—that the job loser rates and job leaver rates should be higher for recently arrived foreign-born men—are not supported.

There are two important reasons why we should not jump to this conclusion, however. First is the greater probability of labor force nonparticipation for foreign-born men. We could reasonably assume that movements out of the labor force are not likely to be from labor force entry unemployment; thus most men out of the labor force are probably there because of leaving or losing their jobs (or, for foreign-born men, because they recently arrived in the U.S.). So much of job loser and job leaver unemployment for foreign-born men is actually disguised in the higher rates of labor force nonparticipation. Second, if foreign-born men find jobs at a faster rate than native-born men, the duration of unemployment for foreign-born job losers and job leavers would be less, and the probability of being captured in those states in any given sample would be smaller. We test for this latter possibility in Chapters 10 and 11.

CHAPTER 10

Search Duration—Weeks Looking for Work

Chapters 8 and 9 analyzed the effects of the basic model variables and the foreign-born and YSM variables on the probabilities of being in the states of employment, unemployment, and out of the labor force, and within unemployment the probabilities of being a job loser, lob leaver, or labor force entrant. The underlying objective, however, is identifying the determinants of *entering* these states. The results of Chapters 8 and 9, however, only indicate determinants of the probabilities of being in the states. But if foreign-born men are less likely to be unemployed, is it because they are less likely to become unemployed, or because they spend less time in the job search process after they become unemployed? Unless we can estimate the probability of exit, we cannot make inferences about the probability of entry.

10.1 DESCRIPTION OF MODEL, AND PROBLEMS

Chapter 10 examines the determinants of search duration while unemployed, as measured by the time spent looking for work. The intent is to eventually use the estimates as proxies for what has been previously discussed in this book as the *job finding rate*, or *exit rate* or *escape rate* (Heckman and Singer, 1984), which can be considered as the inverse of the probability of continuing in unemployment once unemployed. There are several problems in making this leap, which will be discussed in this section.

The question is asked "How long have you been looking for work?" only of persons who are unemployed and looking for work Information is only available on incomplete spells of unemployment—

there is no information about persons who have recently been unemployed but have already exited unemployment, or completed their spells. This aspect of the CPS data causes two important problems. First, the data are a perfect example of *length-biased* sampling (Salant, 1977), wherein spells of greater than average duration theoretically have a higher probability of being in the sample, since persons of less than average duration are more likely to have already exited unemployment. This would mean that, *ceteris paribus*, actual completed spells should be shorter than our estimates of them using only uncompleted spells. The second problem is that, on average, each uncompleted spell is only half of its expected completed spell length, a situation called *interruption bias*; thus completed spells should be greater than our estimates of them using uncompleted spells, by a factor of 2, but only under steady-state conditions (Sider, 1985).

A third problem arises if there is *duration dependence*. There is positive duration dependence if the probability of exit increases as spell length increases, which is the classical assumption of search theory—as spells lengthen, searchers lower their reservation wages, increasing the size of the offer distribution. Negative duration dependence can also occur if, for example, there is a signaling effect, making searchers less attractive to employers if they have had a long duration of unemployment.

The general approach in economics has increasingly relied upon the use of hazard function models to minimize the above problems with the data. There is a large literature on estimating unemployment duration, many using hazard functions; surveys are provided in Lippman and McCall (1976), Mortensen (1986), and Devine and Kiefer (1991). A good summary of hazard function models is given in Kiefer (1988).

It is not necessary to define hazard functions here, however, as they cannot be adequately estimated with the data available. In order to adequately estimate a hazard function model, we need to be able to estimate a baseline hazard, which requires information about persons who have already experienced and exited unemployment. As noted by Lancaster (1979), without such information, estimating such a function requires making some strong assumptions about flows into unemployment; Nickell (1979) estimates such a function by first making an estimate of flows into unemployment. Unfortunately, the variable of interest in this analysis *is* the differences in flows into unemployment (or the types of unemployment). Data with information on completed spells is normally longitudinal data. There are no longitudinal studies of adequate size which include information on the foreign born. It is planned for future work to develop a longitudinal data set from matched samples of the CPS, which should give us enough information to estimate a baseline hazard.

The analysis in this book will take a simple approach to estimating exit probabilities, and make allowances for possible errors later. Most of the studies using hazard functions to estimate duration are interested in the duration variable itself, such as in estimating the effect of unemployment insurance benefits on duration (Lancaster, 1979). The variable of interest in this book is the probability of entering the state, and we are interested only in the differences between groups in determining this probability. In Chapter 11 we estimate a crude proxy for the percent differential between foreign-born and native-born men in this probability of entry, using a proxy for the percent differential in the probability of remaining unemployed in time t conditional on being unemployed at time $t\text{-}j$. In this chapter we estimate one of the inputs to Chapter 11, the percentage differential in the *duration of incomplete spells* for men who are unemployed and looking for work at the time of the survey.

In order to maintain consistency with the models in previous chapters, the model parameters for foreign-born men and native-born will be estimated first separately to assess differences in the basic model variables, the jointly, with dummy variables for nativity and/or YSM variables entered into the estimating equation. Thus, we define W_i , weeks looking for work for person i, as $Wi = f(X_i, F_i, Y_i)$ where X_i is a vector of "basic model" variables as used in Chapters 8 and 9, F is a dummy variable indicating foreign-born status, and Y_i is a vector of YSM variables, either continuous or incremental. The functional form is defined as:

$$W_i = e^{\beta_{1i}X_i + \beta_2 F + \beta_{3i}Y_i + e_i} , \qquad\qquad 10.1$$

and the estimating equation is:

$$\ln W_i = \beta_{1i}X_i + \beta_2 F + \beta_{3i}Y_i + e_i . \qquad 10.2$$

Several measures of the duration variable were contemplated, including the raw measure of weeks looking for work and a ratio of the individual's weeks looking to the mean weeks looking for all searchers. The semi-log form of equations 10.1 and 10.2 was chosen for two main reasons. First, the data appear to be non-normally distributed. Hurst (1997) includes graphs in Appendix C which show the histograms and normal probability plots for native-born men, for the raw weeks looking data and the log of the weeks looking data. The histograms show that the raw data appears to be distributed more or less exponentially, but the log data has a more normal bell shape. The normal probability plots show that the raw data (asterisks) stray from the benchmark line (plus marks), while the log data track nearly perfectly. Thus using the raw weeks looking data would violate the OLS assumption of normal error terms.

Perhaps more important however, is the fact that with a semi-log form the coefficients from the output, $\beta_{ji} = dlnW / dX_{ji}$, can interpreted directly as percentage differentials.[5] Thus the output parameter b_2 tells us directly the percent differential in weeks looking for work between foreign-born men and native-born men, and the output parameter b_{3i} tells us directly the percentage differential due to duration in the U.S. Since this is the input we will use in Chapter 11, it is convenient to produce it directly in this form.

There are two other problems with the duration data that should be pointed out. Figures 10.1 and 10.2 show the frequency distribution of weeks looking for work for native-born men and foreign-born men respectively. First, the data end at 99 weeks, and there is a large spike at that level. This is an artifact of the questionnaire, which topcodes anyone who reports a duration greater than 99. Second, there are other large spikes at key points, such as 4 week intervals, 26 weeks, and 52 weeks. These spikes are caused by *digit preference* and for greatest efficiency should probably be smoothed using some method such as proposed by Baker (1992). The end distribution should also be refitted in some fashion. Again, however, the accuracy of the predictions about weeks looking for work is not a major issue in this analysis. What is most important is the differentials between various groups. If the digit preference effect and the spike at 99 weeks were different for foreign-born men, it would be of greater concern, but from the graphs we can see that these effects are very similar for foreign-born men and native-born men. A t-test for differences in proportions show that the only significant differences between native-born men and foreign-born men

Figure 10.1 Frequency of Weeks Unemployed, Native Born

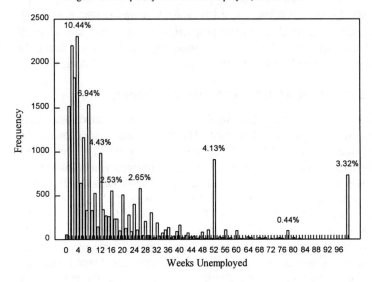

Figure 10.2. Frequency of Weeks Unemployed, Foreign Born

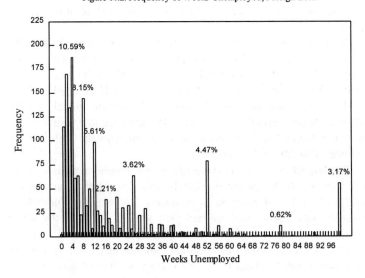

in the proportions are at 6 weeks (1.6%, t = 2.99), 12 weeks (-1.2%, t = -2.28), 15 weeks (0.5%, t = 2.10), and 26 weeks (1.0%, t = -2.43). Because the differences in the proportional distribution are so small and so rarely significant, and since smoothing the data would introduce a different kind of error, the data are not smoothed in this analysis.

10.2. EMPIRICAL RESULTS—BASIC MODEL

Table 10.1 shows the results of the basic model for native-born adult men and foreign-born adult men. The basic model variables will be analyzed in both Tables 10.1 and 10.2. Table 10.1 shows the differences between the three measures of unemployment considered for this analysis—the raw weeks looking for work variable, the weeks ratio (the individuals weeks divided by the mean of all men within the same survey year), and the log of weeks looking for work. Although the magnitudes of the coefficients are different because of the different units, the signs and t-ratios are nearly identical between the three measures. The main exception is in the survey year dummy variables for the weeks ratio; clearly dividing by the mean in the survey year creates an endogeneity problem with the survey year dummies. Another interesting point to note is the closeness of the weeks ratio coefficients to the Ln Weeks coefficients. From Table 10.1, however, it seems that the choice of Ln Weeks as the main variable of analysis is the best.

Table 10.2 presents the results of the pooled analysis and the analysis of foreign-born men; in the pooled model native-born men are 9 times more numerous than foreign-born men. The first model in each section adds the foreign-born dummy variable (in the pooled models) and the years since migration variables. The second model in each section adds two variables to measure the difference in unemployment duration between the three categories of unemployment—job leavers, job losers, and labor force entrants.

The impact of schooling on duration of unemployment is curious. In the foreign-born sample the coefficients are positive and highly significant. A 1 year increase in schooling increases the duration of unemployment among foreign-born men looking for work by about 4%, thus an increase in the level of schooling to 16 years from the mean of 11.8 years would increase the duration of unemployment for foreign-born men by about 18%. This is not a result of collinearity

Table 10.1. Regression Analysis of Weeks Unemployed, Weeks Ratio, and Ln Weeks Basic Model, Native Born and Foreign Born Adult Men

Variables	Native Born			Foreign Born		
	Weeks Unemp.	Weeks Ratio	Ln. Weeks	Weeks Unemp.	Weeks Ratio	Ln. Weeks
Schooling	0.0686	0.0051	0.0023	0.6040	0.0281	0.0400
	(0.81)	(1.25)	(0.55)	(3.75)	(3.64)	(4.91)
Potential Experience	0.6649	0.0324	0.0354	0.7623	0.0390	0.0349
	(8.36)	(8.54)	(9.15)	(3.43)	(3.65)	(3.09)
Exper. Squared	-0.0080	-0.0004	-0.0005	-0.0059	-0.0003	-0.0003
	(-5.26)	(-5.32)	(-6.29)	(-1.47)	(-1.78)	(-1.29)
Married (Sp Pres.)	-3.2588	-0.1532	-0.1207	0.1128	-0.0080	0.0692
	(-7.41)	(-7.29)	(-5.64)	(0.08)	(-0.12)	(1.02)
Metrop. Area	-0.1560	-0.0140	-0.0138	2.4194	0.0899	0.2473
	(-0.33)	(-0.62)	(-0.60)	(1.00)	(0.77)	(2.02)
South	-4.3321	-0.2003	-0.2049	-5.4551	-0.2521	-0.2085
	(-9.38)	(-9.08)	(-9.12)	(-3.61)	(-3.48)	(-2.73)
Agriculture	-6.9542	-0.3233	-0.2803	-8.6877	-0.4170	-0.3734
	(-5.11)	(-4.97)	(-4.23)	(-3.37)	(-3.37)	(-2.86)
November 1979	-10.7947	-0.0730	-0.6620	-9.5265	-0.1067	-0.7098
	(-10.25)	(-1.45)	(-12.92)	(-2.90)	(-0.68)	(-4.26)
April 1983	-1.8545	-0.2061	-0.0757	0.2927	-0.0965	-0.0731
	(-2.24)	(-5.21)	(-1.88)	(0.13)	(-0.88)	(-0.64)
June 1986	-3.6749	-0.0898	-0.2731	-5.5930	-0.1766	-0.3762
	(-4.57)	(-2.33)	(-6.98)	(-2.27)	(-1.49)	(-3.01)

Table 10.1 (continued)

Variables	Native Born			Foreign Born		
	Weeks Unemp.	Weeks Ratio	Ln. Weeks	Weeks Unemp.	Weeks Ratio	Ln. Weeks
June 1988	-4.2304	-0.0245	-0.3190	-6.4801	-0.1541	-0.4155
	(-4.64)	(-0.56)	(-7.19)	(-2.15)	(-1.07)	(-2.72)
November 1989	-7.8967	-0.0283	-0.5337	-3.2291	0.1979	-0.4370
	(-8.72)	(-0.65)	(-12.11)	(-1.13)	(1.44)	(-3.02)
June 1991	-5.6750	-0.0633	-0.2827	-5.9019	-0.0920	-0.3716
	(-7.06)	(-1.65)	(-7.23)	(-2.59)	(-0.84)	(-3.21)
February 1994	1.4804	0.1298	-0.0640	6.6838	0.3783	0.1166
	(1.35)	(2.47)	(-1.20)	(2.58)	(3.04)	(0.89)
Area Unemp. Rate	0.6954	0.0309	0.0350	0.5521	0.0253	0.0346
	(8.85)	(8.23)	(9.16)	(2.31)	(2.21)	(2.86)
Seas/Occ Adjust. Fact.	-0.3033	-0.0127	-0.0076	-0.2334	-0.0099	-0.0087
	(-9.83)	(-8.61)	(-5.04)	(-3.26)	(-2.89)	(-2.39)
Average, Occ. Wages	-0.3849	-0.0182	-0.0166	-0.6535	-0.0264	-0.0192
	(-3.73)	(-3.70)	(-3.32)	(-2.02)	(-1.70)	(-1.17)
Variance, Occ. Wages	-0.1577	-0.0067	-0.0050	-0.1160	-0.0051	-0.0067
	(-8.69)	(-7.76)	(-5.68)	(-1.96)	(-1.78)	(-2.25)
Constant	48.8351	2.0069	2.9612	25.6520	0.9859	2.1167
	(15.20)	(13.07)	(18.94)	(3.13)	(2.50)	(5.10)
Sample Size	13,430	13,430	13,430	1,332	1,332	1,332
Adjusted R Square	0.0731	0.0514	0.0728	0.1044	0.0779	0.1135

Sources: Current Population Survey, various supplements, 1979-94; Survey of Income and Education, 1976.
Notes: t-ratios in parentheses.

Table 10.2. Regression Analysis of Ln Weeks Unemployed Pooled and Foreign Born Samples of Adult Men

Variables	Pooled		Foreign Born	
	(1)	(2)	(1)	(2)
Schooling	0.0096	0.0117	0.0410	0.0435
	(2.63)	(3.19)	(4.87)	(5.16)
Potential Experience	0.0344	0.0325	0.0341	0.0301
	(9.43)	(8.89)	(3.01)	(2.64)
Exper. Squared	-0.0004	-0.0004	-0.0002	-0.0002
	(-6.16)	(-5.65)	(-1.16)	(-0.86)
Married (Sp Pres.)	-0.1042	-0.1105	0.0645	0.0543
	(-5.11)	(-5.42)	(0.95)	(0.80)
Metrop. Area	-0.0068	-0.0105	0.2504	0.2552
	(-0.30)	(-0.47)	(2.04)	(2.08)
South	-0.1998	-0.1937	-0.2156	-0.2214
	(-9.29)	(-9.01)	(-2.81)	(-2.88)
Agriculture	-0.3240	-0.3167	-0.3688	-0.3729
	(-5.55)	(-5.43)	(-2.82)	(-2.86)
November 1979	-0.6679	-0.6733	-0.7230	-0.7091
	(-13.68)	(-13.80)	(-4.33)	(-4.26)
April 1983	-0.0775	-0.0985	-0.0771	-0.0983
	(-2.06)	(-2.61)	(-0.67)	(-0.85)
June 1986	-0.2859	-0.3023	-0.3832	-0.3789
	(-7.69)	(-8.11)	(-3.05)	(-3.03)
June 1988	-0.3311	-0.3431	-0.4186	-0.4176
	(-7.80)	(-8.07)	(-2.74)	(-2.74)
November 1989	-0.5266	-0.5417	-0.4424	-0.4356
	(-12.55)	(-12.89)	(-3.06)	(-3.01)
June 1991	-0.2988	-0.3135	-0.3752	-0.3784
	(-8.12)	(-8.51)	(-3.24)	(-3.28)
February 1994	-0.0392	-0.0508	0.1029	0.0762
	(-0.80)	(-1.03)	(0.78)	(0.58)
Area Unemp. Rate	0.0353	0.0337	0.0340	0.0341
	(9.73)	(9.29)	(2.81)	(2.82)
Seas/Occ Adjust. Fact.	-0.0078	-0.0079	-0.0088	-0.0080
	(-5.65)	(-5.73)	(-2.41)	(-2.21)
Average, Occ. Wages	-0.0173	-0.0197	-0.0194	-0.0261
	(-3.63)	(-4.11)	(-1.19)	(-1.57)

Table 10.2 (continued)

Variables	Pooled		Foreign Born	
	(1)	(2)	(1)	(2)
Variance, Occ. Wages	-0.0051	-0.0050	-0.0067	-0.0058
	(-6.07)	(-5.93)	(-2.25)	(-1.91)
Foreign Born	-0.2218	-0.2041	(a)	(a)
	(-3.27)	(-3.01)		
Years Since Mig. (YSM)	0.0138	0.0123	0.0105	0.0090
	(1.79)	(1.60)	(1.33)	(1.13)
YSM Squared	-0.0002	-0.0002	-0.0003	-0.0002
	(-1.25)	(-1.09)	(-1.43)	(-1.23)
Leaver	(a)	-0.0366	(a)	-0.1355
		(-0.96)		(-1.05)
Loser	(a)	0.1231	(a)	0.1704
		(5.00)		(2.20)
Constant	2.8868	2.8494	2.0644	1.9509
	(19.92)	(19.62)	(4.95)	(4.67)
Sample Size	13,430	13,430	1,332	1,332
Adjusted R Square	0.0657	0.0657	0.1135	0.1188

Sources: CPS, various supplements, 1979-94; Survey of Income and Education, 1976.

Notes: t-ratios in parentheses; (a)—variable not entered.

with the occupational variables—removing the variables for occupational wage, occupational variance, and seasonal adjustment factors do little to change the coefficients or significance levels on the schooling variable, and if anything, make it more positive.

Why schooling would increase the duration of uncompleted spells is not clear, nor is it clear why the schooling variable only affects foreign-born men. In a previous analysis similar to Chapter 9, it was found that additional schooling increased the probability of being out of the labor force for men who were not working, so one possible explanation is that this effect may be an example of the effect of length bias. Perhaps this result is due to offsetting effects. Higher levels of schooling act to increase reservation wages, thus increasing the duration of unemployment; suppose that this effect were the same for native-born and foreign-born men. We would also expect that higher levels of schooling would increase the offer distribution, reducing duration, but perhaps the lower transferability of skills negates this for foreign-born men. In addition, increased schooling increases the opportunity cost of time, and increases search efficiency, both of which would reduce unemployment duration, and perhaps the lower effect of schooling noted in Chapter 8 reduces this impact on foreign-born men.

Experience increases the duration of incomplete spells of unemployment, for both native-born and foreign-born men, which is consistent with other studies testing age rather than potential experience (Kooreman and Ridder, 1983; Lancaster, 1979). Although the coefficients on the square of experience are statistically significant for the pooled sample, their size is so small that we can say that the effect of experience in this data set is practically linear—at 10 years of experience the partial effect is 2.7% for an additional year of experience; it is still 1.1% after 30 years experience. The quadratic terms are not significant for foreign-born men.

Two other results are difficult to explain. Marriage reduces the duration of incomplete spells of unemployment by about 11% for native-born men, but not for foreign-born men. Why marriage has no effect on reducing the duration of unemployment for foreign-born men is not clear. This result could be related to the higher NILF probability of foreign-born men—perhaps the value of non-market time relative to market time is higher for foreign-born men, reducing the degree of specialization between foreign-born husbands and wives. On the other hand, foreign-born men, but not native-born men, who live in a metropolitan area are unemployed longer (about 28% more weeks) than nonmetropolitan foreign-born men. This result is counter to expectations, as expressed in Chapter 7, but could be a result of higher labor force participation for foreign-born men in metropolitan areas. Thus there are some significant and inexplicable differences in the determinants of the duration of incomplete spells of unemployment between foreign-born men and native-born men.

The trend variables are consistent with expectations. The duration of incomplete spells of unemployment is significantly lower than in the benchmark year of 1976, for native-born men, in every survey year except 1994. We might expect 1983 to be higher, and it is lower, but the percent differentials and t-ratios are much lower than in other years, and only marginally significant. The pattern holds for foreign-born men, with the exception of an insignificant coefficient in 1983.

Higher area unemployment rates increase unemployment duration, as expected, by about 3-4% on average for each percentage point increase in the average rate. The occupational/seasonal adjustment factor reduces unemployment duration with an elasticity of about -0.8—a 1% increase in the adjustment factor decreases the duration of incomplete spells by about 0.77% for native-born men and about 0.88% for foreign-born men. One possible explanation for this effect is that persons with high seasonal factors are more likely to be employed in low seasonal factor periods; but in high seasonal factor periods they may have more recently begun their unemployment—are closer to the beginning of the unemployment season—whereas men with low seasonal factors who are unemployed are equally likely to be unemployed in all seasons. In other words, there may be less length bias for men in high seasonality occupations. Another explanation arises from the fact that this result only applies to job losers; as explained below, this is an indication that the persons in highly seasonal occupations are experiencing frictional or seasonal unemployment, compared to structural unemployment for men in less seasonal occupations.

The average of occupational wages acts as expected for native-born men—a dollar increase in the average occupational wage for native-born men reduces the duration of incomplete spells of unemployment by about 1.7% on average. Higher occupational wages increase the cost of continued job search, so would be expected to reduce search time. The coefficients on average occupational wage are not significant for foreign-born men, but have the expected sign. On the other hand, increases in the variance of occupational wages tend to decrease spell duration as well, for both native-born and foreign-born men. This is contrary to what we would expect from search theory—as the variance of wages increases, the probability of finding a job with a higher wage improves with longer search time, so should lead to a higher average duration of unemployment. The reason for this result is unclear.

Finally, in Table 10.2 the last two variables in the second model of each section show the differential impact of reason for being unemployed (job losers or job leavers, compared to the benchmark labor force entrants) on the duration of incomplete spells of unemployment. Job leavers have the lowest unemployment duration on average, for both native-born men and foreign-born men, although the t-ratios indicate that job leavers are not significantly different from

Table 10.3. Regression Analysis of Ln Weeks Unemployed Pooled Samples of Adult Men, by Racial Group

Variables	White	Black	Hispanic	Other Minority
Schooling	0.0022	0.0085	0.0162	0.0364
	(0.50)	(0.72)	(1.40)	(2.70)
Potential Experience	0.0379	0.0220	0.0247	0.0245
	(8.99)	(2.19)	(1.73)	(1.66)
Exper. Squared	-0.0005	-0.0003	-0.0004	-0.0001
	(-5.88)	(-1.38)	(-1.38)	(-0.46)
Married (Sp Pres.)	-0.1166	-0.0876	0.0750	0.0459
	(-4.86)	(-1.61)	(0.96)	(0.52)
Metrop. Area	-0.0209	-0.0743	0.1119	0.0386
	(-0.83)	(-0.98)	(0.98)	(0.34)
South	-0.2328	-0.2326	-0.1473	-0.1947
	(-8.97)	(-3.95)	(-1.87)	(-1.76)
Agriculture	-0.2208	-0.5820	-0.2146	-0.6248
	(-2.81)	(-3.54)	(-1.62)	(-3.09)
November 1979	-0.6646	-0.4296	-1.0586	-0.6910
	(-11.95)	(-3.09)	(-5.43)	(-2.97)
April 1983	-0.0996	0.0819	-0.1816	-0.1019
	(-2.24)	(0.81)	(-1.28)	(-0.64)
June 1986	-0.3091	-0.0677	-0.4529	-0.3942
	(-7.03)	(-0.68)	(-3.29)	(-2.57)
June 1988	-0.3426	-0.0560	-0.6138	-0.4370
	(-6.89)	(-0.48)	(-3.96)	(-2.36)
November 1989	-0.5988	-0.1409	-0.7291	-0.5918
	(-12.08)	(-1.26)	(-4.78)	(-3.18)
June 1991	-0.3132	-0.1451	-0.3900	-0.3261
	(-7.28)	(-1.43)	(-2.84)	(-2.01)
February 1994	-0.0342	0.0082	-0.1630	0.2113
	(-0.57)	(0.06)	(-0.99)	(1.23)
Area Unemp. Rate	0.0327	0.0463	0.0318	0.0563
	(7.86)	(4.56)	(2.21)	(3.13)
Seas/Occ Adjust. Fact.	-0.0105	-0.0012	-0.0036	-0.0099
	(-6.16)	(-0.31)	(-0.87)	(-1.97)
Average, Occ. Wages	-0.0180	-0.0317	-0.0257	-0.0031
	(-3.31)	(-2.16)	(-1.25)	(-0.16)

Table 10.3 (continued)

Variables	White	Black	Hispanic	Other Minority
Variance, Occ. Wages	-0.0045	-0.0041	-0.0081	-0.0016
	(-4.56)	(-1.91)	(-2.41)	(-0.42)
Foreign Born	0.2244	0.0921	-0.3958	-0.4251
	(1.73)	(0.36)	(-2.94)	(-3.05)
Years Since Mig. (YSM)	-0.0303	-0.0132	0.0405	0.0721
	(-2.38)	(-0.39)	(2.99)	(4.25)
YSM Squared	0.0007	0.0002	-0.0009	-0.0015
	(2.55)	(0.23)	(-2.73)	(-3.21)
Constant	3.2243	2.4301	2.4745	2.2364
	(18.29)	(6.19)	(5.13)	(4.03)
Sample Size	10,920	2,106	1,008	726
Adjusted R Square	0.081	0.058	0.0893	0.1431

Sources: CPS, various supplements, 1979-94; Survey of Income and Education, 1976.

Notes: t-ratios in parentheses.

t-ratios indicate that job leavers are not significantly different from labor force entrants in unemployment duration. Job losers, on the other hand, have significantly longer durations of incomplete spells than labor force entrants—13% longer for native born men and 19% longer for foreign-born men. The involuntarily unemployed either have a more difficult time finding work, or may be less inclined to leave the labor force after becoming unemployed.

Table 10.3 shows differences in incomplete unemployment spell duration by racial/ethnic group. The positive impact of the schooling variable affects only other minorities, while experience is significant for all races, except marginally for other minorities. Marriage does not have an effect on the duration of unemployment for Hispanic or other minority men, and working in the agricultural sector reduces unemployment duration for all races, marginally for Hispanic men. The impact of the yearly trend variables appears to be about the same for all racial groups except for blacks, who show little significant difference in the duration of unemployment between 1976 and most other years. The area unemployment rate increases duration for all races, and the seasonal adjustment factor reduces unemployment duration for whites and other minorities, but not for blacks or Hispanics. The effect of average occupational wages is to reduce unemployment duration for whites and blacks, while the variance of occupational wages reduces duration for all except other minorities.

Table 10.4 shows the basic pooled analysis run separately for each of the three categories of unemployment. The first point to note is that for job leavers the effects of the basic variables are almost always negative; the only significant variable that increases incomplete unemployment spell duration for job leavers is the area unemployment rate. Also, when variables have negative impacts on the other categories of unemployment, the impacts are generally less strong for job leavers than for the other categories. Thus job leavers, having the choice whether or not to enter unemployment, have more control over their search process, and tend to be less affected by demographic, geographic, or other exogenous influences. This pattern is generally similar, but to a lesser extent, for the other voluntary unemployment category, labor force entrants, with a few notable exceptions. Older labor force entrants (potential experience) spend a longer time in the job search process than younger labor force entrants. This result would be understandable if older labor force entrants tend to be men with lower recent labor force attachment, such as persons who have been disabled or sick, in jail, on welfare, changing occupations, or men who have recently been discouraged workers. It is reasonable to expect that persons who have been out of the labor force at an older age in general have a more difficult time locating employment. Labor force entrants appear to be less affected in their unemployment duration by the area unemployment rate. Finally, men who entered the labor force in 1994 experienced a longer duration of incomplete unemployment spells than entrants in other years, for which there is no ready explanation.

An interesting observation is that the impact of schooling on increasing unemployment duration only affects job losers. It would seem, therefore, that the effect of schooling works through increasing reservation wages. Voluntary entrants into unemployment—job leavers and labor force entrants—have more control over their labor force situation, probably made preparations for their unemployment, and higher levels of schooling improves the potential distribution of job offers. But involuntarily unemployed men made fewer preparations for their unemployment, and their higher initial expectations would reduce

Table 10.4. Regression Analysis of Ln Weeks Unemployed Pooled Samples of Adult Men, by Category of Unemployment

Variables	Job Losers	Job Leavers	Labor Force Entrants
Schooling	0.0164	0.0138	0.0074
	(3.65)	(1.13)	(0.91)
Potential Experience	0.0288	-0.0033	0.0466
	(6.32)	(-0.26)	(5.75)
Exper. Squared	-0.0003	0.0004	-0.0008
	(-3.69)	(1.62)	(-5.11)
Married (Sp Pres.)	-0.1195	-0.0545	-0.0658
	(-4.92)	(-0.84)	(-1.29)
Metrop. Area	0.0024	-0.1621	-0.0672
	(0.09)	(-2.26)	(-1.18)
South	-0.1814	-0.1589	-0.2221
	(-7.02)	(-2.41)	(-4.20)
Agriculture	-0.3670	-0.1559	-0.3938
	(-5.07)	(-0.83)	(-3.27)
November 1979	-0.8224	-0.4603	-0.4542
	(-13.59)	(-3.09)	(-3.98)
April 1983	-0.0978	-0.0479	-0.2221
	(-2.20)	(-0.34)	(-2.27)
June 1986	-0.3363	-0.1902	-0.2814
	(-7.46)	(-1.54)	(-3.03)
June 1988	-0.4091	-0.2440	-0.2220
	(-7.78)	(-1.88)	(-2.20)
November 1989	-0.6428	-0.3761	-0.3928
	(-12.65)	(-2.95)	(-3.85)
June 1991	-0.3876	-0.2600	-0.1712
	(-8.70)	(-2.13)	(-1.98)
February 1994	-0.1593	-0.0240	0.2407
	(-2.64)	(-0.16)	(2.21)
Area Unemp. Rate	0.0310	0.0517	0.0154
	(7.49)	(3.62)	(1.55)
Seas/Occ Adjust. Fact.	-0.0103	-0.0038	-0.0021
	(-6.01)	(-0.82)	(-0.71)

Table 10.4 (continued)

Variables	Job Losers	Job Leavers	Labor Force Entrants
Average, Occ. Wages	-0.0256	0.0121	-0.0192
	(-4.42)	(0.83)	(-1.70)
Variance, Occ. Wages	-0.0064	-0.0036	-0.0036
	(-6.23)	(-1.33)	(-1.82)
Foreign Born	-0.0470	-0.5089	-0.4753
	(-0.54)	(-1.99)	(-3.62)
Years Since Mig. (YSM)	-0.0060	0.0389	0.0409
	(-0.62)	(1.32)	(2.59)
YSM Squared	0.0002	-0.0007	-0.0008
	(1.00)	(-0.96)	(-2.30)
Constant	3.3248	2.2964	2.4007
	(18.26)	(4.58)	(7.73)
Sample Size	10,143	1,419	2,565
Adjusted R Square	0.0872	0.0627	0.0497

Sources: CPS, various supplements, 1979-94; Survey of Income and Education, 1976.

Notes: t-ratios in parentheses.

the potential distribution of acceptable job offers. In addition, higher levels of schooling increase the cost of dropping out of the labor force, as the value of home production may be less than the value of market production for higher levels of schooling. Finally, there may be a wealth effect, wherein job losers with greater wealth are able to search longer, although we would expect a wealth effect to apply to job leavers and labor force entrants as well.

Finally, job losers have a reduction in their incomplete unemployment spell duration for a higher occupational/seasonal adjustment factor—about 1 to 1 for percentage increases in the adjustment factor, compared to insignificant changes for job leavers or labor force entrants. We can surmise that persons who are unemployed because they left their jobs or entered the labor force are less sensitive to seasonal fluctuations in their occupations. But for men who lost their jobs, those who are in higher seasonal occupations or high seasonal periods will likely be recalled to their previous jobs or to other jobs in their occupation, while for others in nonseasonal occupations the possibility of recall is smaller. In other words, unemployment in seasonal occupations is frictional or seasonal unemployment, resulting in lower duration, while unemployment in nonseasonal occupations is more structural, with longer duration.

10.3. THE FOREIGN-BORN VARIABLES

The lower portion of Tables 10.2-10.4 show the percentage differential in incomplete spell duration between foreign-born men at arrival in the U.S. and native born men (the Foreign-born variable); the percentage differential for each additional year of residence in the U.S. (YSM); and the quadratic effect, or percentage differential for the square of each additional year. Model 1 in the pooled sample in Table 10.2 shows that foreign-born men upon arrival in the U.S. spend about 19.9% less time unemployed (as measured by incomplete spells) than similar native born men, after adjusting for the demographic, geographic, and period variables above. The average time unemployed increases with duration in the U.S. by about 1% for each additional year, marginally significant. The YSM adjustment appears to be linear, as the coefficient on YSM squared is not even marginally significant ($t = -1.25$); a separate test shows that a linear YSM variable is slightly more significant ($t = 1.86$). In the foreign-born model, the evidence for increasing unemployment duration with additional years residence is weak ($t = 1.33$), but this may be an artifact of the smaller sample size; a linear YSM variable is negative with an even smaller level of significance ($t = -0.96$).

Table 10.3 shows that the lower incomplete spell duration for foreign-born men is not consistent across the races. Black foreign-born men are not significantly different from native born black men in their unemployment duration, neither upon arrival in the U.S. nor at any time thereafter. White foreign-born men at arrival actually spend more time searching for employment than native born men, by about 25%, which decreases quadratically to the white native born norm at about 11-12 years.

It is Hispanic and other minority foreign-born men who cause the negative differential for foreign-born men in Table 10.2—their percent differentials with native born men in their own racial/ethnic group at arrival are -32.7% and -34.6% respectively, both of which rise quadratically toward the native born norm in their racial/ethnic group, crossing over the native born norm at about 12 years.

These last two results, although they appear to be very similar, are actually part of two separate dynamics. Although other minority foreign-born men are less likely to be employed than their native-born counterparts shortly after arrival (Table 8.6), the difference is small in terms of unemployment probabilities; instead, they are much more likely to be out of the labor force (9.9% vs.3.2%). On the other hand, Hispanic foreign-born men are *less* likely (2.7%) to be out of the labor force at arrival into the U.S. than native born Hispanic men (4.8%), as well as less likely than foreign-born other minority men; in contrast, they are less likely to be unemployed and more likely to be employed. Thus for persons who are out of work at any point in time, Hispanics are likely to return to work sooner than other minorities, while other minorities are more likely to drop out of the labor force. The causes are not clear, but it is possible that there is a difference in the quality or availability of ethnic networks, or lower "ethnic capital" for other minority foreign born, who come mostly from Asia. There may also be a wealth effect, increasing the ability of other minorities to search for work longer (passively or actively) than Hispanics. Similarly, social benefits are more available to refugee groups from Asia, and less available to illegal aliens, which comprise a greater proportion of Hispanic foreign-born men than other minorities.

The results of the previous paragraph are illustrated further in Table 10.4. Among job leavers and labor force entrants, foreign-born men at arrival in the U.S. have a duration of incomplete spells of unemployment 38-40% less than native-born job leavers or labor force entrants. There is no significant difference in unemployment duration between foreign-born and native-born men in the case of job losers. Earlier it was shown that job losers have a substantially higher duration of incomplete unemployment spells, and foreign-born men are less likely to be job losers. In addition, not only are foreign-born men more likely to be in the categories of unemployment that have lower duration—job leavers and labor force entrants—but the unemployment duration is even lower for foreign-born men than for native-born men *within* these categories.

Finally, Table 10.5 shows that the continuous duration variables used in the previous tables smoothes over an important discontinuity. Incomplete unemployment spell duration is lower for foreign-born men compared to native-born men only within the first two increments—0 to 4 years—in the pooled sample and for Hispanics, and marginally significant only in the first 2 years for blacks and other minorities. Foreign-born other minorities have a longer unemployment spell duration than native-born other minorities after about 10 years, but for other races there is no significant difference for longer years since migration. Thus it appears that foreign-born men are making labor market adjustments rapidly after they arrive in the U.S., a result that is not being picked up with the continuous duration variable. This provides further evidence of greater voluntary turnover among newly arrived foreign-born men.

10.4   SUMMARY OF CHAPTER 10

Chapter 10 analyzed the determinants of differentials in incomplete spells of unemployment duration. As in previous chapters, separate runs were made on native-born and foreign-born men to analyze the basic model variables. Then pooled models and foreign-born models were run with a foreign-born dummy variable and/or continuous or incremental variables to measure the effects of duration in the U.S. Separate analyses were done for the three categories of unemployment that were analyzed in Chapter 9, and each was also added as dummy variables within the pooled and foreign-born sample. In Chapter 10 the methodology was ordinary least squares applied to a semi-log equation on the number of weeks looking for work.

Unlike Chapters 8 and 9, the effects of the basic model variables on incomplete spell duration was remarkably similar between native-born and foreign-born men. The most notable exception is that higher levels of schooling increased spell duration for foreign-born men, but not for native-born men. Other notable exceptions were the effects of being married, which reduced spell duration for native-born men but not foreign-born men, and metropolitan residence, which increased spell duration for foreign-born men but not native-born men. More highly seasonal occupations reduced spell duration significantly for both groups, as did average occupational wages and wage variances, except that average wages were not significant for foreign-born men. The period dummy variables showed lower spell duration in the 1980s and 1990s compared to 1976, with little difference between native-born men and foreign-born men in the trend effects.

Table 10.5. Regression Analysis of Ln Weeks Unemployed, Duration Variables Only Shown, Pooled and Foreign Born Samples of Adult Men, and by Unemployment Category

	Pooled	Foreign Born	White	Black	Hispanic	Other Minority	Job Losers	Job Leavers	Lab.Force Entrants
YSM 25 Years +	-0.0307	-0.0968	0.0221	-0.0511	0.0061	0.4244	-0.0210	0.0917	-0.0804
	(-0.42)	(-0.86)	(0.23)	(-0.15)	(0.04)	(1.81)	(-0.24)	(0.42)	(-0.48)
YSM 20-24 Years	0.0042	0.0026	-0.0286	-0.2105	0.1066	0.1992	-0.0052	-0.1364	0.0195
	(0.05)	(0.02)	(-0.23)	(-0.49)	(0.70)	(0.78)	(-0.05)	(-0.43)	(0.09)
YSM 15-19 Years	-0.0266	-0.0474	-0.0234	-0.1531	-0.0424	0.5613	0.0270	0.0842	-0.1970
	(-0.26)	(-0.36)	(-0.11)	(-0.34)	(-0.27)	(2.53)	(0.22)	(0.25)	(-0.76)
YSM 10-14 Years	-0.1244	-0.0571	-0.1708	-0.1883	-0.1155	0.2964	-0.1468	-0.2549	-0.0357
	(-1.76)	(-0.55)	(-1.01)	(-0.83)	(-0.99)	(1.88)	(-1.80)	(-1.03)	(-0.20)
YSM 7-9 Years	-0.1147	(a)	-0.1142	0.1221	-0.1679	0.0594	-0.1232	-0.2413	-0.2644
	(-1.41)		(-0.72)	(0.45)	(-1.17)	(0.36)	(-1.25)	(-0.85)	(-1.39)
YSM 5-6 Years	-0.0507	0.0506	0.4063	0.3955	-0.1939	-0.0161	-0.0925	0.1853	-0.0160
	(-0.52)	(0.41)	(1.47)	(1.34)	(-1.16)	(-0.10)	(-0.84)	(0.33)	(-0.07)
YSM 3-4 Years	-0.2349	-0.1598	0.1126	0.0543	-0.4571	-0.2127	-0.1231	-0.4735	-0.3349
	(-2.14)	(-1.18)	(0.49)	(0.18)	(-2.37)	(-1.03)	(-0.91)	(-0.99)	(-1.31)
YSM 2 Years or Less	-0.2950	-0.2332	0.2891	-0.5664	-0.4936	-0.2414	-0.0915	-0.2365	-0.4521
	(-2.96)	(-1.84)	(1.53)	(-1.43)	(-2.48)	(-1.60)	(-0.59)	(-0.66)	(-2.96)
Constant	2.8826	2.1607	3.2295	2.4289	2.5534	2.0986	3.3255	2.3057	2.3859
	(19.89)	(5.13)	(18.29)	(6.18)	(5.26)	(3.68)	(18.25)	(4.57)	(7.65)
Sample Size	14,763	1,332	10,920	2,106	1,008	726	10,143	1,419	2,565
Adjusted R Square	0.0751	0.1130	0.0806	0.0579	0.0876	0.1345	0.0870	0.0599	0.0473

Sources: CPS, various supplements, 1979-94; Survey of Income and Education,1976.

Notes: t-ratios in parentheses; (a)—variable not entered.

Lob leavers had slightly lower durations of incomplete spells of unemployment than labor force entrants for both foreign-born men and native-born men. Job losers, on the other hand, had significantly longer spell durations, and this effect was stronger for foreign-born men. Thus foreign-born men were less likely to be job losers than native-born men on average, but foreign-born job losers were unemployed longer than native-born job losers.

After holding constant the basic model variables, the duration of incomplete spells of unemployment was significantly lower for foreign-born men upon arrival in the U.S. but then increased rapidly to approach the native-born norm after a few years. The convergence was nearly linear. In the incremental models, the convergence was complete after 4 years between foreign-born and native-born men in the pooled model, and after 2 years in the foreign-born model.

Finally, in a separate analysis by job category, it was shown that foreign-born labor force entrants and job leavers had significantly shorter unemployment spells than native-born labor force entrants or job leavers. The job leaver difference remained constant despite increased duration in the U.S., but the labor force entrant difference diminished asymptotically with duration in the United States.

The results of Chapter 10 support Hypothesis number 4. We might infer that lower reservation wages for foreign-born men have a strong effect in reducing unemployment duration, or that they are affected by a stronger proclivity to work or by an inability to claim unemployment insurance. Another explanation may be simply that foreign-born men who become unemployed may simply drop out of the labor force sooner than native-born men. This is a difficult conclusion to support if we compare the racial groups in Tables 8.6 and 10.3(for other minorities, lower unemployment duration is matched by a lower rate of labor force participation, but for the other racial groups the relationship is reversed.

CHAPTER 11

Adjusting Unemployment Probabilities for Duration of Unemployment

So far this book has focused on two aspects of the unemployment and labor force dynamics of native-born and foreign-born men: the probability of being in the states of unemployment, employment, or out of the labor force, or the various categories of unemployment; and the duration of time spent looking for work. But these are only two pieces of the puzzle. The probability of being in the states is a complex interplay of the probability of entering the states and the probability of exiting the states. We have focused upon the areas above because that is what the data gives us. But the variable of greatest interest for this book is the probability of entry. Part of the assimilation hypothesis assumes that foreign-born men, in attempting to acquire destination-specific human capital, will experience many firms, will move freely in and out of the market, and will have higher rates of turnover, and two of our hypotheses propose higher quit rates and layoff rates, and higher rates of entering unemployment.

For an adequate test of these hypotheses, we would ideally produce estimates of rates of entering unemployment and job loser, job leaver, and labor force entrant status. Unfortunately, as will be shown, a reasonably accurate estimate of entry probabilities would require longitudinal data. Still, suppose we know that foreign-born men at arrival are 14% less likely to be unemployed at time t than are native-born men. Is this result because they spend less time in searching for employment, or because they are less likely to become unemployed? If we know that their duration of job search is significantly higher while unemployed, then we can surmise that a lower probability of unemployment is likely due to a lower probability of entry. But if their duration of job search is lower, we cannot make inferences about their entry probabilities. What we should be able to do, however, is to adjust the state probabilities by the duration of unemployment while in the state, and the result should be a reasonable first approximation of the probability of entering the state.

This chapter will attempt to produce adjusted state probabilities by synthesizing the results of Chapters 8-10. The results are presented in section 11.2 and 11.3 below, but first the estimating logic and methodology will be derived.

11.1. DERIVATION OF THE ESTIMATING EQUATIONS

This section will derive the methodology used for the estimates in this chapter, and will specify two key assumptions. While we will not call the end result the "probability of entry", the fundamental logic derives from the relationship between the entry probability, search duration, and state probabilities. To start, define the following terms:

U_t = a state of unemployment, or type of unemployment, at time t.

$P(E_{t-s-1})$= probability of entering a state of unemployment, or type of unemployment, at time t-s-1, where s is the number of periods of unemployment including t.

$P(U_t) \mid U_{t-s-1}$ = probability of being in a state of unemployment, or type of unemployment, at time t, conditional on being unemployed at time t-s-1, where s is the number of periods of unemployment including t.

As described in Chapter 7, we can define the probability that a man is in a state of unemployment at any time as the product of the probability of entry into unemployment and the probability of remaining unemployed after entry. First, consider a two-period model:

$$P(U_t) = P(E_{t-1})[P(U_t)|U_{t-1}] + P(E_t)[P(U_t)|U_t], \qquad \textbf{11.1}$$

where $U_t \mid U_t = 1$. Similarly, a three-period model would be:

$$P(U_t) = P(E_{t-2})[P(U_t)|U_{t-2}] + P(E_{t-1})[P(U_t)|U_{t-1}] + P(E_t)[P(U_t)|U_t]. \qquad \textbf{11.2}$$

In general, the overall probability of unemployment at any time t is the sum of all of the product terms; the equation for an s period model:

$$P(U_t) = \sum_{j=0}^{s-1} P(E_{t-j})[P(U_t) \mid U_{t-j}].$$ *11.3*

Equation 11.3 is essentially the same as equation 8 in Nickell (1979), page 1255. Nickell's task was to estimate $P(U_t) \mid U_{t-j}$. Our goal is to estimate $P(E_{t-j})$. To convert this formula, we will make one simplifying assumption. We assume that $P(E_{t-j})$ is not a function of j, in other words, the probability of entering a state of, say, unemployment is not a function of the duration of unemployment, or time between the entry date and t. In other words, the probability of a person becoming unemployed is not a function of how long he will eventually stay unemployed. $P(E)$ may be a function of t, and could conceivably be different at different periods because of seasonality, but the data set used in this analysis uses samples taken at different times during the year—February, June, November; plus the basic model equation includes additional controls for seasonality. But we assume only that $P(E)$ is not a function of $t - j$. Then we can specify $P(E)$ as constant over all j, after controlling for seasonal and cyclical unemployment factors.

For example, suppose that our system is characterized by positive duration dependence, so that $P(U_t) \mid U_{t-j}$ declines by 90% for larger j, such as 1 for j=0, .9 for j=1, .81 for j=2, etc. Suppose also that on average the probability of becoming unemployed at any time is .01, holding seasonality factors constant. Then the probability of being unemployed at time t in a 3 period model is .01(.81) + .01(.9) + .01(1) = .027. For a ten period model this equation would yield an unemployment rate of 6.5%. With $P(E)$ constant over all j, equation 11.3 leads to:

$$P(E_t) = \frac{P(U_t)}{\sum_{j=0}^{s-1} P(U_t) \mid U_{t-j}}.$$ *11.4*

Since we have $P(U_t)$ from Chapters 8 and 9, if we had the probability of unemployment at time t conditional on all previous s periods (the denominator in equation 11.4), we could estimate $P(E_t)$ directly. Unfortunately, we cannot realistically estimate such a conditional probability without longitudinal data. What we have to work with is the duration of incomplete spells of unemployment for persons unemployed at the time of the survey. Define W^F_t as the duration of incomplete spells for foreign-born men at time t; in addition, to simplify the equations define C^F_t as the conditional probability (the denominator from equation 11.4) call it the "continuation probability". It is reasonable to assume some functional relationship (say f) between C^F_t and W^F_t, essentially that there should be some functional relationship between the determinants of the length of incomplete spells and the determinants of the length of completed spells. The exact relationship would depend on factors such as interruption bias, length bias, and duration dependence, as described in Chapter 10. We may overestimate or underestimate C^F_t by using W^F_t, depending on which of these factors is dominant. But we can reasonably define the continuation probability, C^F_t as

$$C^F_t = \lambda^F(W^F_t),\qquad\qquad 11.5$$

where λ^F is an error function. If our estimate of C^F_t is too high, i.e. if we overestimate the true probability of a completed spell from fW^F_t, then λ_f is less than 1. Similarly, for native-born men,

$$C^N_t = \lambda^N(W^N_t).\qquad\qquad 11.6$$

Next define the percentage differential in the continuation probabilities between foreign-born men and native-born men as

$$pd^{FN}C_t = \frac{C^F_t}{C^N_t} - 1 = \frac{\lambda^F(W^F_t)}{\lambda^N(W^N_t)} - 1.\qquad\qquad 11.7$$

and if we define $pd^{FN}W_t$ as the percentage differential in the duration

$$pd^{FN}C_t = \frac{\lambda^F}{\lambda^N} \cdot pd^{FN}W_t + \frac{\lambda^F}{\lambda^N} - 1.\qquad\qquad 11.8$$

Equation 11.8 defines the percentage differential in the conditional probability of unemployment between foreign-born and native-born men as a function of the percentage differential in the duration of incomplete spells plus an error function, l. If $\lambda_f = \lambda_N$, in other words if our functional error in estimating continuation probabilities from incomplete spells is the same for the foreign-born and native-born calculations, then the percentage differential in continuation probabilities would be accurately estimated by the percentage differentials in incomplete spell duration.

The lambda parameters represent differences between the two groups due to such influences as interruption bias and length bias as described above. Since we don't know how these biases differ between the two groups, we cannot make direct estimates of the relative magnitudes of the lambdas. Salant (1977) shows that much depends on the variance of completed spells—if the variance of completed spells is high, then length bias dominates interruption bias, and we would overestimate the length of completed spells. He also shows that if duration dependence is negative, i.e., if the probability of escape falls with greater time unemployed, we will also tend to overestimate completed spells.

We can't at this point make accurate guesses as to the magnitudes of the lambdas. It is difficult to conceive of a theoretical justification for differences in interruption bias between foreign-born and native-born men. Nor is it clear what differences there would be in duration dependence. Would foreign-born men adjust their reservation wages at a faster or slower rate than foreign-born men? Would signaling effects be greater for foreign-born men? At this point we will assume that duration dependence is the same for both groups. We might make a theoretical justification for greater length-bias for foreign-born men: because of substantial differences in transferability of skills between foreign-born men from different backgrounds, we might expect greater variance in their completed spells of unemployment, particularly in the early adjustment period. More importantly, however, is one of the key results from Chapters 8 and 9: the probability of escape out of the labor force appears to be much higher for foreign-born men. Although spells of *nonemployment* might actually be higher, the spells of *unemployment* that we observe for immigrants are more likely to be from a distribution of greater completed duration. We might then guess that we are overestimating the completed duration for foreign-born men relative to native-born men, i.e., that $\lambda_F < \lambda_N$. However, as a point of departure, we make the second key assumption of this section: we will assume that the lambdas are equal for foreign-born and native-born men.

Finally, from equation 11.4 we can derive our final estimating equation. Let $pd^{FN}E_t$ be the percent differential between foreign-born men and native-born men in the probability of entry into

$$pd^{FN}E_t = \frac{E_t^F}{E_t^N} - 1 = \frac{U_t^F / C_t^F}{U_t^N / C_t^N} - 1 = \frac{U_t^F}{U_t^N} \frac{C_t^N}{C_t^F} - 1 \quad . \qquad 11.9$$

unemployment, defined as:

Then it is straightforward to show that the percent differential between foreign-born men and native-born men in the probability of entry is:

$$pd^{FN}E_t = \frac{pd^{FN}U_t + 1}{pd^{FN}C_t + 1} - 1 \quad , \qquad 11.10$$

and, substituting in equation 11.8 and setting $\lambda_F = \lambda_N$,

$$pd^{FN}\hat{E}_t = \frac{pd^{FN}U_t + 1}{pd^{FN}W_t + 1} - 1 \quad . \qquad 11.11$$

Equation 11.10 gives us a formula for estimating the percent differential between foreign-born men and native-born men (actually between any two groups) in the probability of entering unemployment from the percent differentials in the probabilities of being in the state of unemployment and the percent differentials in the probabilities of continuing in unemployment once unemployed. We can easily estimate the percent differentials in the probabilities of being unemployed, job losers, job leavers, and labor force entrants between any of the basic model variables and the reference, by simple calculations in the tables in Chapters 8 and 9.

Then equation 11.11 gives us a formula for calculating the probability of unemployment, adjusted for a proxy for the conditional continuation probability, which gives us a better idea of the direction at least, if not the exact magnitude, of the entry probabilities. For our immediate purpose, it is not important from this formula that we have a perfect estimate of the lambdas. If we knew their relative magnitudes we would know how close the proxy for the continuation probability comes. For the purposes of this book, however, we will estimate merely that $\lambda_F = \lambda_N$. With this assumption, we can provide an estimate for the probability of entering one of the states of unemployment, since we have $pd^{FN}W_t$ from Chapter 10. Since we are guessing about the lambdas, we can't place too much emphasis on the magnitudes of the actual estimates, nor will we call the results entry probabilities. But the logic is fairly straightforward—if a variable, such as the foreign-born variable, produces an increase in unemployment, but the same variable results in a lower duration of unemployment for those who are unemployed, then the probability of entry into unemployment must be higher for that variable. The signs and the direction of change from $P(U)$ to $P(E)$ should still be informative.

11.2. THE BASIC MODEL

Table 11.1 calculates the adjusted differentials described above—we'll call them adjusted probability differentials. The numbers are calculated by estimating the percent differentials in the probabilities of the various unemployment states—unemployment in total, job losers, job leavers, and labor force entrants—from Chapters 8 and 9, and applying them to the duration differentials from Chapter 10, via equation 11.11.

As an illustration, from the results in Chapter 8 (from the pooled model, shown in Table 9.4) increasing schooling from the mean of 12.7 years to 16 years was found to reduce the probability of unemployment from 3.6% to 2.4%, a differential of about -32%; then in Chapter 10 we showed that schooling increased the duration of unemployment. Since men with 16 years of schooling would be unemployed about 3% longer than men with only 12.7 years of schooling, the fact that they had a 32% lower probability of being unemployed means that they must have a probability of entering unemployment even less than -32% after adjusting for the lower duration. Applying the results of our previous calculations, we estimate that men with 16 years of schooling should have about a 34%

Table 11.1. Percent Differentials in Unemployment Probabilities Adjusted for Percent Differentials in Unemployment Duration

VARIABLES	POOLED—BY UNEMP. TYPE				BY RACE—OVERALL			
	Unemp.	Job Leavers	Job Losers	Lab Force Entrants	White	Black	Hispanic	Other Minority
Schooling = 16 Yrs	-34.1	-14.8	-41.6	-19.9	-31.3	-42.3	-28.6	-23.6
Schooling = 9 Yrs	58.9	31.3	68.0	36.4	64.4	30.9	7.5	64.6
Potential Exper. = 36	-24.6	-45.2	-34.7	-0.1	-18.2	-39.8	-23.5	-32.0
Potential Exper. = 12	56.4	83.3	31.0	85.9	58.8	58.9	36.1	27.8
Unmarried	85.2	133.8	69.4	136.9	148.2	74.5	9.4	29.3
Non-Metrop. Residence	2.6	2.9	0.9	-0.3	17.2	3.0	-17.7	60.5
South	8.4	35.4	-0.2	26.2	4.1	-4.2	8.0	14.6
Agriculture	0.7	-4.1	-4.7	48.4	-26.4	39.8	38.7	104.4
November 1979	12.0	-1.7	35.5	-28.7	18.7	-20.4	94.7	30.6
April 1983	6.7	-31.6	25.9	-45.3	16.3	-15.9	13.9	1.1
June 1986	25.6	-6.6	47.4	-31.1	21.9	1.7	47.3	72.3
June 1988	22.3	-1.3	44.5	-31.2	28.8	-13.7	53.7	46.6
November 1989	49.9	16.4	85.1	-23.3	58.3	14.2	77.2	84.4
June 1991	34.9	0.9	61.2	-19.4	47.1	8.8	28.7	42.2
February 1994	-17.2	-35.0	-3.1	-42.0	-18.0	-17.5	-6.3	-27.1
Area Unemp. Rate=11.5%	52.5	11.7	67.8	50.3	52.1	46.5	35.0	48.6
Seas. Adjust. = 110%	26.4	12.0	27.8	8.0	33.4	1.1	15.6	15.7

Table 11.1 (continued)

	POOLED—BY UNEMP. TYPE				BY RACE—OVERALL			
	Unemp.	Job Leavers	Job Losers	Lab Force Entrants	White	Black	Hispanic	Other Minority
Avg. Occ. Wages = $10	45.5	11.7	53.9	9.0	49.7	29.5	38.6	22.8
Var. Occ. Wages x 2	-43.2	-36.8	-43.7	-45.4	-46.7	-37.9	-15.8	-38.8
Foreign Born at Entry	7.1	-12.8	-29.7	206.0	-11.9	-34.2	4.4	81.3
YSM = mean	-1.1	2.7	4.3	-15.4	3.6	-10.7	-22.2	-39.3
YSM = mean + 10	0.5	14.1	9.6	-32.2	-0.4	10.5	-18.0	-57.0
YSM 25 Years or More	15.7	54.5	7.2	26.6	3.5	62.8	8.5	-48.7
YSM 20-24 Years	3.1	25.5	5.9	-9.5	1.6	-7.4	-7.9	-41.4
YSM 15-19 Years	-9.6	-2.3	-17.3	13.0	-11.5	-32.6	-14.2	-56.7
YSM 10-14 Years	8.8	16.7	11.1	2.9	-3.9	26.5	0.8	-41.4
YSM 7-9 Years	-8.7	10.6	-14.2	36.6	30.0	-38.7	-22.8	-30.7
YSM 5-6 Years	3.3	-73.6	11.3	18.7	-51.5	-35.4	4.7	19.3
YSM 3-4 Years	-2.3	-12.0	-15.9	42.6	-21.6	7.4	10.9	-25.3
YSM 2 Years or Less	33.2	14.9	-37.9	376.1	1.4	-1.4	26.7	70.0

Source: Unemployment probabilities in Tables 9.4, 8.5, and B.3 (Hurst 1997); percent differentials from Tables 10.2-10.4.

lower probability of being unemployed adjusted for unemployment duration. We also should feel reasonably confident that these adjusted differentials from higher schooling fairly well approximate the entry rate differentials. Otherwise λ for persons with college degrees would have to be significantly different from the λ for those with only high school degrees. Would their variance of completed spells be different, or their degree of duration dependence? It is difficult to know, but the guess here is that these are fairly close estimates. In addition, these estimates are consistent across unemployment types, although schooling affects job losers more than job leavers, and are also consistent across the various racial groups.

Most of the rest of the basic model variables are consistent with theory. Experience reduces overall unemployment as well as each category of unemployment—older workers have greater investments in firm-specific human capital so are less likely to quit and have greater value to their employer. Unmarried workers are more likely to be unemployed after adjusting for duration in any of the categories of unemployment. Southern men are more likely to be job leavers or labor force entrants; in Table 9.5 it was shown that Southern men have a 16.8% lower probability of being a job loser on average, but after adjusting for their lower duration, there is no real difference for Southern men. Living in a non-metropolitan area has little effect on the adjusted probabilities in any of the states of unemployment; non-metropolitan men are 21% more likely to be unemployed job leavers on average (Table 9.5), but after adjusting for a higher duration of unemployment this differential falls to about 3%.

One interesting result is that nearly all of the survey year dummy variables show a consistently higher adjusted probability of being a job loser or of being unemployed than in 1976, in spite of the *lower* probability calculations in Table 9.5. This is almost entirely because in the survey years after 1976 the duration of unemployment was consistently and substantially lower. This could indicate a general trend toward higher turnover but higher job finding rates in general but it may also reflect a trend in the 1980s toward tighter unemployment compensation eligibility requirements and lower benefits in many states.

Earlier we noted that a higher occupational wage seemed to cause an increase in the probability of being unemployed, 32.7% as shown in Table 9.5. In Table 11.1 we can see that after adjusting for lower duration, the differential is even greater—46%. We can conclude that higher wages cause a higher probability of entering unemployment, and the cause seems to be higher job loss rates. In the case of duration we know theoretically that higher wages would reduce search time by raising search costs, which was substantiated in Chapter 10. We can also see that a higher wage encourages layoffs much more than quits. This result would be consistent with a model in which higher wages acted as efficiency wages on the one hand but increased the probability that wages would be above marginal costs.

11.3. THE FOREIGN-BORN VARIABLES

Chapter 8 showed that the probability of being unemployed was lower, by about 14%, for foreign-born men at arrival in the U.S. compared to native-born men. This result is counter to the hypotheses being tested in this book, particularly Hypothesis number 6. Chapter 10, however, showed that the average duration of incomplete spells of unemployment for foreign-born men was about 20% lower than for native-born men. Table 11.1 shows the net result: recently arrived foreign-born men are more likely to be unemployed (by about 7%) than native-born men after adjusting for lower duration; if we could accept these results as differentials in entry probabilities, foreign-born men can, on average, be expected to enter unemployment at a slightly higher rate than native-born men, *ceteris paribus*. This higher adjusted differential falls with duration in the U.S. but does not seem to cross the norm of native-born men and in fact rises after a period of time. Thus Hypothesis 6 (that recently arrived foreign-born men would have higher unemployment rates) is supported, but just barely.

There are, however, three particularly interesting results from the adjustment made in this chapter, two of which are not at all expected. First, the probability of being a job loser is still *lower* for foreign-born men than for native-born men in the early years after arrival, even after adjusting for unemployment duration. The percentage is calculated as 30% lower and, even though we can't be sure how accurate this figure is, it is large enough that we can probably feel confident about the direction. This result translates directly into a 33% lower probability of being a job loser for foreign-born men than for native-born men (Table 9.5), or about 30% lower from table 11.1, since there is no significant difference between foreign-born men and native-born men in the duration of unemployment for job losers.

The second interesting result is that the probability of being a job leaver is also *lower* for foreign-born men than native-born men, by about 13%. In this case the probability of being an unemployed job leaver at any point in time is about 48% lower than for native-born men, but this is mainly caused by a 40% shorter duration while unemployed. We can guess from Table 11.1 that the probability of quitting is not much lower for foreign-born men, in spite of the results shown in Table 9.5.

The third interesting observation is the size of the differential in the probability of entering the labor force. We expect recently arrived foreign-born men to enter the labor force at a higher rate than native-born men, for a number of reasons, including that the main reason to migrate is for greater employment prospects. In addition there is a definition problem, since many men may have been in the origin labor force prior to emigrating, but may not report that experience on the questionnaire because it was not in the U.S. But the size of the estimate is interesting—foreign-born men in their first two years after arrival in the U.S. are over 3.0 to 4.7 *times* as likely to be labor force entrants than native-born men, after adjusting for duration of unemployment. This is also a combination effect—a 90-200% higher probability of being in a job entrant state combined with a 38% lower duration of incomplete spells of unemployment after entry into the labor force.

11.4 SUMMARY OF CHAPTER 11

We have now seen two results which run counter to some of the basic tenets of the assimilation hypothesis. First, in Chapter 8, we saw that foreign-born men do have a lower employment probability than native-born men in their first few years after arrival in the U.S. But we showed that this is less a result of higher rates of unemployment than of much higher rates of being out of the labor force. Then we showed that foreign-born men had lower probabilities of being job leavers or job losers, but we surmised that this might be explained by a shorter duration of unemployment for job losers or leavers among foreign-born men. Our estimates show that this hypothesis is true for job leavers but not for job losers. We show that adjusted unemployment probabilities are higher for foreign-born men for the first couple of years after arrival, but this is not because of higher turnover—instead it is more the result of foreign-born men entering the labor force at a higher rate. It appears that the greatest difference between foreign-born men and native-born men is that foreign-born men flow more freely in and out of the labor force.

CHAPTER 12

Summary, Conclusions, Policy Implications

12.1 THE ASSIMILATION HYPOTHESIS

As the number of persons from other countries who migrate to the United States continues to increase, the issues surrounding immigration continue to be a part of the public agenda. An important part of the debate has focused on the process of assimilation and economic adjustment of immigrants, both in the early years after arrival and over the long term.

Two key hypotheses have energized this debate. The *assimilation hypothesis* proposes that many immigrants will arrive in the U.S. with differences in their human capital characteristics which put them at an early disadvantage in the labor market compared to native-born workers. Many will have lower absolute levels of human capital, in such areas such as education and work experience. But even for those with equal amounts of schooling and experience, many will still be at a disadvantage because their human capital may not be easily transferable to the U.S. labor market. Poor English language ability, less information about the job market, and fewer firm-specific or labor market-specifc skills result in a lower employment probability and lower earnings shortly after arrival. Important determinants of these differences include the transferability of skills between countries and the motive for migration—economic or noneconomic. The payoff in investments in human capital will be higher for these immigrants, however, so their degree of investment will be greater. As they improve their language skills and acquire market and firm-specific skills, their earnings increase at a faster pace than that of native-born workers.

The second hypotheses is the *self-selection hypothesis*. This hypothesis says that not only will the earnings of immigrants converge toward the native-born norm over time in the U.S. but that in many cases immigrant earnings will surpass those of similar native-born workers. This is explained by the concept that in general it is persons with the most human capital, the most innate ability, the most motivated, or perhaps the most physical capital who will have the most incentive to migrate. All may still be at a disadvantage in regards to destination-specific human capital, but once such human capital is obtained, the higher ability eventually results in higher earnings.

These two hypotheses are important for public policies dealing with immigrants, particularly admission policies. If immigrants assimilate over time, then even low-skilled immigrants can be expected to provide positive net benefits to society, as lifetime earnings will be substantially greater than initial earnings, and highly skilled immigrants will contribute greatly. If, however, immigrants are not able to assimilate, then they will compete with economically disadvantaged native-born workers, add additional burdens on social services, and increase income inequality. These are the some of the arguments in favor of restricting immigration, proposing that recent immigrants are of lower quality and are less likely to assimilate in the future. Since important public policies are currently being set on the basis of these arguments, it is important that we keep working to improve our knowledge of the subject.

12.2. LABOR FORCE HYPOTHESES, AND STUDY DESIGN

Most previous studies about this issue have analyzed primarily earnings, and the bulk have found that earnings of immigrants are lower upon arrival in the U.S. but do converge to, and eventually surpass, the norms of the native born over time. Other studies have shown this effect to be lower in recent years. But a part of the changing pattern has been shown to be because of changing skill prices. Thus earnings tests can only be an indirect, albeit important, test of the assimilation hypotheses.

Assimilation adjustments also imply some important differences between foreign-born and native-born workers in terms of labor force processes and outcomes. Immigrants of course would be expected to have higher probabilities of labor force entry, since they are out of the U.S. labor force prior to arrival. An important hypothesis proposes that turnover will also be higher—both in terms of job loss, because of poor job matches during the early adjustment period, and in terms of job quits, because of the desire of immigrants to acquire more labor market-specific skills early implies a greater propensity for experiencing many employers. These processes are similar to those of native-born youth. But as firm-specific skills are acquired, such differences in turnover rates should diminish, according to familiar labor market theory.

The net result of higher turnover and higher probabilities of labor force entry implies a higher rate of unemployment for recent immigrants. We would also expect a higher rate of turnover in and out of the labor force beyond the initial increase in labor force entry. Recent immigrants are generally less eligible for unemployment compensation during the first few years after arrival, they may have higher rates of participation in the underground economy, and ethnic networks may relieve some of the pressure when not employed. These and other factors should make immigrants more likely than native-born workers to drop out of the labor force when unemployed. The flip side of this is that they will become labor force entrants again later. Thus the immigrant nonemployment experience is likely to be peppered with multiple spells of unemployment and labor force nonparticipation.

Finally, because of higher unemployment and lower labor force participation, we expect that immigrants would have lower employment rates shortly after arrival. All of these effects are expected to diminish and converge to the norm of the native born over time.

Very little work has been done on these underlying notions of the assimilation hypotheses. A couple of studies have focused on weeks worked during the year, and found that weeks worked were significantly lower for recent immigrants but converged to the native-born norm over time; these studies were robust across the 1970 and 1990 censuses. One also looked at unemployment rates and found higher rates in the first 3 years in one specification (OLS) and lower rates in another (Logit). One study found lower employment probabilities but less consistent results in terms of unemployment.

This is the first study to directly examine the probabilities of being in, or of entering, the states of job loser unemployment, job leaver unemployment, labor force entry, and not-in-labor-force (NILF). Previous studies have been hampered by a lack of information. The detail on unemployment is not available on the most commonly used data source on the foreign born, the U.S. Census. They are available on the Current Population Survey (CPS) but on very few and irregular supplements. With the recent additions of 1991 and 1994, and with the addition of the 1976 Survey of Income and Education (SIE), this book was able to analyze a data set that had enough observations to make reasonably precise calculations, spanned a period of 18 years, and included the key questions about labor force and employment turnover. The analysis was limited to men between the ages of 25 and 64.

The analysis covered four chapters. First, a multinomial logit analysis was performed on the simultaneously-determined state odds and probabilities of employment, unemployment, and NILF. A set of base variables was held constant, to filter out the effects of pre-migration human capital, demographic characteristics, differential effects across geographic areas, cyclical, seasonal, and time trends, and variables to control for expectations of wages. Then variables were added to test the differential impacts of being a foreign-born man at entry into the U.S. and of duration of time in the U.S. after arrival. The second part of the analysis ran a similar multinomial logit analysis on the group of men who are unemployed—job losers, job leavers, and labor force entrants, and the probabilities calculated from the first 2 analyses were combined to get total probabilities of being in each of the 5 states (job loser, job leaver, labor force entrant, NILF, and employed).

The third part of the analysis used a multiple regression equation to analyze the duration of incomplete spells of unemployment for men unemployed at the time of each survey. The natural log of weeks unemployed was used as the dependent variable, allowing the interpretation of the results as percentage differentials. Finally, an algorithm was developed to adjust the percentage differentials in the state probabilities from the first two analyses by the percentage differentials in the duration of incomplete spells of unemployment in the third analysis, interpreting the results as potential indicators of percentage differentials in the probabilities of entry. Each of the separate chapters provided results for a pooled sample, a separate foreign-born sample, and separate analyses for each of four racial/ethnic groups.

12.3. SUMMARY OF FINDINGS, BASE VARIABLES

The empirical analyses in each chapter had two basic sections: a section describing the results relating to the base variables, and a section describing the differences attributed to the foreign-born variables. This section will summarize the results by each of the variables, synthesizing across the four chapters.

The level of schooling is one of the most important, and most widely studied, of the base variables tested here. Schooling was found to reduce unemployment and increase employment for both native-born and foreign-born workers, with higher labor force participation for more educated foreign-born men; these results were consistent across the four racial groups. Among the unemployed, higher levels of schooling had little effect on job leaver or labor force entry probabilities, but reduced the probability of being a job loser, thereby increasing the leaver/loser ratio. Higher levels of schooling also increased the duration of unemployment for those unemployed, so after adjusting for duration, it was inferred that higher levels of schooling reduce probabilities of job quits, job layoffs, and labor force entry. Thus higher levels of schooling reduce employment turnover, but for those out of work may lead to less labor force participation.

Potential labor market experience, primarily an age effect beyond school, had the expected results for all groups. More experience increased the probability of being out of the labor force, a likely artifact of greater retirement and disability probabilities for older men. More experience also reduced turnover, reducing overall unemployment and the probabilities of being job losers or job leavers, with little difference between 24 years and 36 years in the probability of being a labor force entrant. Marriage had the same stabilizing effect as experience on employment turnover, but also increased labor force participation. Metropolitan residence had little effect overall on employment turnover although it increased labor force participation for foreign-born men. Southern residence reduced labor force participation of native-born men but increased labor force participation of the foreign born.

There are a few trend effects worth noting. Compared to the base year of 1976, employment turnover is generally higher, more so for job losers. In the pooled sample the probability of being out of the labor force is lower, of being employed higher, with each trend diminishing in strength as the years progress from 1979 to 1994. For the foreign born, there is a greater probability of being out of the labor force in the

1980s and 90s, and a reduction in the probability of employment. If these probabilities are indicators of immigrant "quality", then there is some indication that quality has declined from 1976. It should be noted however, that these trends also apply to each of the racial groups other than white, and are strongest for blacks, who have a small percentage foreign born, so these trend effects may be more racial effects rather than immigrant effects, perhaps reflecting reduced demand for low skilled labor, rather than changes in the relative skill levels. If recent immigrants tend to be concentrated in low-skilled industries, their labor market status could be affected negatively even if their innate abilities were not changed.

The area unemployment rate consistently performs as expected, increasing probabilities of job loss, reducing the probability of job quits, with a net effect of increasing unemployment, while also reducing employment and labor force participation. The only unexpected result is the increase in labor force entry in higher unemployment areas, which may be a problem of reverse causality.

A higher seasonal adjustment factor slightly increased the probability of being a job loser job leaver, labor force entrant, or of unemployment in general, which are consistent with theory, with little impact on the overall probability of being a job leaver. But the largest impacts were on increasing labor force participation, and on reducing the duration of unemployment for job losers, but not for job leavers or labor force entrants. In other words, men in more seasonal occupations are more likely to become unemployed for any of the three reasons examined here, but their unemployment is of shorter duration despite their higher labor force participation rates. Thus men in more seasonal occupations seem to have greater attachments to the labor force, largely because their unemployment is seasonal or frictional as opposed to structural.

Higher average occupational wages tended to increase job loss probabilities the most, with a small reduction in the probability of being a job leaver or labor force entrant. Most consistent with theory are that higher average wages reduced the duration of unemployment, because of a higher cost of job search, and that higher average wages increased labor force participation. Higher occupational wage variances had even stronger effects on increasing labor force participation and employment and reducing unemployment, of all three types.

12.4. SUMMARY OF FINDINGS, FOREIGN-BORN VARIABLES

The main focus of this book is on the differences in the labor force and employment adjustments between foreign-born and native-born men. After holding constant the base variables mentioned above, a dummy variable was added in one model to measure the effect of immigration at entry, plus continuous years since migration (YSM) variables were added that measure the quadratic adjustment over time in the U.S.; in a second model, incremental YSM variables replaced the foreign-born dummy and continuous YSM variables.

The first result, from Chapter 8, was that foreign-born men, at entry in the continuous model or over the first 2-4 years in the incremental model, were less likely to be employed and more likely to be out of the labor force. Thus the first results support Hypothesis 5 (higher NILF probabilities) and Hypothesis 6 (lower employment probabilities), and the employment result is consistent with previous studies. In both cases the trends reversed after a few years, and after about 6-9 years immigrant men had higher probabilities of employment and labor force participation, again consistent with the hypotheses. These results hold in the separate model for the foreign born—at entry immigrants had lower employment probabilities and labor force participation probabilities than they had at later stages after an early adjustment period. There were a couple of notable differences among the racial groups—black and Hispanic foreign-born men at entry had higher probabilities of employment, with employment for black immigrants increasing over time, for Hispanics decreasing over time. In addition, Hispanics had a much higher labor force participation probability, both at entry and in later years.

The first contradiction in the analysis occurs around unemployment. In the continuous model the unemployment probability for immigrant men at entry was lower (3.1%) than for native-born men (3.6%); the change over time was also increasing, not decreasing as proposed in Hypothesis 6. The incremental model suffered from inconsistent results because of insignificant coefficients. By racial group these results are driven by Hispanics and blacks, whereas whites and other minorities match the pattern proposed in the hypothesis. The results from Chapter 8 suggest a different interpretation of coefficients that show lower weeks worked or employment ratios for recent immigrants. Such results are not indicative of higher unemployment, but in fact can be explained almost completely by lower probabilities of labor force participation.

By unemployment type, we saw that foreign-born men upon arrival had higher probabilities of labor force entry than native-born men, as expected, but these probabilities did not diminish over time as suggested in Hypothesis 5. The other two unemployment categories—job losers and job leavers—showed substantially lower probabilities for foreign-born men at arrival, which converged to the loser and leaver probabilities of native-born men after a few years, but did not differ substantially from the native-born probabilities in later years.. These results are also contrary to Hypotheses 1 and 2. These results are consistent across the racial groups, except that the job loser probability was not substantially different for white foreign-born men, and the labor force entry probability is not substantially different for Hispanic men.

Furthermore, the leaver/loser ratio was not significantly different for foreign-born men at arrival, contrary to Hypothesis 3. Although this hypothesis was not a direct statement about the assimilation hypothesis, the implication is that unemployment is no more or less voluntary for foreign-born men than for native-born men.

Although the turnover hypotheses at this point were not supported, the results applied only to state probabilities, not flows. Chapter 10 was the first step in converting those probabilities into "entry" probabilities. Foreign-born men had a substantially lower duration of incomplete spells of unemployment, about 20% on average, shortly after arrival. This lower duration increased over time, but linearly in the continuous model, not quadratically as hypothesized. In the incremental model it was shown that the lower duration was even more pronounced in the first two years, about 26%, but reached convergence after only 4 years. Hypothesis Number 4 is supported by these results. These results held for Hispanics and other minorities, but black foreign-born men were no different in their unemployment probabilities than black native-born men, and the trend for white native-born men was just the reverse of the pooled results. It was also shown that job leavers and labor force entrants had about the same duration of unemployment on average, but that job losers were unemployed about 12% longer on average. In addition, the reduction in unemployment duration for the foreign born applied strongly to job leavers and labor force entrants, about 38-40% lower duration, but foreign-born job losers are no different from other job losers in their unemployment duration.

Thus, it would appear that the lower probability of being a job leaver may be partially a result of lower time spent in the state, and that the higher probability of being a labor force entrant is underestimated, considering the lower time spent in that state. But the lower probability of being a job loser is not affected by the duration of unemployment. To get a more accurate reading, however, the probability results regarding the unemployment categories from Chapters 8 and 9 were adjusted for the duration of incomplete spells of unemployment from Chapter 10, using an algorithm that converted the probabilities into percent differentials and making the assumption that percent differentials between foreign-born and native-born men in the length of uncompleted spells of unemployment should reasonably well proxy for percent differentials in completed spells.

There were three key results from this final conversion. First, after adjusting for lower unemployment duration, the adjusted state probability, an indicator of probability of "entering" the state of unemployment, was higher for foreign-born men upon arrival, but only slightly, and this rate fell, then rose over time. In the incremental model, however, the adjusted unemployment probability was 33% higher in the first 2 years after arrival, with very small differences after the first 2 years. This final result thus supports Hypothesis Number 6, higher unemployment probabilities, and shows that relying on state probabilities can be misleading.

Second, even after adjusting for lower unemployment duration, the probability of being a job loser was still about 30% lower for foreign-born men upon arrival, and the adjusted probability of being a job leaver was about 13% less for foreign-born men upon arrival. These probabilities still converged and eventually surpassed the probabilities of native-born men. This result refutes Hypotheses 1 and 2. From this result it appears that the hypothesis of higher employment turnover of recent immigrants is not supported. There are at least two reasons why this test is still not complete, however, which will be discussed further in the next section.

Finally, the probability of being a labor force entrant, after adjusting for lower unemployment duration, was 206% to 376% higher for the foreign born in the first couple of years after arrival, *ceteris paribus*, but then converged quickly to the native-born norm. This provides further strong support for Hypothesis Number 5, higher labor force turnover. More importantly, it shows that again we must be precise in our interpretation of higher unemployment probabilities for recent immigrants—the higher probabilities are not due to higher quit rates or layoff rates, but can be explained entirely by the higher probabilities of recent immigrants entering the labor force.

12.5. DISCUSSION

The primary stated goal of this book is to test the basic premises of the assimilation hypothesis. We have attempted to do so by testing six related underlying hypotheses about employment/unemployment and labor force turnover. What do the results of this book tell us about the overall assimilation hypothesis?

It appears that the overall hypothesis is supported, but at first glance we must withhold total support, because of some mixed results. Hypothesis Number 6 is supported, showing that recent immigrants have lower employment probabilities, which converge to the native-born norm after a few years in the U.S. At first the hypothesis of higher unemployment probabilities for recent immigrants is not supported, but is supported after we adjust for lower duration of unemployment spells.

Hypothesis Number 5 is strongly supported, with recent immigrants having substantially higher probabilities of both being out of the labor force and of being labor force entrants. These trends diminish and converge to the native-born norm after a few years. This result indicates that there is substantial movement in and out of the labor force for recent immigrants, but also that this movement stabilizes over time.

Hypothesis Number 4 is also strongly supported, with recent immigrants having substantially lower duration of incomplete spells of unemployment. Lower unemployment duration is consistent within the context of needing to experience many employers to gain market-specific and firm-specific skills.

Hypothesis Number 3, a higher leaver/loser ratio, is not supported, but does not directly address the assimilation hypothesis. There seems to be little difference between native-born and foreign-born men in their relative voluntary/involuntary types of unemployment.

The major question arises around the first two hypotheses, of higher rates of job quitting or job loss, neither of which are supported by the tests in this analysis. This is troubling for the assimilation hypothesis, since it implies that probabilities of job quitting and/or job losing are not higher for recent immigrant men than they are for native-born men, and in fact are substantially lower.

It is also. clear, however, that the tests in this book do not completely address these flows. There are at least two major reasons why the loser or leaver probabilities are underestimated here. The first reason regards the lambdas as set forth in Chapter 10. We made the explicit assumption that the lambdas, which would account for our error in computing lengths of completed spells from uncompleted spells, were equal for native-born men and foreign-born men. However, we should modify that assumption, based upon the results regarding Hypothesis Number 5. Since recent immigrants have such high probabilities of leaving and entering the labor force, it is possible that their variance of completed spells is therefore higher, since they are more heterogeneous in their means of exiting unemployment. As Salant showed, this implies that $\lambda_F < \lambda_N$, in other words, we are probably overestimating the length of actual completed spells of unemployment for foreign-born men, or underestimating the negative differential between foreign-born and native-born men. From another perspective, a higher probability of leaving the labor force for those not working would imply greater length bias, so that those who are most likely to exit unemployment early, either into employment or out of the labor force, are likely to have already done so, so that those that are still unemployed are likely to be persons with normally longer duration. Again, we have probably overestimated the true length of completed spells for foreign-born men. Therefore our adjustment for unemployment duration in Chapter 11 was probably understated.

The second reason we may have underestimated loser or leaver probabilities is that the only adjustment we have made to the state probabilities is through unemployment duration. But the higher probabilities of being out of the labor force and of being labor force entrants have important implications themselves beyond what was stated in the previous paragraph. In reality, while a few of the men who are out of the labor force may have dropped out after entering without intervening employment, or may have never entered the labor force after immigration, the bulk of those out of the labor force are previously job losers or job leavers.

Summers and Clark (1990b) suggest that the distinction between unemployment states and NILF states is artificial for youth, and that the two should be considered together when assessing the nonemployment experiences of youth. They also show (Summers and Clark, 1990a) that for young men ages 16-19 who are out of school, half of all flows out of employment are directly out of the labor force, and 37% of flows out of unemployment are out of the labor force. They also show that for men ages 16-19 the probability of leaving employment by leaving the labor force is 11.6%, compared to 0.4% for men ages 25-69.

In our case we are talking about adults, although upon arrival in a new country immigrants bear many resemblances to native-born youth in their labor force situations. Also, the increase in the labor-force-eligible population is much higher for immigrants and must be considered. Still, if the probability of leaving the labor force were the same for foreign-born and native-born men, then the probabilities of job loser unemployment or job leaver unemployment would be much higher for foreign-born men. Would that be enough to account for the 30% lower adjusted loser probabilities or 13% lower leaver probabilities for the foreign born? It is hard to tell with the data we have, but it seems possible. About 10.1% of foreign-born men and about 10.8% of native-born men are out of the labor force in the data set we used, compared to 4.2% and 3.4% job losers, and 0.5% and 0.4% job leavers, respectively. Thus either nativity group is 2 to 3 times more likely to be out of the labor force than to be in one of the unemployment states. Yet foreign-born men in their first couple of years in the U.S. are either 55% or 124% more likely to be out of the labor force than native-born men, depending upon whether we use the continuous model or the incremental model (Table 8.3). The 30% lower loser probability or 13% lower leaver probability for foreign-born men actually seems quite small compared to the large percentage increase in the probability of being out of the labor force. So if we could count even half of those out of the labor force as job losers or leavers, it seems likely that the probability of quits or layoffs would indeed be higher for foreign-born men in their first couple of years after arrival. Therefore, although our loser or leaver calculations refute Hypotheses 1 and 2, combined with the NILF probabilities it is probably safe to conclude that they should be supported.

12.6. POLICY IMPLICATIONS AND CONCLUSION

In considering public policy focused on the immigrant issue, it is useful to divide such policy into two variants, *immigration* policy and *immigrant* policy. Immigration policy deals with the number of immigrants admitted, the characteristics of those admitted, the reasons for admitting immigrants, and efforts to stop illegal immigration.

Immigrant policy deals with immigrants after they have migrated—social benefits, labor laws, naturalization policy, and policies to foster assimilation.

Three common threads bind the four chapters analyzing the assimilation of foreign-born men in this book, and each has implications for public policy. The first commonality is that the labor market situation does seem to be somewhat worse for foreign-born men in the 1980s compared to 1976, relative to native-born men, after controlling for seasonality factors and geographic unemployment rates. This could at least partly be a result of the increase in immigration flows—differences between foreign-born men and native-born men in unemployment and labor force status are more pronounced in the early years after arrival, and the increase in immigration flows (legal and illegal) increases the proportion of immigrants who are recent arrivals. There are no differences in trends in the proportions of unemployment attributable to job losers, job leavers, or labor force entrants, nor in the duration of unemployment for those who become unemployed.

Public policy to deal with the worsening labor market situation would be of two types—reducing the flow, and altering the immigrant characteristics. Reducing flows is problematic, given the increases in illegal immigration; setting lower limits will be ineffective until illegal immigration is better controlled. Increasing the proportion of legal flows that are skill-based rather than family reunification-based would help, since it has been shown that higher skill levels, as measured by schooling, increase employment and labor market participation and reduce unemployment among the foreign born.

A second common result is that immigrants do assimilate. Regardless of which labor market outcome we consider, or whether the initial difference with native-born men is higher or lower, there is an adjustment process within the first 10 years that brings the status of foreign-born men close to the status of native-born men. The adjustment process is also rapid in many cases. And in many cases there is an actual crossover, where foreign-born men eventually exceed the status of native-born men.

It would seem, therefore, that much of the concern about the effect of immigrants on the economy of the United States is exaggerated. There may be other valid concerns, such as those caused by the concentration of immigrants in a few geographic areas, or the impact on population growth or on the ethnic composition of the U.S. because of a higher fertility rate of some immigrant groups (Clark, 1996; Clark and Schulz, 1996). But any differences in economic outcomes between foreign-born and native-born persons are temporary; over the long run foreign-born persons tend to resemble native-born persons in their labor market status. Recent hysteria surrounding the immigration issue may be a result of the recent increase in flows, which increase the proportion of foreign-born persons who are newly arrived. If increases in flows subside, concerns may abate.

A third common theme throughout the analysis is that the basic model variables used to control for demographic, geographic, and wage effects had less effect on the labor market situations of foreign-born men than they did for native-born men. One conclusion from this result is that public policies aimed at altering the known characteristics of immigrants may end up having less impact than desired. In terms of immigration policy, attempts to change the characteristics of those admitted may have little effect in changing the long run labor market status of foreign-born persons. Immigrant policy that tries to alter the characteristics of immigrants after arrival may actually backfire if such policies have to be applied equally to foreign-born and native-born persons, since the effects are stronger for native-born persons.

It is important that we specify the problem clearly when discussing the labor force adjustment processes of foreign-born men. Clearly employment ratios are lower for foreign-born men shortly after arrival in the U.S. But the flip side of employment is not unemployment, but nonemployment. Nonemployment consists of unemployment plus labor force nonparticipation and while in many cases they may and have been considered functionally equivalent, there are important distinctions. Nonemployment is clearly higher for foreign-born men shortly after arrival in the U.S. But that is primarily because labor force nonparticipation is higher. Unemployment is more ambiguous. In terms of unemployment rates, they have been shown in previous studies to be higher for foreign-born men shortly after arrival. But unemployment ratios—unemployment as a percent of the population—such as considered in this book, are not substantially higher, and may even be lower for foreign-born men shortly after arrival.

Therefore it is contended here that unemployment is not such a serious policy problem in relation to the economic adjustment of foreign-born men. Concerns about increased flows of immigrants draining the unemployment insurance trust funds or increasing local unemployment rates are exaggerated.

Labor force nonparticipation, on the other hand, may be a legitimate public policy issue. Concerns include increased use of welfare and other public benefits, increased use of job training and job placement services, and possibly increased crime according to a recent article by Richard Fry (1996). Others are concerned with rising poverty rates (Clark and Schulz, 1996). One important problem is that we don't fully know what foreign-born men are doing when they are not in the labor force. Many, apparently, are enrolled in school. Fry's tables show that foreign-born men in 1990 were more likely than native-born men to be enrolled in school—1.5 times as likely for prime age (25-44) males and that about 8% of prime age immigrant men who arrived between 1985 and 1990 were enrolled in school in 1990, 6.6 percentage points above the rate for native-born men. Over a third of prime age foreign-born males who were not employed, unemployed, or institutionalized (i.e., were either NILF or enrolled in school) were enrolled in school. Similarly, a recent report on high school graduates ages 18-24 showed that foreign-born youth, relative to native-born youth, return to school faster, stay in longer, spend more of their nonemployment time in school, and spend more time in a combination of school and employment (Quigley, 1996). Thus in terms of public policy, efforts to limit immigrants' access to public education would be misguided, given the eventual payoff in terms of labor market participation and employment. On the other hand, Quigley concludes that efforts to promote more schooling for immigrants, or to assist them further in their school-to-work transitions, would appear to be unnecessary. Immigrants appear to be doing just fine on their own.

Interestingly, a recent paper (White and Kaufman, 1997) finds that immigrant youth are more likely than native-born youth to drop out of high school, even after controlling for influences such as socioeconomic status, test scores and grades, ethnicity, and language usage. And the more recent the immigration, the more likely the propensity to drop out. Although this is not in direct contrast to Quigley, who focused on high school graduates, it offers a different view recent immigrants. The dynamic is likely different, as immigrant youth probably came as tied movers, and do not have the self-selection advantage of economic migrants. The implications are different as well: immigrant high school dropouts are likely to experience the disadvantages of low human capital to an even greater extent than ordinary economic migrants. It might be worthwhile, therefore, to target high school-age immigrants for assistance.

Finally, Fry's paper emphasizes the increasing rates of immigrant idleness in the past few decades. Yet even his own tables show basically the same results as in this book—that the higher rate of labor force nonparticipation is a temporary situation attached to only newly arrived immigrants, and that after 6-10 years foreign-born men have higher rates of labor force participation. Given the positive effects of immigration on the U.S. economy as a whole, it would be wise to keep the long run perspective in mind. Other than getting flows under control and stemming illegal immigration, and possibly increasing the skill-based criteria of immigration, the best public policy solution may indeed be hands-off.

Notes

1. Both of the expected wage variables were calculated in sample, although data on wages are available for only about 25% of the sample. In addition, data on occupation are only available for about 25% of men out of the labor force; these men were given the average wage for persons out of the labor force.

2. A weight variable is provided in the CPS samples to normalize each individual household's effect on the sample to represent its expected proportion in the population as a whole. Each individual on this data set is assigned an individual weight, ranging from an average of about 493 in the 1976 survey to an average of about 1,908 in the 1994 survey. Individual weights will sum to a close approximation of the entire population. The weights are applied in a weighted least squares fashion to all analyses. Weighting each observation by the individual weights, however, will produce unbiased estimates but heavily deflated standard errors in regression analyses. The weights could be used directly in the OLS regression and the results would be valid, except for exaggerated sums of squares, which are not a problem. But in a logistic model, the standard errors of the slope coefficients would be reduced by a factor of about 100, greatly increasing the probability of a Type I error. To keep the relative weights intact but not distort the standard errors, individual weights were standardized by dividing by the average weight in each sample, so that the individual weights sum to about 1.

3. Tests show a consistently higher variance for the native-born across surveys, and shows that the foreign-born are somewhat more concentrated in occupations with lower variances.

An early analysis showed that the native-born variance was unreasonably large. The reason for this huge differential was found to be a set of outliers in the 1976 survey, which had a number of persons in the professional and managerial occupations with very large hourly wages in the hundreds of dollars. This was a big enough difference to affect all of the variances, even though the effect on averages was small. Tests on an adjusted series showed that the impact was limited to the native-born, to working persons, and only affected the occupational variance variable. The occupational wage variance variable was computed after top-coding the maximum houly wage in 1976 to $50 per hour.

4. Note that there are discontinuities in the incremental duration variables, with a steadily increasing percentage being in the country for longer years, except for breaks at 3 to 4 years, 5 to 6 years and at 15-19 years. This is due to differences in the codes assigned by the CPS in different years, particularly in 1976 and 1979. In 1976, one increment was entry in 1960-64, for an average duration of 14 years, and an assigned increment of 10 to14 years. The next group immigrated from 1950-59, with an average duration of 21.5 years; these were assigned to the increment 20 to 24 years, thus there was nobody assigned to the increment 15 to 19 years. Similar problems occurred for 1979 in the 3 to 4, 5 to 6, and 20 to 24 years categories.

5. More precisely, percentage differentials are computed with the formula $[e^b-1]*100$.

Appendices

APPENDIX A. DEFINITION OF DEPENDENT VARIABLES

This book focused on the estimation of the effects of several independent variables on 7 dependent variables: employment, unemployment, not-in-labor-force (NILF); within unemployment, job losers, job leavers, and labor force entrants; and weeks unemployed looking for work. At the heart of the definition of each of these variables are several specific questions in the questionnaire. This appendix defines the dependent variables by first describing the questions, then describing how each determination is made based on the answers to the questions. Since the question numbers change from survey to survey, they will be numbered here simply from 1 to 8.

Q1. *What was ... doing most of LAST WEEK?*
1. Working
2. With a job but not at work
3. Looking for work
4. Keeping house
5. Going to school
6. Unable to work
7. Retired
8. Other

Q2. Did ... do any work at all LAST WEEK, not counting work around the house?
1. Yes
2. No

Q3. How many hours did ... work last week at all jobs?

Range = 0-99

Q4.   Why was ... absent from work last week?
    1. Own illness
    2. On vacation
    3. Bad weather
    4. Labor dispute
    5. New job to begin within 30 days
    6. Temporary layoff (under 30 days)
    7. Indefinite layoff (30 days or more, no definite recall date)
    8. Other

Q5.   When did ... last work at a full-time job or business lasting 2 consecutive weeks or more?
    1. In last 5 years
    2. Before last 5 years
    3. Never worked full-time 2 weeks or more
    4. Never worked at all

EMPLOYED. Any person who, in the survey week, is in the civilian labor force (age 16 and over) and who:

1)   did any paid work, including self-employment—answered Q1-a, and Q2-a;

2)   had a job but was not at work—answered Q1-b, Q2-b, and any of Q4-1 through Q4-4.

3)   if a member of the family has a farm or business, worked in this business unpaid for 15 hours or more.

UNEMPLOYED. A person who, in the survey week, is in the civilian labor force (age 16 and over) and who:

1)   is not working and is looking for work—answered Q1-c and Q2-b; this person was further asked:

Q6.   What has ... been doing in the last 4 weeks to find work?
    a. Checked with public employment agency
    b. Checked with private employment agency
    c. Checked with employer directly
    d. Checked with friends or relatives
    e. Placed or answered ads
    f. Nothing
    g. Other

A person would be considered unemployed if he/she answered affirmatively to any of the options in Q4. If a person did not answer affirmatively to Q4, he/she would be considered unemployed if on temporary or indefinite layoff, or with a new job to begin within 30 days—answered Q4-5 through Q4-7 and Q5-1 through Q5-2.

NOT IN LABOR FORCE (NILF). All civilians ages 14 and above who are not classified as employed or unemployed—answered Q1-d through Q1-h and Q2-b.

Categories of unemployment. If a person is classified as unemployed according to the above criteria, he/she is asked the following question:

Q7. At the time ... started looking for work, was it because he/she lost or quit a job or was there some other reason?
   1. Lost job
   2. Quit job
   3. Left school
   4. Wanted temporary work
   5. Change in home or family responsibilities
   6. Left military service
   7. Other

JOB LOSERS. A person is considered a job loser if he/she is classified as unemployed as above and lost their previous job—answered Q7-1; in addition, he/she would be considered a job loser if on temporary or indefinite layoff—answered Q4-6 through Q4-7 and Q5-1 through Q5-2.

JOB LEAVERS. A person is considered a job leaver if he/she is classified as unemployed as above and quit their previous job—answered Q7-2.

LABOR FORCE ENTRANTS. A person is considered a labor force entrant if he/she otherwise is classified as unemployed as above but is not a job leaver or job loser. A **new entrant** is an entrant who answered Q5-3 or Q5-4; a **reentrant** is an entrant who answered Q5-1 or Q5-2.

WEEKS LOOKING FOR WORK. Persons who were classified as unemployed as above were further asked:

Q8. 1. How many weeks has . . . been looking for work?
     2. *How many weeks ago did . . . start looking for work?*
     3. *How many weeks ago was . . . laid off?*

These questions are all considered equivalent and result in the number of weeks unemployed and looking for work. The answer is topcoded at 99 weeks.

Cited References

Aigner, D., & Cain, G. (1977). Statistical Theories of Discrimination in Labor Markets. *Industrial and Labor Relations Review, 30*(2), 175-87.

Akerlof, G., & Main, B. (1980). Unemployment Spells and Unemployment Experience. *American Economic Review, 70*(5), 885-93.

Akerlof, G., & Main, B. (1981). An Experience Weighted Measure of Employment Durations. *American Economic Review, 71*(5), 1003-11.

Akerlof, G. A. (1982). Labor Contracts as Partial Gift Exchange. *Quarterly Journal of Economics, 97*(4), 543-69.

Akerlof, G. A. (1984). Gift Exchange and Efficiency Wage Theory: Four Views. *American Economic Review, 74*(2), 79-83.

Albrecht, J., & Axell, B. (1984). An Equilibrium Model of Search Generated Unemployment. *Journal of Political Economy, 92*(5), 824-40.

Alchian, A. A. (1970). Information Costs, Pricing, and Resource Unemployment. In E. S. Phelps (Eds.), *Microeconomic Foundations of Employment and Inflation Theory* . New York: W. W. Norton & Company, Inc.

Altonji, J. G., & Spletzer, J. R. (1991). Worker Characteristics, Job Characteristics, and the Receipt of On-the-Job Training. *Industrial and Labor Relations Review, 45*(October), 58-79.

Atkinson, A. B., & Micklewright, J. (1991). Unemployment Compensation and Labor Market Transitions: A Critical Review. *Journal of Economic Literature, 29*(December), 1679-1727.

Baker, M. (1992). Unemployment Duration: Compositional Effects and Cyclical Variability. *American Economic Review, 82*(March), 313-21.

Ballen, J., & Freeman, R. B. (1986). Transitions between Employment and Nonemployment. In R. B. Freeman & H. J. Holzer (Eds.), *The Black Youth*

Unemploynment Crisis (pp. 75-114). Chicago: The University of Chicago Press.

Bean, F. D., Cushing, R.G., Haynes, C.W., and Van Hook, J. V. W. (1997). Immigration and the Social Contract, *Social Science Quarterly, 78*(2), 433-49.

Bean, F. D., Edmonston, B., & Passel, J., S. (Ed.). (1990). *Undocumented Migration to the United States: IRCA and the Experience of the 1980s.* Washington, D.C.: The Urban Institute Press.

Bean, F. D., Van Hook, J. V. W., Glick, J.E. (1997). Country of Origin, Type of Public Assistance, and Patterns of Welfare Recipiency among U.S. Immigrants and Natives, *Social Science Quarterly, 78*(2), 249-68.

Becker, G. S. (1975). *Human Capital* (2nd ed.). Chicago: University of Chicago Press.

Bell, B. D. (1997). The Performance of Immigrants in the United Kingdom: Evidence from the GHS. *Economic Journal, 107*(441), 333-44.

Benhabib, J., & Bull, C. (1983). Job Search: The Choice of Intensity. *Journal of Political Economy, 91*(5), 747-64.

Blau, F., & Kahn, L. (1981). Race and Sex Differences in Quits by Young Workers. *Industrial and Labor Relations Review, 34*(4), 563-77.

Blau, F. D. (1979). Immigration and Labor Earnings in Early Twentieth Century America. In J. L. Simon & J. da Vanzo (Eds.), *Research in Population Economics* (pp. 21-41). Greenwich: JAI Press.

Blaustein, S. J. (1993). *Unemployment Insurance in the United States.* Kalamazoo: W.E. Upjohn Institute for Employment Research.

Borjas, G. J. (1985). Assimilation, Changes in Cohort Quality, and the Earnings of Immigrants. *Journal of Labor Economics, 3*(4), 463-489.

Borjas, G. J. (1994). The Economics of Immigration. *Journal of Economic Literature, 32*(4), 1667-1717.

Bose, G. (1997). Nutritional Efficiency Wages: A Policy Framework, *Journal of Development Economics, 54*(2), 469-78.

Briggs, V. M. (1992). *Mass Immigration and the National Interest.* Armonk: M.E. Sharpe, Inc.

Briggs, V. M., & Moore, S. (1994). *Still an Open Door? U.S. Immigration Policy and the American Economy.* Washington, D.C.: The American University Press.

Burdett, K., & Judd, K. (1983). Equilibrium Price Dispersion. *Econometrica, 51*, 955-70.

Burton, J. F., & Parker, J. E. (1969). Interindustry Variations in Voluntary Labor Mobility. *Industrial and Labor Relations Review, 22*(2), 199-216.

Cafferty, P. S. J., Chiswick, B. R., Greeley, A. M., & Sullivan, T. A. (1984). *The Dilemma of American Immigration: Beyond the Golden Door.* New Brunswick: Transaction Books.

Camarota, S. A., (1997). The Effect of Immigrants on the Earnings of Low-Skilled Native Workers: Evidence from the June 1991 Current Population Survey. *Social Science Quarterly, 78*(2), 417-31.

Campbell, C. M. (1993). Do Firms Pay Efficiency Wages? Evidence with Data at the Firm Level. *Journal of Labor Economics, 11*(3), 442-70.

Carliner, G. (1980). Wages, Earnings, and Hours of First, Second, and Third Generation American Males. *Economic Inquiry, 18*(January), 87-102.

Chiswick, B. R. (1977). A Longitudinal Analysis of the Occupational Mobility of Immigrants. In B. D. Dennis (Ed.), *Proceedings of the Thirtieth Annual Winter Meeting of the Industrial Relations Research Association,* (pp. 20-27). New York City: Industrial Relations Research Association.

Chiswick, B. R. (1978). The Effect of Americanization on the Earnings of Foreign-born Men. *Journal of Political Economy, 86*(5), 897-921.

Chiswick, B. R. (1979). The Economic Progress of Immigrants: Some Apparently Universal Patterns. In W. Fellner (Eds.), *Contemporary Economic Problems* 1979: AEI.

Chiswick, B. R. (1980). *An Analysis of the Economic Progress and Impact of Immigrants* No. NTIS PB80-200454). Employment and Training Administration.

Chiswick, B. R. (1982). *The Employment of Immigrants in the United States.* Washington, D.C.: American Enterprise Institute for Public Policy Research.

Chiswick, B. R. (1986a). Is the New Immigration Less Skilled Than the Old? *Journal of Labor Economics, 4*(2), 168-192.

Chiswick, B. R. (1986b). Statement of Barry R. Chiswick, Research Professor, Department of Economics and Survey Research Laboratory, University of Illinois at Chicago. In *Economic and Demographic Consequences of Immigration: Hearings Before the Subcommittee on Economic Resources, Competitiveness, and Security Economics,* (pp. 234-236). Washington, D.C.: U.S. Government Printing Office.

Chiswick, B. R. (1988). Differences in Education and Earnings Across Racial and Ethnic Groups: Tastes, Discrimination, and Investments in Child Quality. *The Quarterly Journal of Economics,* August, 572-97.

Chiswick, B. R., Cohen, Y., & Zach, T. (1997). The Labor Market Status of Immigrants: The Roles of Unemployment at Arrival and Duration of Residence. *Industrial and Labor Relations Review, 50*(2), 289-303..

Chiswick, B. R., & Hurst, M. E. (1998a). The Employment, Unemployment, and Unemployment Compensation Benefits of Immigrants. *Research in Employment Policy,* Vol. II, forthcoming.

Chiswick, B. R., & Hurst, M. E. (1998b). The Labor Market Status of Immigrants: A Synthesis. In Hermann Kurthen, et. al., Eds., *Immigration, Citizenship, and the Welfare State: Germany and the United States in Comparison*, Greenwich, Connecticut, JAI Press (forthcoming)

Chiswick, B. R., & Miller, P. W. (1992). The Endogeneity Between Language and Earnings. In *European Research Conference on Migration and Development*, December. Davos Platz, Switzerland.

Clark, W. A. V. (1996). Scale Effects in International Migration to the United States. *Regional Studies, 30*(6), 589-60.

Clark, W. A. V., & Schulz, F. (1996). Mass Migration, Dependency, and Poverty in the United States. In H. Kurthen, J. Fijalkowski, & G. G. Wagner (Ed.), *Immigration and the Welfare State: Germany and the United States in Comparison*, Berlin, forthcoming.

Clark, W. A. V., & Schultz, F. (1997). Evaluating the Local Impacts of Recent Immigration to California: Realism versus Racism. *Population Research and Policy Review, 16*(5), 475-91.

Cornelius, W. A. (1982). *America in the Era of Limits: Nativist Reactions to the 'New' Immigration* ,Working Paper, Center for U.S.-Mexican Studies.

Davidson, C. (1990). *Recent Developments in the Theory of Involuntary Unemployment*. Kalamazoo, Michigan: W.E. Upjohn Institute for Employment Research.

Davidson, C., & Woodbury, S. A. (1995). *Wage Subsidies for Dislocated Workers* (Staff Working Paper No. 95-31). W.E. Upjohn Institute for Employment Research.

Devine, T. J., & Kiefer, N. M. (1991). *Empirical Labor Economics: The Search Approach*. New York: Oxford University Press.

Dickens, W. T., & Katz, L. F. (1987). Inter-industry Wage Differences and Industry Characteristics. In K. Lang & J. S. Leonard (Eds.), *Unemployment and the Structure of Labor Markets* New York: Basil Blackwell.

Dorantes, C. A., & Huang, W. (1997). Unemployment, Immigration and NAFTA: A Panel Study of Ten Major U.S. Industries. *Journal of Labor Research, 18*(4), 613-19.

Duleep, H. O., & Regets, M. C. (1995). Measuring Immigrant Wage Growth Using Matched CPS Files, *Demography, 34*(2), 239-49.

Duleep, H. O., & Regets, M. C. (1996). *The Elusive Concept of Immigrant Quality: Evidence from 1970-1990*. The Urban Institute, Program for Research on Immigration Policy, January.

Ehrenberg, R. G. (1980). The Demographic Structure of Unemployment Rates and Labor Market Transition Probabilities. In *Research in Labor Economics* (pp. 241-291). Greenwich: JAI Press.

Ehrenberg, R. G., and Smith, R.S. (1994). *Modern Labor Economics: Theory and Public Policy* (5th ed.). New York: HarperCollins.

Ehrenberg, R. G., & Oaxaca, R. L. (1976). Unemployment Insurance, Duration of Unemployment and Subsequent Wage Gains. *American Economic Review, 66*(5), 754-766.

Eichengreen, B., & Gemery, H. A. (1986). The Earnings of Skilled and Unskilled Immigrants at the End of the Nineteenth Century. *Journal of Economic History, 46*(2), 441-54.

Enchautegui, Mariq E. (1997). Immigration and County Employment Growth. *Population Research and Policy Review, 16*(5), 493-511.

Feldstein, M. (1973). The Economics of the New Unemployment. *Public Interest, 33*(Fall), 3-42.

Ferrie, J. P. (1995). *Immigrants and Natives: Comparative Economic Progress in Two Centuries: 1840-1860 and 1960-1980* ,Working Paper, Northwestern University.

Ferrie, J. P. (1997). The Entry into the U.S. Labor Market of Antebellum European Immigrants, 1840-1860. *Explorations in Economic History, 34*(3), 295-330.

Fix, M., & Passel, J. S. (1994). *Immigration and Immigrants*. Washington, D.C.: The Urban Institute Press.

Fry, R. (1997). The Increase in Idleness of Immigrant Arrivals: The Role of Age at Arrival, Refugees, and Country of Origin. *Quarterly Review of Economics and Finance*, forthcoming.

Funkhouser, E., & Trejo, S. J. (1995). The Labor Market Skills of Recent Male Immigrants: Evidence From the Current Population Survey. *Industrial and Labor Relations Review, 48*(4), 792-810.

Galor, O. (1986). Time Preference and International Labor Migration. *Journal of Economic Theory, 1*(20), 1-20.

Greene, W.H. (1993). *Econometric Analysis* (2nd Ed.). New York: Macmillan Publishing Company.

Greene, W.H. (1995). *LIMDEP, Version 7.0*. New York: Econometric Software, Inc.

Greenwood, M. J., & McDowell, J. M. (1982). The Supply of Immigrants to the United States. In B. R. Chiswick (Eds.), *The Gateway: U.S. Immigration Issues and Policies* (pp. 55-83). Washington, D.C.: American Enterprise Institute for Public Policy Research.

Gronau, R. (1971). Information and Frictional Unemployment. *American Economic Review, 61*, 290-301.

Hatton, T.J. (1997). The Immigrant Assimilation Puzzle in Late Nineteenth-Century America. *Journal of Economic History, 57*(1), 34-62.

Hashmi, A. (1987) *Post-Migration Investment In Education By Immigrants In The United States.* Ph.D. Thesis, University of Illinois at Chicago.

Heckman, J. J., & Singer, B. (1984). Econometric Duration Analysis. *Journal of Econometrics, 24*, 63-132.

Hoffman, E. P. (1991). Estimation of Length of Job Search by Survival Analysis. *Eastern Economic Journal, 17*(4), 393-401.

Holzer, H. J. (1986). Black Youth Nonemployment: Duration and Job Search. In R. B. Freeman & H. J. Holzer (Eds.), *The Black Youth Unemploynment Crisis* (pp. 75-114). Chicago: The University of Chicago Press.

Hurst, M. (1997) *Always in Motion: A Close Examination of the Assimilation Process of Immigrants In The United States.* Ph.D. Thesis, University of Illinois at Chicago.

Jasso, G., & Rosensweig, M. (1990). Self-selection and the Earnings of Immigrants: a Comment. *American Economic Review, 80*, 298-304.

Jovanovic, B. (1979). Job Matching and the Theory of Turnover. *Journal of Political Economy, 87*(5, pt 1), 972-990.

Karras, G., & Stone, L. (1994). Determinants of the Natural Rate and Persistence of Unemployment: Evidence from a Panel of U.S. States. Presented at: Midwest Economics Association Meeting, March. Chicago, Illinois.

Kieffer, N. M. (1988). Economic Duration Data and Hazard Functions. *Journal of Economic Literature, 26*(June), 646-679.

Kooreman, P., & Ridder, G. (1983). The Effects of Age and Unemployment Percentage on the Duration of Unemployment. *European Economic Review, 20*, 41-57.

Kreuger, A. B., & Summers, L. H. (1987). Reflections on the Inter-industry Wage Structure. In K. Lang & J. S. Leonard (Eds.), *Unemployment and the Structure of Labor Markets* New York: Basil Blackwell.

LaLonde, R. J., and Topel, Robert H. (1991). Immigrants in the American Labor Market: Quality, Assimilation, and Distributional Effects. *AEA Papers and Proceedings, 81*(2), 297-302.

LaLonde, R. J., & Topel, R. H. (1992). The Assimilation of Immigrants in the U.S. Labor Market. In G. J. B. a. R. B. Freeman (Eds.), *Immigration and the work force: Economic consequences for the United States and source areas* Chicago: University of Chicago Press.

Lancaster, T. (1979). Econometric Methods for the Duration of Unemployment. *Econometrica, 47*(4), 939-956.

Leonard, J. S. (1987). Carrots and Sticks: Pay, Supervision, and Turnover. *Journal of Labor Economics, 5*(4, pt. 2), S136-52.

Light, A., & Ureta, M. (1990a). Gender Differences in Wages and Job Turnover Among Continuously Employed Workers. *American Economic Review, 80*(2), 293-87.

Light, A., & Ureta, M. (1990b). Panel Estimates of Male and Female Job Turnover Behavior: Can Female Nonquitters Be Identified? *Journal of Labor Economics, 10*(2), 156-81.

Lippman, S. A., & McCall, J. J. (1976). The Economics of Job Search: A Survey. *Economic Inquiry, 14*, 155-89 and 347-68.

Long, J. (1980). The Effect of Americanization on Earnings: Some Evidence for Women. *Journal of Political Economy, 88*(3), 620-29.

Marston, S. T. (1976). Employment Instability and High Unemployment Rates. *Brookings Papers on Economic Activity, 1976*(1), 169-203.

Mattila, J. P. (1969). Quit Behavior in the Labor Market. *American Statistical Association Procedings*(August), 697-701.

McCafferty, S. (1990). *Macroeconomic Theory.* New York: Harper & Row.

McCall, J. J. (1965). The Economics of Information and Optimal Stopping Rules. *Journal of Business, 38*, 300-17.

McCall, J. J. (1970). The Economics of Information and Job Search. *Quarterly Journal of Economics, 84*(1), 113-126.

McLaughlin, K. J. (1991). A Theory of Quits and Layoffs with Efficient Turnover. *Journal of Political Economy, 99*(1), 1-29.

Meitzen, M. E. (1986). Differences in Male and Female Job-Quitting Behavior. *Journal of Labor Economics, 4*(2), 151-167.

Mortensen, D. T. (1970). Job Search, the Duration of Unemployment, and the Philips Curve. *American Economic Review, 60*(December), 847-862.

Mortensen, D. T. (1986). Job Search and Labor Market Analysis. In O. Ashenfelter & R. Layard (Eds.), *Handbook of Labor Economics* (pp. 849-919). Amsterdam: North-Holland.

Muller, T., & Espenshade, T. J. (1985). *The Fourth Wave.* Washington, D.C.: The Urban Institute Press.

Nam, C. (1959). Nationality Groups and Stratification in America. *Social Forces, 37*(4).

Nasar, Z. M. (1997). *The Effect of Naturalization on the Earnings Profiles of Young Workers.* Ph.D. Thesis, Kansas State University.

Nelson, P. (1970). Information and Consumer Behavior. *Journal of Poltical Economy, 78*(2), 311-29.

Nickell, S. (1979). Estimating the Probability of Leaving Unemployment. *Econometrica, 47*(5), 1249-66.

North, D. S., & Houstoun, M. F. (1976). *The Characteristics and Role of Illegal Aliens in the U.S. Labor Market: An Exploratory Study* . Employment and Training Administration.

Parsons, D. (1972). Specific Human Capital: An Application to Quit Rates and Lay-off Rates. *Journal of Political Economy, 80*(November), 1120-1143.

Parsons, D. O. (1977). Models of Labor Market Turnover: A Theoretical and Empirical Survey. In R. Ehrenber (Eds.), *Research in Labor Economics* (pp. 185-223). Greenwich: JAI Press.

Passel, J. S., & Edmonston, B. (1994). Immigration and Race: Recent Trends in Immigration to the United States. In B. Edmonston & J. S. Passel (Eds.), *Immigration and Ethnicity* Washington, D.C.: The Urban Institute Press.

Pencavel, J. H. (1970). *An Analysis of the Quit Rate in American Manufacturing Industry.*

Pindyck, R.S. & Rubinfeld, D.L. (1991). *Econometric Models & Economic Forecasts*, New York: McGraw-Hill, Inc.

Pischke, J., & Velling, J. (1997). Employment effects of Immigration to Germany: An Analysis Based on Local Labor Markets. *Review of Economics and Statistics, 79*(44), 594-604.

Quigley, D. D. (1996). Native and Immigrant School-to-Work Transitions: The Case of the United States. Presented at: Immigration and the Welfare State: Germany and the United States in Comparison, Berlin.

Reinganum, J. (1979). A Simple Model of Equilibrium Price Dispersion. *Journal of Political Economy, 87*, 851-58.

Salant, S. W. (1977). Search Theory and Duration Data: A Theory of Sorts. *Quarterly Journal of Economics, 91*, 39-57.

Salop, S. (1973). Systematic Job Search and Unemployment. *Review of Economic Studies, 40*(April), 191-201.

Sattinger, M. (1993). Assignment Models of the Distribution of Earnings. *Journal of Economic Literature, 31*(2), 831-880.

Schmidt, P., & Strauss, R. P. (1975). The Prediction of Occupation Using Multiple Logit Models. *International Economic Review, 16*(2), 471-86.

Schultz, T. W. (1975). The Value of the Ability to Deal with Disequilibria. *Journal of Economic Literature*, September, 827-846.

Schwartz, A. (1976). Migration, Age, and Education. *Journal of Political Economy, 84*(4), 701-719.

Sehgal, E. (1985). Foreign born in the U.S. labor market: the results of a special survey. *Monthly Labor Review*, July, 18-24.

Shapiro, C., & Stiglitz, J. E. (1984). Equilibrium Unemployment as a Worker Discipline Device. *American Economic Review, 74*(June), 433-44.

Sider, H. (1985). Unemployment Duration and Incidence, 1968-82. *The American Economic Review, 75*(3), 461-72.

Sjaastad, L. A. (1962). The Costs and Returns of Human Migration. *Journal of Political Economy, 70*(5, pt. 2), 80-94.

Smith, J. (1992). *Hispanics and the American Dream: An Analysis of Hispanic Male Labor Market Wages* , Rand Corporation.

Stigler, G. (1962). Information in the Labor Market. *Journal of Political Economy, 70*(pt. 2), 94-105.

Stoikov, V., & Raimon, R. L. (1968). Determinants of Differences in the Quit Rate Among Industries. *American Economic Review, 58*(4), 1283-98.

Summers, L. H., & Clark, K. (1990a). Labor Market Dynamics and Unemployment. In L. H. Summers (Eds.), *Understanding Unemployment* (pp. 3-47). Cambridge: The MIT Press.

Summers, L. H., & Clark, K. B. (1990b). The Dynamics of Youth Unemployment. In L. H. Summers (Eds.), *Understanding Unemployment* (pp. 48-85). Cambridge: The MIT Press.

Summers, L. H., & Clark, K. B. (1990c). Unemployment Insurance and Labor Market Transitions. In L. H. Summers (Eds.), *Understanding Unemployment* (pp. 188-226). Cambridge: The MIT Press.

Swan, N. (1991). *Economic and Social Impacts of Immigration: A Research Report Prepared for the Economic Council of Canada* . Economic Council of Canada.

Tandon, B. B. (1973). Earnings Differentials Among Native-Born and Foreign-Born Residents of Toronto. *International Migration Review, 12*(3), 406-10.

Topel, R. H., & Ward, M. P. (1992). Job Mobility and the Careers of Young Men. *Quarterly Journal of Economics, 107*(May), 439-79.

Topel, R. H. (1997). Factor Proportions and Relative Wages: The Supply-Side Determinants of Wage Inequality. *Journal of Economic Perspectives, 11*(2), 55-74.

Vedder, R., Galloway, L., and Moore, S. (1990). Do Immigrants Increase Unemployment or Reduce Economic Growth? *Congressional Record* (26 September).

Warren, R. (1993). *Estimates of the Resident Illegal Alien Population,* October Immigration and Naturalization Service.

Weiss, A. (1980). Job Queues and Layoffs in Labor Markets with Flexible Wages. *Journal of Political Economy, 88,* June, 526-38.

Weiss, A. (1984). Determinants of Quit Behavior. *Journal of Labor Economics, 2*(3), 371-87.

White, M. J., & Kaufman, G. (1997). Language Usage, Social Capital, and School Completion among Immigrants and Native-Born Ethnic Groups. *Social Science Quarterly, 78*(2), 385-98.

Woodbury, S. A., & Spiegelman, R. (1987). Bonus to Workers and Employers to Reduce Unemployment: Randomized Trials in Illinois. *American Economic Review, 77,* 513-30.

Yellen, J. L. (1984). Efficiency Wage Models of Unemployment. *American Economic Review, 74*(2), 200-205.

Yuengert, A. M. (1991). *Self-employment and the earnings of male immigrants in the U.S.* (Working Paper No. 9105). Federal Reserve Bank of New York.

Yuengert, A. M. (1994). Immigrant Earnings, Relative to What? The Importance of Earnings Function Specification and Comparison Points. *Journal of Applied Econometrics, 9,* 71-90.